PRAYERBOOK OF THE KING: THE PSALMS

Dedication

Msgr. John R. Portman
who has always generously shared
his theological insights
with ecumenical enthusiasm

PRAYERBOOK OF THE KING:
THE PSALMS

Msgr. Charles Dollen

ALBA·HOUSE NEW·YORK

SOCIETY OF ST. PAUL, 2187 VICTORY BLVD., STATEN ISLAND, NEW YORK 10314

ST PAULS

Library of Congress Cataloging-in-Publication Data

Prayerbook of the King: the Psalms / [compiled by] Charles Dollen.
     p.   cm.
   Includes indexes.
   ISBN 0-8189-0751-7
   1. Bible. O.T. Psalms — Criticism, interpretation, etc.
   2. Spiritual life — Catholic Church.   I. Dollen, Charles.
   BS1430.2.P73   1997
   223'.206 — dc21   97-20173
                                    CIP

Produced and designed in the United States of America by the
Fathers and Brothers of the Society of St. Paul,
2187 Victory Boulevard, Staten Island, New York 10314,
as part of their communications apostolate.

ISBN: 0-8189-0751-7

Printing Information:

Current Printing - first digit   1   2   3   4   5   6   7   8   9   10

Year of Current Printing - first year shown

1998   1999   2000   2001   2002   2003   2004   2005

TABLE OF CONTENTS

Book Four: Psalms 90 - 106

Book Five: Psalms 107 - 150

FOREWORD

There are several reasons for calling this work, "Prayerbook of the King."

The most obvious is that so many of the psalms in the Psalter are attributed to King David or related to him. Reading between the lines in these psalms, he is seen as a very complex man. His successes and his sins, his triumphs and his set-backs, his spiritual vision and his psychological depths are inviting and inspirational, but also cautionary. His understanding of true human values that transcend time and culture make his work a valued part of world literature.

Perhaps the reason that is most moving is that the Psalter as a prayer book formed the human spirituality of Christ, the God-man. This was how Jesus, who spent many hours in prayer, learned to pray both at home in Nazareth with Mary and Joseph, and in the synagogue which he attended so faithfully.

The fact that the psalms are used so much in the Liturgy of the Catholic Church is also persuasive. Christians who are called to share the Christ-life through Baptism and are joined to him "as priest, prophet and king" have their prayer life molded by the Psalter, more so than most imagine.

Eusebius of Caesarea writes in the fourth century about the joy felt by Christians when they were finally freed to worship:

"Our bishops performed religious rites with full ceremonial, priests officiated at the liturgy — the solemn ritual of the Church, chanting psalms, proclaiming the other parts of the God-given Scriptures, and celebrating the divine mysteries" (*Ecclesiastical History*, Bk. 10).

St. Ambrose, writing later in that century, says:

"In the Book of Psalms there is profit for all with healing power for our salvation. There is instruction from history, teaching from the law, prediction from prophecy, chastisement from denunciation and persuasion from moral teaching... All with eyes to see can discover in it a complete gymnasium for the soul, a stadium for all virtues, equipped with every kind of exercise. It is for each to choose the kind he judges best to help him gain the prize" (*On Psalm 1*).

Quite to the point, on a wider scale, St. Jerome states, "Ignorance of Scripture is ignorance of Christ" (From the *Prologue on Isaiah*).

Closer to modern times, Cardinal Manning taught that:

"The divine office is a part of the divine tradition. It is a perpetual witness for God and for the Faith. It has been put together by the hands of men, but these men were saints... The materials of which it is composed are the words of the Spirit of God... The psalms and scriptures of inspired men under the old law and the new, with the writings of the saints, are all interwoven into a wonderful texture of prayer and praise, of worship and witness of the kingdom of God and of the communion of saints" (*The Eternal Priesthood*).

Abbot Columba Marmion, O.S.B., of Maredsou Abbey echoes these sentiments:
⌐Belgium.

"With wonderful and great variety of expression, the psalms sing by turns the power, magnificence, holiness, goodness, mercy and beauty of God... At the same time as they celebrate the Divine perfections, the psalms wonderfully express the sentiments and needs of our souls. The psalms know how to weep and rejoice; to desire and supplicate. There is no inward disposition of our souls that they cannot express" (*Christ the Life of the Soul*, p. 309 ff.).

Among the many contemporary scripture scholars we could quote, listen to Father Carroll Stuhlmueller, C.P.:

"Every great movement of salvation-history is relived in the psalms. If we lost the entire Bible except the book of Psalms, we would possess enough material, if not to rewrite the Scriptures, at least to reconstruct Bible history.

"Because the psalms are so very human, they can bring the spirit of God, or might we say, the beat of God's heart into every moment of human activity. When this is finally achieved, then the eternal liturgy of the new heaven and the new earth will absorb all the elect in the fullness of life" (*The Bible Today Reader*, pp. 256ff.).

The *Constitution on the Sacred Liturgy* of the Second Vatican Council proclaims that the Liturgy is the "fount from which all of (the Church's) spiritual power flows" (#10). After commenting extensively on the value and importance of the divine office for priests and religious, with its mixture of scripture readings, psalms and writings, the Council states, "And the laity, too are encouraged to recite the divine office, either with the priests, or among themselves, or even individually" (#100).

This popular look at the individual psalms is particularly written for the laity who choose this powerful form of liturgical prayer. If it also explores some of the riches of the Psalter to help priests and religious, that will indeed be a bonus.

The plan, quite briefly, is this. First, a commentary on the psalm after consulting writings of contemporary biblical scholars. In some cases individual verses may be singled out. Throughout this work we will look for the Christian dimension in the psalms. We must also remember to allow the psalmist the poetic license that all poets have. We will look at the rich Catholic tradition of the ages for more insight into the ideas sparked by the psalms. Finally there may be a brief interpretation or essay in which I will share whatever insights I may have on the psalm after fifty years of praying them.

I have relied heavily on *The Jerome Biblical Commentary, The Collegeville Biblical Commentary, A New Catholic Commentary on Holy Scripture, The Liturgy of the Hours* and *Harper's Bible Commentary*. Father John McKenzie's *Dictionary of the Bible* was also most helpful. Of great use for the Christian dimension was *The Six Version Parallel New Testament* (Creation House, Carol Stream, IL).

Also of great help was my volume, *The Book of Catholic Wisdom* (Our Sunday Visitor Press) and *Augustine Day by Day* compiled and edited by Father John E. Rotelle, O.S.A. (Catholic Book Publishing Co.). The meditations on the Psalms in various issues of *God's Word Today*, a monthly publication from P.O. Box 64088, St. Paul, MN 55164, were useful.

Note: The Psalms are divided by many experts into five "books:" Psalms 1-41; Psalms 42-72; Psalms 73-89; Psalms 90-106; and Psalms 107-150.

Biblical Abbreviations

OLD TESTAMENT

Genesis	Gn	Nehemiah	Ne	Baruch	Ba
Exodus	Ex	Tobit	Tb	Ezekiel	Ezk
Leviticus	Lv	Judith	Jdt	Daniel	Dn
Numbers	Nb	Esther	Est	Hosea	Ho
Deuteronomy	Dt	1 Maccabees	1 M	Joel	Jl
Joshua	Jos	2 Maccabees	2 M	Amos	Am
Judges	Jg	Job	Jb	Obadiah	Ob
Ruth	Rt	Psalms	Ps	Jonah	Jon
1 Samuel	1 S	Proverbs	Pr	Micah	Mi
2 Samuel	2 S	Ecclesiastes	Ec	Nahum	Na
1 Kings	1 K	Song of Songs	Sg	Habakkuk	Hab
2 Kings	2 K	Wisdom	Ws	Zephaniah	Zp
1 Chronicles	1 Ch	Sirach	Si	Haggai	Hg
2 Chronicles	2 Ch	Isaiah	Is	Malachi	Ml
Ezra	Ezr	Jeremiah	Jr	Zechariah	Zc
		Lamentations	Lm		

NEW TESTAMENT

Matthew	Mt	Ephesians	Eph	Hebrews	Heb
Mark	Mk	Philippians	Ph	James	Jm
Luke	Lk	Colossians	Col	1 Peter	1 P
John	Jn	1 Thessalonians	1 Th	2 Peter	2 P
Acts	Ac	2 Thessalonians	2 Th	1 John	1 Jn
Romans	Rm	1 Timothy	1 Tm	2 John	2 Jn
1 Corinthians	1 Cor	2 Timothy	2 Tm	3 John	3 Jn
2 Corinthians	2 Cor	Titus	Tt	Jude	Jude
Galatians	Gal	Philemon	Phm	Revelation	Rv

BOOK ONE: PSALMS 1 - 41

The lot of good & wicked

The commentators consider Psalm 1 to be something like a preface to the Psalter. There is a way to perfection and a way to perdition and with the gift of free will, we are asked to cooperate in our salvation.

As St. Augustine remarked, "God who created us without our cooperation, will not save us without our cooperation." Faith and good works are intimately bound together in the work of salvation. Faith is the beginning, a free gift from God, but it comes alive through works of charity.

The older translation, with a phrase so familiar, began "Happy the man who..." Now translators are using "happy the one," or, as here, "Happy those who do not follow..." If it does not alter the sense or the image, the gender-free form is preferable.

There is an interesting blend of the appeal for individual justification and the notion of the community involved in the work. It is difficult, if not impossible, to understand the Old Testament without a knowledge of the words "covenant" and "community" and their wide application.

In Christ, what was symbolized in the Old Testament by those notions, is now fulfilled. "It has pleased God to make men holy and save them not merely as individuals, without bond or link between them, but by making them into a single people" (*Lumen Gentium*, #9).

Of this people, Christ is the head; we, the baptized followers of Christ, are the members. "The law of the Lord is their joy; God's law they study day and night." It is one thing to be incorporated into the Church; it is another thing to grow to full maturity in Christ.

Palestine, like Southern California, would be a desert without additional water. Therefore, it is no surprise that there are many allusions to trees planted near running streams that can withstand the rigorous sun.

Early Christian writers saw the Cross in the tree of this psalm and every mention of <u>running water</u> was, for them, a sign of the saving waters of <u>Baptism</u>.

PSALM 2: *"Why do the nations protest..."*

This is the <u>first of the Messianic Psalms</u> and it was used in the early Church as a proclamation of the divinity of Jesus. "You are my Son; this day I have begotten you." The concept, "today I am your Father," was applied literally to him. What the Davidic kings were symbolically, Christ was actually.

Plotting against "the anointed of the Lord" was equivalent to rebelling against God himself. "The anointed" gives us the word "Messiah" from the Hebrew and "Christ" from the Greek. St. Theophilus of Antioch would write to Autolycus in the second century, "We are called Christians on this account, because we are anointed with the oil of God."

Francis X. Durrwell in *The Resurrection*, writes:

"For Christians Christ was this divine King-Messiah. The earliest Palestinian communities called him *'Maran'* (Our Lord) and the Greek communities proclaimed him *'Kyrios.'*

"In the first public proclamation of faith in Christ we read, 'Let all the house of Israel know most certainly that God has made both Lord and Christ this same Jesus whom you have crucified' (Ac 2:36)."

In St. Peter's mind the two terms are closely joined: God has made Jesus the "Lord-Messiah."

Zion and Jerusalem are often used by ancient authors as symbols of the heavenly Jerusalem when Christ's Kingdom will be perfected, and as a figure of the Church in which it is being completed. Thus St. Athanasius:

"If we follow Christ closely, we shall be allowed, even on this earth, to stand as it were on the threshold of the heavenly Jerusalem and enjoy the contemplation of the everlasting feast..." (*Letter 14*).

But Christ had to suffer to enter into his royal kingdom as St. Paul insists:

> Though he was in the form of God,
> Jesus did not deem equality with God
> something to be grasped at.
> Rather he emptied himself
> and took the form of a slave,
> being born in the likeness of men.
> He was known to be of human estate,
> and it was thus that he humbled himself,
> obediently accepting even death,
> death on a cross!
> Because of this,
> God highly exalted him
> and bestowed on him the name
> above every other name,
> So that at Jesus' name
> every knee must bend
> in the heavens, on the earth,
> and under the earth,
> and every tongue proclaim
> to the glory of God the Father:
> JESUS CHRIST IS LORD (Ph 2:6-11).

PSALM 3: *"How many are my foes, O Lord..."*

Considered by many a "morning prayer," Psalm 3 is tied to the following which is considered an "evening prayer." This is the first of the many Psalms attributed to David, or to a Davidic Guild.

It is also typical of the many Psalms of Lamentation in which three characters appear: God, who is addressed, the petitioner protesting his innocence and "the enemy."

They are a direct cry to God in time of a very specific complaint such as a military need, agricultural distress, sickness, treachery, the consequences of sin, etc. Except in the last case, the one praying usually claims innocence.

Then follows the expression of hope that God will act and the confidence that faith in God gives the petitioner. With true Semitic vehemence, this is often coupled with a plea for the enemies' destruction. This part is replete with words of assurance, that God does hear prayers.

The lament usually ends with the a serene statement of God's ability to arrange the things of the world, collectively for the community or singly for the individual.

The particular Christian significance of this psalm, and all Psalms of Lamentation, is that Christ has overcome the world (Jn 16:33) and shares his victory with us. The Incarnation has made visible the hope we have as we make our way on our earthly pilgrimage. The Passion and Death of Christ have won us the graces we need. The Holy Spirit has been given to enkindle those graces in us.

St. Paul reminds us: "Who will separate us from the love of Christ? Trial, or distress, or persecution, or hunger, or nakedness, or danger, or the sword? Yet in all this we are more than conquerors because of him who loved us" (Rm 8:35, 37).

St. Bernard expressed it this way:

"The whole of the spiritual life consists of these two elements. When we think of ourselves we are perturbed and filled with a salutary sadness. When we think of the Lord we are revived to find consolation in the joy of the Holy Spirit. From the first we derive fear and humility and from the second hope and love" (*Misc. Sermons*, 5).

PSALM 4: *"Answer when I call, my saving God..."*

Used as an evening prayer by devout Jews, probably in Temple worship also, the Church uses this psalm to begin the series of Night Prayers in *The Liturgy of the Hours*. Calling on his past experiences, the poet serenely asks for God's continuing help in times of trouble.

After an aside to the faithless who do not honor God in prayer and deed, he announces with great trust that the Lord works wonders for the faithful. This is most likely a reference to salvation history, always close to Jewish spirituality, which testifies to the great signs and wonders in the lives of the patriarchs, prophets and kings.

"Tremble and do not sin," suggests a justifiable anger with sin, not the sinner. St. Paul quotes this verse in his rules of life for the Ephesians: "Be angry but do not sin; do not let the sun set on your anger" (Eph 4:26).

"Pondering on your beds in silence" may well refer to the many times that God has revealed himself during dreams. Abram (Gn 15) and the patriarch Joseph (Gn 37) come to mind immediately. In the Infancy Narratives in Matthew, the angel appears to St. Joseph in a dream, to tell him of the miraculous conception (Mt 1:20), to order the Holy Family to Egypt (Mt 2:13) and their return (Mt 2:19). The Magi were also warned about Herod in a dream (Mt 2:12).

"Offering fitting sacrifice" to the Lord results in a sublime confidence that God will respond. Of course, for Christians this is the Sacrifice on Calvary and its continuance in the Sacrifice of the Mass.

The conclusion is a mature prayer for better times. For those who trust in the Lord, there is a harvest feast of grain and wine already prepared for them. This a reflection of the wisdom literature in which evil is immediately punished and virtue is rewarded immediately.

It remained for the Christian revelation to seek perfect rewards in heaven and to call to rise above the materialism of the world. "For the world and its enticements are passing away. But whoever does the will of God remains forever" (1 Jn 2:17). "And the victory that overcomes the world is this faith of ours" (1 Jn 5:4). "He is always able to save those who approach God through him, since he lives forever to make intercession for them" (Heb 7:25).

For St. Augustine, the final remark about a peaceful sleep was a reference to Christ's Death ("falling asleep" in the ancient writers) and Resurrection. In that connection he exults, "The Resurrection of Christ was God's supreme and wholly marvelous work!"

PSALM 5: *"Hear my words, O Lord..."*

In ancient times, unless you were very rich, life was hard and difficult. There are many references in the Old Testament to prayers with tears and so this petitioner speaks directly, "Hear my word, O Lord; listen to my sighing."

The plea is made as a morning prayer, probably at the time of sacrifice. It is something of the equivalent of our Morning Offering, setting the tone for the day. The Wise Man says, "... one must give you thanks before the sunrise, and turn to you at daybreak" (Ws 16:28).

The psalm proceeds with a view of the company of evildoers. False speech and deceit are particularly singled out because of the harm they can do in a closed community. They are formidable foes of interpersonal relationships.

God does not delight in evil and shuns the company of evil people unless and until they evidence a true conversion of heart. These people are to be excluded from the true Temple worship. Because the sinners mentioned here lack sincerity they are, in fact, rebels who have turned their backs on God and his Temple.

"Their throats are open graves" because they deny God in speech as well as deed. St. Paul quotes this verse as part of his catalogue of the bondage of sin (Rm 3:13).

The psalmist, however, delights in the liturgical celebrations of Temple service. He concludes with the assurance that God will protect his friends and be their sure refuge. The prayer of St. Richard of Chichester shows the Christian dimension of this song, "O most merciful Friend, may I know you more clearly, love you more dearly, and follow you more nearly, day by day, day by day."

PSALM 6: *"Do not reprove me in your anger, Lord..."*

Since the end of the Patristic period, the seven Penitential Psalms have been used by the Church to express repentance. They are Psalms 6, 32, 38, 51, 102, 130 and 143. They express repentance for one's personal sins and the social evils of the community.

It was widely believed that illness was a punishment for personal sins and the incursions of enemies a retribution for the sins of society, Israel in this case. The writer says he has wept a river of tears over the sickness that afflicts him. Even with the advancement of modern medical science, there are many crippling and disabling ills that afflict us and we need to pray for help. It would be impossible to say that these are punishment for sin, but it would be equally impossible to deny that it might be, in some cases.

Here the sinner entrusts himself to the mercy of God. He uses a Hebrew word, *hesed*, which does not have an exact English translation. Some render it "kindness," which does not seem strong enough. It is more like "merciful love," or "loving mercy." The word is used often in the Old Testament.

The mention of Sheol brings up the subject of life after death. For the ancient Israelites life after death was a loveless, shadowy existence. It was akin to the Hades of classical literature. In popular folklore, they spoke of Enoch, "who walked with God and was seen no more" (Gn 5:24), of the witch of Endor who conjured the ghost of Samuel (1 S 28:8-25) and the ascension of Elijah (2 K 2:11).

It wasn't until a few centuries before Christ that belief in a personal and loving existence of the soul after death became popular among the Jews, as seen in passages from Daniel, Wisdom, and 2 Maccabees. With the Christian revelation, of course, belief in a true spiritual paradise was realized. Christ could say with certitude to the good thief, "This day you will be with me in paradise" (Lk 23:43), and St. Paul would maintain, "Eye has not seen, and ear has not heard, and it has not entered the human heart what God has prepared for those who love him" (1 Cor 2:9).

The Christian applications of this psalm are many and varied. The Church itself, the New Israel, is beset with troubles from within and without. The many wounds of the Church we ask God to heal by the power of the Risen Christ so that we can return to praising God.

Since repentance always includes the notion of conversion of life, the saints treasured the virtue of repentance. Pope St. Clement I wrote at the end of the first century:

"Let us fix our attention on the blood of Christ and recognize how precious it is to God his Father, since it was shed for our salvation and brought the gift of repentance to all the world" (*Letter to the Corinthians*, #30).

St. Augustine wrote:

"When we transform our old life and give our spirit a new image, we find it very hard and tiring to turn back from the darkness of earthly passions to the serene calm of the divine light. Therefore, we ask God to help us so that a complete conversion may be brought about in us" (*Commentary on Psalm 6*).

PSALM 7: *"Lord, my God, in you I take refuge..."*

From the inscription for this psalm, the author either is referring to King Saul's unjustified enmity toward David or is using that story as his type of a personal lament. Either view makes it a powerful plea for God's help when one who is innocent of an evil deed is accused of it.

Taking refuge in the Lord, possibly in the Lord's Temple, the poet will have some respite from attacks. The reference to lions reminds us that they roamed Israel as late as the time of the Crusaders.

Standing in the presence of God, the accused protests his innocence with the plea that if he is guilty, then he deserves punishment; if he is truly innocent, the punishment should be meted out to his enemy.

Then the scene becomes very solemn as the plea is taken to the court of God. God cannot be deceived whether it involves individuals or nations. There is no doubt but that God will judge justly.

In verse 10 God is addressed as one who judges "hearts and minds." Actually it reads "hearts and reins (kidneys)," meaning the seats of reason and emotion. Ronald Knox's translation offers "no thought or desire of ours can escape the scrutiny of your divine justice." Critics of Knox charged him with publishing the Psalms as "variations on a Davidic theme"! Actually, his work frequently goes to the heart of the meaning rather than the literal translation.

The themes and examples used in the last few verses are frequent in Old Testament writings: the sharpened sword, the deadly bow and arrow, "pregnant with mischief," and the open pit used to entrap the enemy (cf. Pr 26:27). Thus, Haman the enemy of the Jews who planned to hang Mordecai was hung on the gibbet he had prepared (Est 7:10).

Most psalms of lament end with a ringing celebration of the God who vindicates the just. So this conclusion is typical, "I praise the justice of the Lord; I celebrate the name of the Lord Most High."

Christian belief makes the Last Judgment a certitude where God's own justice will be vindicated to all humankind. The God who "makes his sun rise on the bad and the good and causes rain to fall on the just and the unjust" (Mt 5:45) will sort out all the apparent injustices that occur.

Pope St. Clement I (c. 97 A.D.) concluded his *Letter to the Corinthians* in this way:

"Lord, You created the world according to the eternal decrees now revealed in your works. Faithful through all generations, you are just in judgment, wonderful in power and majesty. You formed your creation with wisdom and established it with prudence. Everything we see proclaims your goodness. You are kind and compassionate and never fail those who put their trust in you."

PSALM 8: *"O Lord, our Lord, how awesome is your name…"*

One of the most beautiful hymns of praise in the psaltery, Psalm 8 has us marvel at the majesty of the God of Creation. Creation great and small praises God by its very being and by the order imposed on it. From babes and infants to the great stars of heaven, all tell the story of God's omnipotence.

Yet, if we are awed by the power of God, we are humbled by his immanence — his presence in us individually and his care for us as the human race. Mere mortals that we are, he has still crowned us with glory and honor, graced us with intellect and free will and in Christ he has made us his sons and daughters.

God has made us the stewards of creation (Gn 1:29-30; 2:15). The sheep and the oxen, the birds of the air and the fishes in the sea, all the works of God's hands are subjected to our care. The awesome vision of the scope of creation reminds us of the proofs for the existence of God, from reason, as taught by St. Thomas Aquinas (cf. Walter Farrell, *Companion to the Summa*, vol. 1, c. 2).

The Christian use and understanding of this psalm is vast. St. Paul refers to it to teach of Christ's exaltation (Heb 2:6-10) and again of the universality of Christ's dominion (1 Cor 15:20-28). He further teaches, "He [God] has put all things under his [Christ's] feet and has given him as head over all things to the Church" (Eph 1:22).

Christ himself referred to this psalm when the chief priests and the scribes objected to the hosannas of Palm Sunday (Mt 21:15-16). The Church uses it for many Christological Feasts to celebrate the majesty of Christ the King. It is also used on the Feast of the Holy Innocents (Dec. 28).

Father Carroll Stuhlmueller, C.P., makes this observation about Psalm 8 in *Harper's Bible Commentary*:

"Humankind, redeemed and lifted up from its lowly state by the Lord, shares in the divine governance of the world. The harmony of nature depends upon the harmony of men and women among themselves and with their God. Ecology belongs to the theology of redemption" (p. 438).

Let St. Paul expand on that thought:

"For creation awaits with eager expectation the revelation of the children of God; for creation was made subject to futility, not of its own accord but because of the one who subjected it, in hope, that creation itself would be set free from slavery to corruption and share in the glorious freedom of the children of God. We know that all creation is groaning in labor pains even now" (Rm 8:19-22).

And in the heavenly vision from the Book of Revelation:

O Lord our God, you are worthy
to receive glory and honor and power.
For you have created all things;
by your will they came to be and were made.
For you were slain;
with your blood you purchased for God
men and women of every race and tongue
of every people and nation.
Worthy is the Lamb that was slain
to receive power and riches,
wisdom and strength,
honor, glory and praise.   (Rv 4:11; 5:9, 11)

PSALM 9: *"I will praise you, Lord, with all my heart..."*

Psalms 9 and 10 are actually one psalm called an acrostic — each verse beginning with the succeeding letter of the Hebrew alphabet. Possibly because of content, in the Hebrew text (Masoretic) it is divided into two separate pieces.

In the ancient Greek and Latin translations (Septuagint and the Vulgate) it is numbered as one psalm, Psalm 9. Modern scripture scholars, in opting for the Hebrew numbering, move the rest of the numbers up by one until Psalms 146 and 147, which are joined in the Hebrew.

This makes for many difficulties in reading and translating the Fathers of the Church and many of their successors, who quote the Psalms by the Greek and Latin numbers. The verse numbers differ as well, since the Masoretic text numbers the choir directions as verse one.

Taking Psalm 9 as we now number the psalms, we have a song of magnificent praise for the help God gives the righteous nation or individual. "Declaring the wondrous works of God" takes in the whole economy of salvation, from the Patriarchs, the Exodus, and for the Christian, free salvation in Christ.

The great nations of ancient times that inspired such terror have been blotted out, their names remembered only by scholars of ancient history. Their cities have been destroyed and are remembered only by archaeologists. Isn't this true even of comparatively recent tyrants and dictators? Hitler, Stalin and Mussolini with all their pomp and might are now just names in history.

"Those who seek you," a phrase used over 150 times in the Old Testament, find in God a just judge who is also the safeguard and defender of the just, the oppressed, and the poor.

"The gates of death" are contrasted to the "gates of Daughter Zion." The gates of death are like a prison's entrance with the words of Dante emblazoned over its portals: "Abandon hope all you who enter here." Those who enter Jerusalem through its gates can hope to find spiritual refreshment in the Temple on Mount Zion and safety in the strength of the city's walls.

Our Lord used this symbol in conferring the primacy on St. Peter, "And I say to you, you are Peter, and upon this rock I will build my church, and the gates of the netherworld shall not prevail against it" (Mt 16:18).

The wicked will be condemned to Sheol where they will suffer final, ultimate defeat. Human tyrants cannot triumph beyond the certitude of mortality which ends in death. Only the just can hope for help from God. For the Christian this includes life after death in an eternal homeland of life and love.

Christ "is the image of the invisible God, the firstborn of all creation... He is the beginning, the firstborn of the dead" (Col 1:15, 18). He is "the firstborn among many brothers" (Rm 8:29).

That is why we proclaim that Jesus Christ "will come to judge the living and the dead" (2 Tm 4:1).

PSALM 10: *"Why, O Lord, do you stand at a distance?"*

Preachers, from time immemorial, have always decried the evils of their time as the worst that has ever happened. That is true in this psalm where the prayer is for protection from scoundrels and schemers. There is an urgency, an immediacy here that cries out almost desperately for attention.

The pride and insolence of the wicked is not their only vice. Their practical atheism makes them proclaim that God doesn't care, that he won't take notice and that he doesn't even exist. How that wounds the hearts of the faithful.

How often, in various private revelations, Our Lord has complained to St. Margaret Mary Alacoque, St. Gertude, St. Mechtilde and others about the coldness of the hearts of even those who say they are Christian. Our Lady spoke of this to St. Catherine Laboure, St. Bernadette, the children at Fatima, at Medjugorje and so forth. The lukewarmness of the many is worse than the practical atheism of the sophisticated.

The psalmist, however, is confident that God will triumph and take care of the poor and oppressed. The Christian praying this psalm feels even stronger confidence: "For the Lamb who is in the center of the throne will shepherd them and lead them to springs of life-giving water, and God will wipe every tear from their eyes" (Rv 7:17).

For Christ, whose spiritual life was nourished on these prayers, it is not a surprise that his social gospel was so concerned with the poor. "Blessed are you who are poor, for the kingdom of God is yours. Blessed are you who are hungry now, for you will be satisfied..." (Lk 6:20-21).

Dorothy Day, who based her whole understanding of Catholicism on the social gospel, would write:

"All men are brothers. How often we hear this refrain, the rallying cry that strikes a response in every human heart. These are the words of Christ, 'Call no man master for all are brothers.' Going to the people is the purest and best act in Christian tradition, and in revolutionary tradition, and is the beginning of world brotherhood" (*The Long Loneliness*, pt. 3).

PSALM 11: *"In the Lord I take refuge..."*

Sublime confidence in God is the theme of this song. During times of political chaos and civil distress, it was common to take to the wilderness for refuge. We read this several times in the Old Testament, such as in the life of King David, in the times of the Maccabees and various of the prophets.

The faithful Jews looked to God for their strength and looked to the Temple in Jerusalem. From his throne in heaven, mirrored in the Temple worship, God judges the just and the unjust and keeps careful watch over the works of men.

The punishment of the wicked is colorfully described, with a reference to Sodom and Gomorrah (Gn 19:23-24), towns which were destroyed by fire and brimstone.

The allusion to the "cup" is a traditional symbol of the cup or lot destined for each individual. Our Lord used it during the agony in the Garden of Gethsemane, "My Father, if it is possible, let this cup pass from me; yet, not as I will, but as you will" (Mt 26:39).

For the Christian, this confidence is based on the power of Christ, the Son of God, to protect us. "For there is one God and one mediator between God and men — the man Christ Jesus, who gave himself as a ransom for all" (1 Tm 2:5-6).

Christ is the great and only Priest of the New Testament:

"We have such a high priest, who has taken his seat at the right hand of the throne of Majesty... He has obtained so much more excellent a ministry as he is mediator of a better covenant, enacted on better promises" (Heb 8:1, 6).

"How much more will the blood of Christ, who through the eternal Spirit offered himself unblemished to God, cleanse our consciences from dead works to worship the living God. For this reason he is the mediator of a new covenant" (Heb 9:14-15).

The Christian martyrs are the heroes and heroines of the Church who expressed their confidence in Christ's promises of eternal life so completely, that they were willing to give their lives in witness. The liturgy uses this psalm in their office, the Common of One Martyr.

PSALM 12: *"Help, Lord, for no one loyal remains..."*

Nothing can disrupt a small town like vicious gossip, and even Jerusalem, not large by our standards, could have felt the scourge of such trouble-makers. In Psalm 12, almost all of the severe troubles are ascribed to sins of the tongue.

St. James goes to great length in his epistle (3:1-12) to warn about the disruptions it can cause in a small Christian community. He says that we put a bit in a horse's mouth to control it, rudders to steer great ships. Yet small as these things are, they have great power.

He says the same thing about the tongue. We use speech to praise God and then curse our fellows. It is a powerful instrument that can be used for good or evil. "If anyone does not fall short in speech, he is a perfect man, able to bridle his whole body also" (v. 2).

So the psalmist cries out in near despair that no one remains loyal and that it seems as if the faithful have vanished from the earth. He demands graphic punishment — cut off the deceitful and boasting lips and tongues — not for vengeance but so that God's justice may be available for all.

Then the Lord speaks, promising to grant safety to those who long for it, and listening to the needy and the weak whose groans he hears. Those who are praying can exult in the certitude that God's promises will be fulfilled, that they are more precious than fire-tried gold and silver. The boastful and the arrogant will remain until the end, plaguing the just, but the word of God is sure to triumph.

The "word of God" always reminds the Christian who uses this psalm, or any other with like expression, that Jesus Christ is the Word of God. The prologue to St. John's Gospel (1:1-18) contains a sublime proclamation of this truth and a vigorous meditation on it.

Origen remarks to Heraclides:

"His Word is the son of God, God and man, through whom all things are made, God according to the spirit, man inasmuch as He was born of Mary."

The "word of God" as a teaching instrument sustains Christians as they travel like pilgrims through the trials of life. The Father "willed to give us birth by the word of truth that we may be a kind of firstfruits of his creatures" (Jm 1:18).

St. Vincent of Lerins writes:

"He is the true and genuine Catholic who loves the truth of God, who loves the Church, who loves the Body of Christ, who esteems divine religion and the Catholic Faith above everything else" (*First Instruction*, #20).

In his *Rule*, St. Benedict of Nursia, the founder of Western monasticism, puts it quite bluntly, "Utter truth from the heart and mouth."

PSALM 13: *"How long, Lord? Will you utterly forget me?"*

With the prevailing philosophy of reward for good deeds and punishment for evil deeds in the immediate "now," sickness and death carry a heavy connotation. There seems little explanation but that they are divinely sent punishment.

Here the sick person is troubled more by God's seeming abandonment of him to the illness and the fact that his enemies will conclude that his virtuous living was not pleasing to God.

The sleep of death was joyless to the Israelite, but the Christian praying this psalm has the certitude of the Resurrection of Jesus that eternal light will be granted. For us, death is a *natalitia*, a birthday to eternal life and love. With Christ we can exclaim, "I have overcome the world!"

The psalm concludes with the conviction that the writer will triumph and be able to cry out, "How good our God has been to me!" This confidence in God, the virtue of hope, sustains the just person in all times of crisis.

St. Paul wrote, "May the God of hope fill you with all joy and peace in believing, so that you may abound in hope by the power of the Holy Spirit" (Rm 15:13). Relying on this hope, we can read, "I will rather boast most gladly of my weaknesses, in order that the power of Christ may dwell with me. Therefore I am content with weakness, insults, hardships, persecutions and constraints for the sake of Christ; for when I am weak, then I am strong" (2 Cor 12:9-10).

An anonymous tract dated from the early second century and attributed to Barnabas says in the first chapter:

"The Lord has given us three basic doctrines: hope for eternal life, the beginning and end of our faith; justice, the beginning and end of righteousness; and love, which bears cheerful and joyous witness to the works of righteousness."

PSALM 14: *"Fools say in their hearts..."*

There is no place for the lukewarm in the mind of the author of Psalm 14. He writes with deep conviction and clear-cut definitions in his mind. Deeply religious, he considers the ultimate in foolishness to be the practical atheist.

For him there are the fools on one side and the just, or the community of the just, on the other. Because the fool despises God, the actions that spring from his depraved condition are "loathsome and corrupt." Our Lord used the figure of the good and bad tree. The good tree bears good fruit; the rotten tree bears bad fruit. "So, by their fruits you will know them" (Mt 7:20).

When St. Paul speaks of the universal bondage of sin, he quotes this psalm: "There is no one who understands, there is no one who seeks God. All have gone astray; all are alike worthless; there is not one who does good, there is not even one" (Rm 3:11-12).

St. Paul reacts to this gloomy assessment with the teaching of grace and life through Jesus Christ: "Where sin increased, grace overflowed all the more, so that, as sin reigned, grace also might reign through justification for eternal life through Jesus Christ, our Lord" (Rm 5:20-21).

The wicked devour the poor; they war against the just, but God, examining them from heaven, is not unmindful of their evil ways and how the good suffer. "But the poor have the Lord as their refuge."

The psalm concludes with a prayer of confident longing that God will strike forth from Zion to deliver Israel. He will come like a mighty, conquering hero to correct all wrongs with true justice.

And we feel confident that he continues that protection for the People of God:

"God has called man, and still calls him, to be united with his whole being in perpetual communion with himself in the immortality of the Divine Life. This victory has been gained for us by the Risen Christ, who by his own death freed man from death... By entering into the Paschal mystery and being made like Christ in death, (we) will also look forward, strong in hope, to the Resurrection" (Vatican II, *Gaudium et Spes*, #20).

The Christian, worshipping God in spirit and in truth, realizes that truth and holiness cannot survive without God's help. Therefore, we beg God to safeguard his Church and make us truly happy in proclaiming the Good News.

As we enter the post cold-war era, it will be interesting to see how historians will evaluate the legacy of atheism that reached its apex in the Soviet Union when Communism dominated everything.

Sir Arnold Lunn pointed out in 1925, that "it is significant that freedom of speech and action has never been more ruthlessly suppressed than in the one great European nation which has officially adopted atheism as the religion of the state" (*Now I See*).

Thomas Merton did well to remind us that "it is in Christ and in his Spirit that true freedom is found, and the Church is his Body, living by his Spirit." And he adds, "Since I am a Catholic I believe that my Church guarantees me the highest spiritual freedom" (*Conjectures of a Guilty Bystander*, pt. 2).

PSALM 15: *"Lord who may abide in your tent?"*

The Temple in Jerusalem was not like a Church, open many hours and available to anyone who wants to enter. It was a sacred place and only those judged to be true Israelites were admitted. Psalm 15 is a "liturgy of entrance."

The question is most logical. "Who may enter your tent?" is a reference to the sanctuary carried about by the Israelites during the Exodus. "Who may dwell on your holy mountain?" is an extension of the question, for those who lived in Jerusalem, Mt. Zion, were expected to reflect the nearness of the Temple in their daily lives.

So the catalogue of virtues in vv. 2-5 shows that the righteous person must have inner integrity as well as ritual purity. What is recommended is a social virtue which takes into account the health and well-being of the community.

Slander, defamation, false oaths, bribery and physical abuse can cause so much heartache in small communities that they hurt far beyond the apparent outward harm.

The need for good companionship and the avoidance of the company of the wicked is a frequent theme throughout the Bible. Today we see it as "peer pressure," especially among the young. But at all ages, the old saying is true, "I can tell who you are from the friends you keep." It was said of President Grover Cleveland, "We love him for the enemies he has made."

The problem of usury in the Old Testament was a serious one. To demand interest from a fellow Israelite was to make a profit from his need (Ex 22:24-25). It was a sin against the extended family in general, and only in exceptional circumstances was it permitted. Before the invention of money, loans were made in kind, and interest rates went anywhere from 33% to 75% (John L. McKenzie, *Dictionary of the Bible*, p. 518).

The psalm concludes with the assertion that those who practice this manner of life shall remain firmly in God. The author of the Epistle to the Hebrews alludes to this psalm when he speaks of the gratitude we should have since God has brought us into intimate contact with himself in the New Covenant. "You have approached Mount Zion and the city of the living God, the heavenly Jerusalem" (Heb 12:22).

The Christian praying this psalm is saying, in effect, "Help me do what is right and speak whatever is the truth." There is in it the echo of the Beatitudes, such as "Blessed are the clean of heart for they will see God" (Mt 5:8). It is because of this that the Church uses this psalm in the Common of Pastors and the Common of Holy Men in *The Liturgy of the Hours*.

PSALM 16: *"Keep me safe, O God"*

Confidence in God, the Supreme Good, is the theme that runs through Psalm 16 and the writer encourages us to take refuge in the Lord, the ultimate defender of the just.

The author, possibly a Levite, looks at the confused state of religion, especially as the Israelites took possession of Canaan. The multitude of local gods and goddesses of fertility, planting, harvesting and the like, were appealing to a nomadic people who now had to settle into an agricultural mode.

The scorn for this false worship is obvious in phrases such as "They multiply their sorrows who court other gods" and "Accursed are all who delight in them," and even to naming them. *Nomen est omen* ("A name is a sign, or omen") said the ancients, so the Baals and Astartes had to go nameless.

The psalmist turns to the very first temporal benefit that God has bestowed, the pleasant land portioned out to the Jews (cf. Joshua, cc. 13-19) and which they were to pass on in their families as an everlasting inheritance.

The second part of this poem is a sublime reference to the spiritual delights of serving the Lord. God is intimately close to the faithful person and always a trusted counselor.

The Apostles used verse 10, "You shall not let your faithful servant see corruption," as a prophecy of the Resurrection of Christ. Both St. Peter (Ac 2:24-32) and St. Paul (Ac 13:35-37) used this quotation, following the Septuagint translation. This psalm is also used in the liturgy of Holy Week and the Octave of Easter.

Abbot Columba Marmion, O.S.B., comments in this way:

"St. Paul says that Christ was 'in all things to be made like his brethren' (Heb 2:17); even in his burial, Jesus is one of us. They bound the body of Jesus, says St. John, 'in linen cloths, with the spices, as the manner of the Jews is to bury' (Jn 19:40). But the body of Jesus, united to the Word, was not 'to suffer corruption.' He was to remain scarcely three days in the tomb; by his own power, Jesus was to come forth victorious over death, resplendent with life and glory..." (*Christ in His Mysteries*, pp. 283-4).

Pope St. Gregory the Great has an interesting passage on "doubting Thomas" and the Resurrection:

"The disbelief of Thomas has done more for our faith than the faith of all the other disciples... As he touches Christ and is won over to belief, every doubt is cast away and our faith is strengthened. The disciple who doubted, but then felt Christ's wounds, becomes a witness to the reality of Christ's Resurrection. Touching Christ he cried out, 'My Lord and My God!'" (*Homily #26*).

PSALM 17: *"Hear, Lord, my plea for justice..."*

The petitioner begs God's help in the midst of the plots of cruel enemies. He asks God to see his innocence and therefore, in justice, come to save him.

So confident is he of his righteousness that he can say that

God has tried him by fire and searched his way of life and that he has not faltered in his religious duties.

The beautiful figures of speech in vv. 6-9 have been used in Christian prayer in many ways. "Show your wonderful love" is a tender appeal to the all-powerful Yahweh. "Keep me as the apple of your eye" reflects the intimate nature of God's strong love. "Hide me in the shadow of your wings" probably referred to the wings of the cherubim who surrounded the throne of God. However, it also evokes images of the mother hen guiding her chicks.

As the song progresses, it turns to look at the insidious enemies who are plotting evil. In their arrogance, they are ready to exult in the defeat of the one praying as if it were already accomplished. A familiar figure for an enemy is the lion on the prowl. In this case, the enemy seems to prosper in all ways with prosperity overflowing into his family.

The final verse simply expresses the complete confidence of the just person who will be filled with the presence of God, and, as a consequence, be assured of victory. The phrase "when I awake" could indicate an overnight stay in the Temple or perhaps, better, a night prayer by anyone in serious trouble.

For the Christian, this psalm was applied to the martyrs who were so confident in God's judgment in their favor that their trust extended even beyond the grave. They were indeed tried by fire, sometimes literally, but while the world seemed to triumph over them, they were awakened to the divine presence in the heavenly kingdom, an eternal reward.

St. Ambrose wrote:

> The world its terrors urged in vain;
> They recked not of the body's pain;
> One step, and holy death made sure
> The life that ever shall endure.
>
> (*Christo profusum sanguinem*)

The mystery of Christ's Passion and Death, he who certainly was "The Just Man," is explained by the author of Hebrews in this way, "In the days when he was in the flesh, he offered prayers and supplications with loud cries and tears to the One who was able to save him from death, and he was heard because of his reverence. Son though he was, he learned obedience from what he suffered" (Heb 5:7-8).

In commenting on this psalm, St. Augustine writes, "Lord, you help those who turn to you. You redeem us so that we may come to you."

PSALM 18: *"I love you, Lord, my strength..."*

Thanksgiving is the theme running throughout this psalm. It applauds the work of God in conquering his people's enemies as well as his care for the individual just man. In 2 Samuel 22, this psalm is repeated with some interesting variations.

The opening verses praise God as deliverer under several typical biblical symbols — the rock upon which the warrior can look down on his enemies, the fortress that is impregnable, the shield to protect and the horn, a symbol of the bull's mighty power as well as a striking fertility symbol. Zechariah uses it when he proclaims, "He has raised up a horn for our salvation within the house of David his servant" (Lk 1:69).

Judging the battles in which the Israelite might be involved from God's point of view, the theophany described in the next section is awesome to repeat. The breakers of death — the cords of Sheol — earthquakes, lightning, storms — all symbolize the mighty power God has at his command. In describing the seven trumpets of God's wrath the Book of Revelation uses this imagery (Rv 11:19).

In the nineteenth century, Robert Grant captured this mood in a hymn used in *The Liturgy of the Hours:*

> O worship the king, all glorious above;
> O gratefully sing his power and his love;
> Our shield and defender, the ancient of days,

Pavilioned in splendor, and girded with praise.
O tell of his might, O sing of his grace;
Whose robe is the light, whose canopy space;
His chariots of wrath the deep thunder-clouds form,
And dark is his path on the wings of the storm.

(*O Worship the Lord*, vv. 1-2)

The cherubim, angels of a high order in the spiritual hierarchy, are mentioned about 75 times in the Old Testament. They are associated with the omnipotence of God and were represented in the Temple in Jerusalem. The letter to the Hebrews, after describing the Holy of Holies in the Temple, states, "Above it (the Ark of the Covenant) were the cherubim of glory overshadowing the place of expiation" (Heb 9:5).

King David acknowledges that he could not have triumphed over Saul, or any of his enemies, without the saving help of Yahweh. There is the tender and humble admission, "He rescued me because he loves me."

For David this was a reward for his faithful following of God's law and plan. "Toward the faithful you are faithful; to the honest you are honest; toward the sincere, sincere; but to the perverse you are devious."

David exults in his physical skills, but these, too, are a gift from God. He has feet swift as a deer's, well trained hands and an arm that can bend a bow of bronze — that is, a bow that is difficult to use, but shoots an arrow much farther than an ordinary one made of wood.

The vengeance worked on various enemies, fellow Israelites who called on God in vain because they were faithless, and foreigners who despised the God of the Hebrews, was a vindication of the justice of God in his dealings with mankind.

The Fathers of the Church interpreted the other nations mentioned as referring to the great Gentile world which would accept the divinity of Christ, "the Son of David." His rule would extend geographically and qualitatively in a way undreamed of by all the writers of the Old Testament.

St. Paul could exult, "Therefore I will praise you among the Gentiles and sing praises to your name" (Rm 15:9). St. Gregory the Great would write,

> That which the prophet-king of old
> Had in mysterious verse foretold,
> Is now accomplished while we see
> God ruling nations from a tree.
>
> *(Vexilla Regis Prodeunt)*

St. Augustine writes a fitting note in his commentary on this psalm:

"Lord, You help us as we move towards you. Grant that we may never attribute to our own wisdom the fact that we are converted to you. Neither let us ever attribute to our strength the fact that we actually reach you. In this way we will avoid being repelled by you who resist the proud."

PSALM 19: *"The heavens declare the glory of God…"*

Two psalms have been joined together to give us the one we here number 19. The first one, vv. 1-7, is an ancient one more than likely dating back to David himself. The second is a late addition that expands the beauty of the first.

The cosmic beauty of the heavens declare the glory of God both by the order demonstrated and by the magnificence of power displayed. Day following day, night following night proclaim the purpose of the Creator in his works. The soundless procession of days and seasons actually speak in a loud voice the message of divine providence, God caring for us.

The psalmist borrows from the ancient Babylonian myth of the Sun God who is portrayed as a judge. He sees everything in his constant journey through the sky. "Nothing escapes" its vision. But it is God (El) who "pitches a tent" for the sun, who is the Creator of that mighty force. Christians saw an extension of this in the words, "But for you who fear my name, there will arise the sun of justice with its healing rays" (Ml 3:20). This "sun of justice" is none other than Christ, the Lord.

The joyful images of the bridegroom coming forth from the bridal chamber and the athlete who rejoices in running the race give a brilliant note of joy to this section. St. Paul used this allusion to great effect with his statement, "Do you not know that the runners in the stadium all run in the race, but only one wins the prize? Run so as to win" (1 Cor 9:24).

The first section praises God, the author of creation. The second section praises God as the author of Israel's Law. There is the same note of joy that God could care so much that he would give the Torah, the Law, the direction that his people needed to adore and serve him as he wished.

Vv. 8-10 give an alternate name to the Law and then an appreciative follow-up. "The Law is perfect... refreshing. The decree is trustworthy... giving wisdom. The precepts are right... rejoicing the heart."

The Law of God is an immense treasure which enriches the race to whom it has been revealed. To observe God's Law brings a reward more valuable than a hoard of gold. Unknown faults and willful transgressions can both be avoided by keeping the Law, leading to external and internal redemption.

In our Christian liturgy both sections of this psalm are used extensively. It is used during the Easter Season, on the Feasts of the Ascension and the Annunciation. In the Office both of Virgins and Holy Women it is applied to them as persons who have profited from observing the will of God.

For the Feasts of the Apostles it was a natural for the Church to use the verse, "Yet their report goes forth through all the earth, their message, to the ends of the world." It was an obvious application and for some authors, a prophetic interpretation of these lines.

If the joyful observance of the Law of the Old Testament was so powerful to save, how much more should the joy be of observing life in Christ in the grace, peace and justice won for us by him.

This is a constant theme in St. Paul's epistles (e.g., Rm 6 and 7).

For the Christian, St. Ephrem, the fourth century deacon, expressed it succinctly: "We have had your treasure hidden with us ever since we received baptismal grace; it grows ever richer at your sacramental table. Teach us to find our joy in your favor, Lord…" (*Third Letter*).

PSALM 20: *"The Lord answer you in time of distress…"*

Israel was encircled in biblical times, as now, by an overwhelming number of fierce enemies. In Psalm 20 the people pray for the victory of the king as he goes off to battle. God, who dwelt in heaven and was also present in the Temple on Mt. Zion in Jerusalem, is asked to remember all the sacrifices and offerings made to him in the Temple.

"The Lord grant your every prayer" is obviously a prayer for victory and the people express confidence that the banners of triumph will be raised at the end of this particular war. They are confident that God will bless his Anointed, the King, with the strength and courage bestowed by God.

The typical parallel is drawn between the horses and chariots of their well appointed enemies and the strength that comes from the Lord. No one can fight the Lord successfully, so the king will win.

In Christian usage, Christ is the Anointed One. "And it shall be that everyone shall be saved who calls upon the name of the Lord" (Ac 2:21). As St. Bernard remarked, "The name of Jesus is honey in the mouth, music to the ear, a cry of gladness in the heart!" (*On the Canticle of Canticles*).

The sacrifices and oblations of the Old Testament have been replaced with the perfect sacrifice of Christ on the Cross and made present for us in each offering of the sacrifice of the Mass. Christ "entered once for all into the sanctuary, not with the blood of goats and calves but with his own blood, thus obtaining eternal redemption" (Heb 9:12).

St. Alphonsus Liguori comments on this fact:

"Jesus Christ has paid the price of our redemption in the Sacrifice of the Cross. But he wishes that the fruit of the ransom given should be applied to us in the Sacrifice of the Altar, being himself in both the chief sacrificer, who offers the same victim, namely his own body and blood," with the only difference being the former was a bloody offering and the latter is an unbloody one ("The Sacrifice of Jesus Christ," in *The Holy Eucharist*).

PSALM 21: *"Lord, the king finds joy in your power..."*

Psalm 21 is a royal psalm that complements and extends the thoughts of Psalm 20. The victories of the king are actually the victories of Yahweh so the power that sustains the king is divine. Not only did the king represent the whole nation, he was a special instrument of God to show God's justice and righteousness to the nations.

Such powerful phrases as "You have granted him his heart's desire," and "You did not refuse the prayer of his lips," were made for personal prayer as well as liturgical prayer, and in Christian prayer they are used often in the offices for the saints.

"He asked life and you gave it to him, length of days forever" was true in a dynastic way, and was fulfilled completely in Christ, the Son of David. This is acknowledged joyfully, even exultantly, in the canticles in the first chapter of St. Luke's Gospel, the *Magnificat*, the *Benedictus*, and by extension, the *Nunc Dimittis*.

The blessings that are acknowledged in the first half of the psalm are reversed for the enemies of the king in the last half of the psalm. The Israelites felt that the military was a necessity to preserve the nation. Even at the time of Christ, most Israelites felt the Messiah would be a savior who would overcome the Romans with a triumphant military campaign.

From the greeting by the angelic choir at the birth of Christ (Lk 2:14) to the usual greeting that Christ used after the Resurrection, "Peace!" (Mt 28:9, Lk 24:36, Jn 20:19-26), the ideal and goal of peace was a central theme in Christianity.

Pope St. Clement I, at the end of the first century A.D. wrote to the Corinthians, "Hasten toward the goal of peace set before us from the very beginning." In the next century, Clement of Alexandria in *Christ the Educator* wrote, "We are educated not for war but for peace." For him, peace and love were "blood sisters."

In *Gaudium et Spes*, the *Pastoral Constitution on the Church in the Modern World*, from Vatican II, we read that "The Church condemns total war" (#80) and adds, "In order to build peace, the causes of war, especially injustice, must be rooted out" (#83).

The Sign of Peace in the Eucharistic Liturgy should help us rededicate ourselves to the cause of peace at each Mass. We find this same devotion to the cause of peace in such recent figures as Dorothy Day, Catherine de Hueck Doherty and Mother Teresa of Calcutta.

PSALM 22: *"My God, my God, why have you abandoned me?"*

"And at three o'clock Jesus cried out in a loud voice, '*Eloi, Eloi, lama sabachthani?*' which is translated, 'My God, my God, why have you forsaken me?'" (Mk 15:34). The use of the opening verse of this psalm on Good Friday has made the whole psalm a vivid expression of the theology of that drama.

The psalm itself is divided into three unequal sections, of personal suffering, the triumph of God's final help, and the expression of appreciation for the deliverance. It may have been composed in sections or may even have been independent poems at one time.

There is no doubt that the original or first section is the lament of a person who has suffered bitterly from ill health, psychological strain and the attacks of enemies. It is a plea for help in a desperate situation. It will end, of course, with the exultation of success.

The fact that Our Lord used the verse in his own native language, shows that Christ identified with the individual sufferer. People may know prayers in various languages, but when we feel most desperate, "Everyone prays in his own tongue." There was no deeper degradation that Christ could have suffered. "I am a worm and no man, scorned... despised... mocked."

The enemies are fierce, like bulls from Bashan, a cattle-raising area across the Jordan. They are like roaring lions or a pack of wild dogs. They expect him to die. Verses 17b-18a have been translated, "They have pierced my hands and my feet; they have numbered all my bones." While this verse is not quoted in the New Testament it has inspired many sermons on the Passion of Christ.

God did not turn his face away but listened when the innocent sufferer cried out. This then is the occasion of a great thanksgiving banquet. Thus, Our Lord's words from the cross are not a cry of despair but a cry from the depths of his heart and soul with the assurance that God will intervene and that there will be a final triumph.

Verse 30 offers some interesting observations. "All who have gone down into the dust will kneel in homage." This seems to indicate a growing understanding of life after death; it is better than the idea of death as a bitter end, a final punishment, or even the shadowy existence of disembodied souls wandering around out there somewhere.

The prophecy of the Suffering Servant of Yahweh so graphically portrayed in Isaiah 53 is seen fulfilled in the Passion and Death of Christ, and this psalm is a fitting companion to the passage in Isaiah.

Verse 19, "They divide my garments among them and for my clothing they cast lots" is recalled in Mt 27:35. Verse 9 is alluded to in Mt 27:43: "He trusted in God; let him deliver him now if he wants him. For he said, 'I am the Son of God.'" There is a parallel use in the Gospels of Mark and Luke and an indication in St. John (19:24) that he also understood this psalm as applying to Christ.

It would be impossible to list all the great art, literature and music that the Passion has inspired through the ages. However, the *Stabat Mater* is a good example:

> Jesus, Lord, condemned, defiled,
> May we, too, be meek and mild
> As we tread your holy way...
> Life eternal, death defiant,
> Bowed his head — the world was silent,
> Through his death came life anew...
>
> Jacopone da Todi (1306)

PSALM 23: *"The Lord is my shepherd..."*

One of the best-loved psalms, one that is used in a wide variety of liturgical settings, Psalm 23 demonstrates God's providential care under the figure of a shepherd and a host, both with a background of Exodus imagery.

If kings in ancient times were complimented by being compared to a good shepherd, it is no wonder that the role of the shepherd would be elevated to describe God's loving care. The figure is very familiar in Old Testament texts but probably reaches its fullest development in Christ's application of it to himself: "I am the good shepherd" (Jn 10:1-18). In St. John's vision of heaven we read, "For the Lamb who is in the center of the throne will shepherd them and lead them to springs of life-giving water and God will wipe away every tear from their eyes" (Rv 7:17).

The shepherd provides what the sheep need — food, water, safety and attention. No matter how difficult the terrain, how unfamiliar the path, the knowledgeable shepherd makes the right decisions for his flock.

The rod or "crook" is there to provide protection by warding off dangers. The staff is there to lean on, to offer support. This is a very comforting use of symbolism.

Then the scene suddenly changes. After Yahweh has led the people through the desert into the Promised Land, there is a celebration of thanksgiving. Now God is seen as the host providing for his guests. The enemies are kept outside, banned and only able to witness the festivities from afar without participating.

The anointing with oil, a well-established practice in both Old and New Testament times, signaled joy at the reception of the guest and the opportunity to refresh him. In Christian devotion, the symbolism reached its climax when Our Lord was anointed at Bethany in preparation for his death (Mt 26:6-13; Jn 12:1-8), an act anticipated by his anointing in the house of Simon the Pharisee (Lk 7:36-50).

This psalm is used in funeral liturgies since it announces the transition from this time of pilgrimage into the Promised Land of heaven. There Christ will be the host at the banquet of life. St. Augustine, in commenting on this psalm, emphasizes the return from exile theme: "Driven out of paradise by you and exiled in a distant land, I cannot return by myself unless you, O Lord, come to meet me in my wandering. My return is based on hope in your mercy during all of my earthly life. My only hope, the only source of confidence and the only solid promise is your mercy."

For Holy Communion, the figure of the banquet is important. St. Thomas Aquinas salutes it with these words, "O sacred banquet, in which Christ is received, the memory of his Passion is renewed, the soul is filled with grace and a pledge of future glory is given to us."

The apostles and bishops have been saluted as shepherds so often in Christian literature that it is difficult to choose just one example. Perhaps Dante's tribute to the Pope will suffice: "You have the New Testament and the Old Testament and the Shepherd of the Church to guide you; let this be enough for your salvation" (*Divine Comedy*, "Paradiso" 5).

PSALM 24: *"The earth is the Lord's and all it holds..."*

Psalm 24 is an entry song, used in various liturgies as the procession approached the Temple gates. It was used in processions with the Ark of the Covenant from which God ruled, invisibly. It was meant to be an occasion of great joy or triumph.

It recalled the Lord leading the Israelites through the desert during the years of the Exodus. His enemies were their enemies and through them he won victories. At length, he led them into the Promised Land, a supreme act of triumph.

There was no mistaking the God who brought them with him. All the wonders of the created world were the work of his hands. The ancient view of the world was that of a fairly flat earth, firmly anchored on pillars that rose over the raging waters of the abyss. Their God had put all this in order, bringing calm into the chaos.

Then the psalmist asks who can approach this Supreme Being. The clean of hand and pure of heart were those whose consciences were clear and whose intentions were spiritual. This idea was used by Christ in the Beatitudes, "Blessed are the clean of heart for they will see God" (Mt 5:8).

The worshipper must have nothing to do with idols, false gods which seemed to abound in Canaan. The true believer must also be a person who did not swear false oaths. As in medieval societies, the sanctity of oaths was a civil as well as a religious standard. The Spanish, for instance, recognized that when Luther called for the abolition of oaths and vows, he was attacking the very basis of their society.

"Seeking the face of God" was a biblical call to worship, first at Shechem, Shiloh, Bethel and then in Jerusalem on Mt. Zion. It also included a spiritual conversion that was necessary to make ritual meaningful.

The concluding section takes on the aspect of a triumphal march after a great victory. "The Lord of hosts is the king of glory," the very one who is saluted as Creator in the opening verses. The gates are to swing open for him and the towers are to bow down before him. It is a colorful exultation. The call of the prophet Isaiah took place, in vision, in such a triumphant scene (Is 6:1-7).

Psalm 24 is very popular with Christian liturgists and so it can be used as an Invitatory call to prayer in the Office. It is used throughout the Church year for such varied occasions as Holy Saturday, the Easter Season, the Common Office for the Blessed Virgin Mary, the Dedication of Churches, and so forth.

The reason is obvious. Christ is the King of Glory who enters into mankind's history as the Son of Mary. He is the King who won Life for his people on Calvary, the first-born from the dead on Easter Sunday and the one who leads us triumphantly into heaven. As St. Irenaeus put it, "Christ opened heaven for us in the manhood he assumed."

Christ's entry into the world through the Blessed Mother is saluted by St. Cyril of Alexandria:

"This is the doctrine which strict orthodoxy everywhere prescribes. Thus shall we find the holy Fathers to have held. So they made bold to call the holy virgin Theotokos (God-bearer, i.e. Mother of God). Not as though the nature of the Word or his godhead had its beginning from the holy virgin, but forasmuch as his holy body, endued with a rational soul, was born of her, to which body also the Word was personally (hypostatically) united, on this account he is said to have been born after the flesh" (*First Letter to Nestorius*).

On a practical note, when the Christians of Corinth had scruples about eating meat that had been sacrificed to idols, St. Paul quoted this psalm, "Eat anything sold in the market without raising questions of conscience, for 'the earth and its fullness are the Lord's'" (1 Cor 10:25-26).

PSALM 25: *"I wait for you, O Lord..."*

The scholars call this an acrostic psalm since each verse begins with successive letters of the Hebrew alphabet. It is a combination of lamentation, cries for mercy and expressions of hope based on God's kindness and constancy.

The expression "to wait on the Lord," has the idea of patiently waiting for God to notice our needs and of being ready to react to his direction. The "ladies in waiting" in European courts are an example of being present to wait for whatever use the queen might need or want.

Therefore, no one can be disgraced who waits for God's inspiration, rather than rushing precipitously into action. In pleading for God's active direction, the psalmist celebrates the ageless compassion and love God has always demonstrated.

Instead of the usual protestations of innocence, the poet acknowledges his sinfulness and begs for forgiveness. The sins and the stupidity of one's youth should be overlooked "because I am alone and afflicted." This could be interpreted "I am an only child," a tragedy that would stand out in a society that was founded on strong and extended family relationships. The terms "brother" and "sister" had a far greater and wider significance than our very narrow, biological definition. In fact, to express our definition some extra words had to be added, such as "brothers of the same womb."

The final verse, "Redeem Israel, God, from all its distress" might well have been an antiphon chanted between each verse. Some modern hymns make good use of this device. Father Lucien Deiss, C.S.Sp., for instance, excels in this in such pieces as "Have Mercy O Lord, Have Mercy on Us!"

In Christian use, this is an expression of the virtue of hope relying on the infinite goodness and kindness of God for the forgiveness of sins, the help of God's grace and life everlasting. This hope is reinforced through Christ's merciful and saving act on Calvary.

St. Paul reminds us:

"We boast in the hope of the glory of God. Not only that but we even boast of our afflictions, knowing that affliction produces endurance, and endurance, proven character, and proven character, hope; and hope does not disappoint, because the love of God has been poured out into our hearts through the Holy Spirit that has been given to us" (Rm 5:2-5).

St. Cyprian tells us:

"We must endure and persevere if we are to attain the truth

and freedom we have been allowed to hope for. Faith and hope are the very meaning of our being Christians, but if faith and hope are to bear fruit, patience is necessary" (*On the Virtue of Patience*).

To hope in time of affliction requires patience, as St. Francis de Sales also notes:

"Be patient with the big afflictions that may come, but also endure the things that accompany them and the accidental circumstances. Many people would be willing to accept trials if it didn't inconvenience them!" (*Introduction to the Devout Life*, Pt. 3, ch. 3).

PSALM 26: *"Grant me justice, Lord…"*

The protestations of innocence that are a part of so many psalms, and start this one, sometimes seem an arrogant proclamation of self-righteousness. On the contrary, they are a legitimate denial of guilt, particularly for one who expected to be judged on grounds of legal purity. For the Christian, this must be elevated to the heights of moral whole-heartedness, of inner conversion and repentance.

The psalmist boldly depicts his ritual purity by comparing the actions of himself and his friends with the "company of evildoers," the deceivers and hypocrites. In his deep-felt opposition to hypocrisy, Christ certainly echoed these statements in his frequent contests with the scribes and Pharisees. In fact, our language has the word "pharisaical" to describe such behavior.

The heart of this moving psalm is in vv. 6-8, used at the Lavabo (the washing of hands) in the Tridentine Rite Mass of the Catholic Church. To wash one's hands in preparation for entering God's service is a ritual act that expresses the liturgical movement of cleansing, purification and preparation.

The psalmist sees it for what it is, an external rite which takes its meaning from the liturgical significance. His love for the Temple is what gives life and meaning to his actions. Anything else makes ritual an empty, perhaps an insulting, religious activity. In

Shakespeare's words, "My words fly up, my thoughts remain below; words without thoughts never to heaven go" (*Hamlet*, Act III, Scene III).

The last verses repeat with sensitive differences the thoughts of the opening ones. The evildoers this time are the violent and those who take bribes. Because the psalmist walks without blame before God, he can expect to stand on level ground, i.e., safe from the danger of tripping and falling, and to take his place in many of the Temple festivities.

St. Paul introduces his words to the Ephesians with like sentiments. "Blessed be the God and Father of our Lord Jesus Christ, who has blessed us in Christ with every spiritual blessing in the heavens, as he chose us in him, before the foundation of the world, to be holy and without blemish before him. In love he destined us for adoption to himself through Jesus Christ" (Eph 1:3-5).

Abbot Columba Marmion, O.S.B., uses this same passage from St. Paul to begin his conference "The Divine Plan of our Adoptive Predestination in Jesus Christ." This grace of adoption is a reality that demands total interior conversion to Christ (*Christ the Life of the Soul*, ch. 1).

The beauty of ritual is sometimes mistaken for the liturgy itself. The Second Vatican Council in its *Constitution on the Sacred Liturgy* carefully defines the relationship:

"The liturgy is considered as an exercise of the priestly office of Jesus Christ. In the liturgy the sanctification of man is betokened by signs perceptible to the senses, and is effected in a way which is proper to each of these signs; in the liturgy full public worship is performed by the Mystical Body of Jesus Christ, that is, by the Head and his members" (#7).

Ritual is important as the "perceptible sign" through which the liturgy is made present to us. However, one must never be mistaken for the other.

PSALM 27: *"The Lord is my light and my salvation..."*

The sublime confidence that David has in God is sung here with great clarity. The symbolic use of "light" has lost some of its obvious significance for us since the first thing we are apt to do when we walk into a room is to turn on the lights.

When Jesus said to the scribes and the Pharisees, "I am the light of the world" (Jn 8:12), they grasped immediately what he meant. He was the shining beacon that could lead them to eternal life and light. We acknowledge this when we light votive candles at shrines. It is the most practical way to beautify a place that would otherwise be dark.

So, calling on the Lord as the light and salvation of the believer is a most optimistic way to start a prayer. With the Lord guiding the way, sinners who want to destroy the psalmist will end up being destroyed themselves.

"To seek the face of the Lord" meant going on pilgrimage to a shrine where the Lord's presence was celebrated. There was special safety in being in the Temple among a brotherhood of believers. There the sacrifices of praise and thanksgiving for deliverance could be made.

The enemies are described in v. 12 as "lying and malicious witnesses." The psalmist follows the same type of thinking that St. Paul did: "If God is for us, who can be against us? ... What will separate us from the love of Christ?" (Rm 8:31-35).

The line that has most intrigued Christian devotion is in v. 13: "But I believe that I shall enjoy the Lord's goodness in the land of the living." Literally, this refers to daily living versus life in Sheol. It may be an assurance that the one praying will live to perform his religious duty in the Temple.

However, Christians have applied this psalm to Our Lord's Resurrection including its use on Holy Saturday. Since Christ is the first-born of the dead and we are to share his Resurrection, then it is a prayer for our own salvation: eternal life in the land of those who truly live forever.

St. Augustine has this meditation on Psalm 27:

"Be my helper and do not abandon me. See, I am on your path. I have asked for only one thing from you: to live in your house all the days of my life, to gaze upon your delight and to be protected in your temple. One thing I have asked for, but to attain it I am on your path."

PSALM 28: *"To you, Lord, I call..."*

Typical of psalms that call upon God in times of great need, this lament obviously comes from a heart filled with sorrows. The depth of the distress is obvious in the words, "Do not be deaf to me." We have all experienced times when it seems that God is deaf to any and all of our pleadings.

The petitioner is in the Temple, lifting up his hands toward the Holy of Holies, "your holy place." Praying with hands uplifted was an ancient practice, also recommended by St. Paul, "It is my wish, then, that in every place the men should pray, lifting up holy hands..." (1 Tm 2:8). The earliest Christian art portrays the *orantes*, people with hands lifted up in prayer, or stretched out in the form of a cross.

The psalm then goes on to contrast the works of God with the works of the wicked. Simple justice demands that they be rebuked or punished publicly and immediately, a truly Semitic notion about justice.

Because of the abrupt change in direction, it is presumed that at this point, the priest gave some assurance of God's fidelity. This type of "interruption" may have occurred often in Temple liturgies, but the priest's part is not recorded. It may have been spontaneous.

This new direction is a fervent act of thanksgiving. There is also a simple justice in giving acknowledgment to God for favors. Even Our Lord did this, as, for instance, in the raising of Lazarus. "Father, I thank you for hearing me. I know that you always hear me; but because of the crowd here I have said this, that they may believe that you have sent me" (Jn 11:41).

The conclusion of the psalm is a prayer expressing confidence in God's work among his people and asking for continued help and protection. In fact, the last verse has been incorporated into the *Te Deum*, the hymn of thanksgiving used in *The Liturgy of the Hours*.

Christianity has transferred this Temple-based confidence into the closeness to God found in the New Jerusalem, the Church. The use of this psalm in Easter week is an expression of that confidence and that the Resurrection is proof that God hears the prayers of his Son, "since he lives forever to make intercession" for us (Heb 7:25).

St. Bede the Venerable tells us:

"The deliverance of the children of Israel and their journey to the long-promised land correspond with the mystery of our redemption. We are making our way toward the light of our heavenly home with the grace of Christ leading us and showing us the way" (*Commentary on 1 Peter*).

PSALM 29: *"Give to the Lord, you heavenly beings…"*

One of the oldest of the psalms, the echo of the Canaanite culture that Israel replaced is evident here. The power of the fertility rites, and the idea of "enthroning" a deity, were both prevalent in Canaanite Baal worship.

All the angels of the heavenly court are urged to give the Lord the glory due his name. The descriptions that St. John uses in the Book of Revelation (cf. ch. 4) of the heavenly worship draw heavily from the Psalter and the Prophets.

The main action in this psalm is the image of a severe thunderstorm, heavy with wind and lightning. "The voice of the Lord" repeated seven times suggests the crashing of lightning and the power this evoked. The Canaanites worshipped a thunder god; the God of the Israelites himself is actually the power above the forces of nature.

The thunder over the waters evokes images of the Flood (cf.

Gn cc. 6-9) while the vision of thunder and lightning covering mountains and deserts tells of the awesome power of God.

Only a true nature-poet could give us lines like: "Makes Lebanon leap like a calf and Sirion (Mt. Hermon) like a young bull." It describes what the viewer would see as lightning rolled over the landscape. It might also suggest an earthquake occurring at the same time.

Above all this display of raw power, Yahweh sits enthroned in immovable glory. The poet prays that God will use this might to bless his people with peace.

Because this psalm so glorifies the power of God in nature, the early Christians used this song to glorify the power that God manifests in his supernatural works, especially in the Feasts of Pentecost, Epiphany and the Transfiguration. The voice of the Lord was also heard in the Baptism of Jesus (Mt 4:17).

The conclusion of Pope St. Clement I's *Letter to the Corinthians* contains this passage:

"Lord, you created the world according to the eternal decree now revealed in your works. Faithful through all generations, you are just in judgment, wonderful in power and majesty. You formed your creation with wisdom and established it with prudence. Everything we see proclaims your goodness."

Dante gave us another aspect of the power of God:

"The infinite and ineffable good that is God goes out toward proffered love as a sunbeam meets a mirror. God gives himself in proportion to the love he finds, so that however far our charity extends, eternal power exceeds it" (*Divine Comedy,* "Purgatorio" 15).

PSALM 30: *"I praise you, Lord, for you raised me up..."*

A psalm that began as a lament from a very sick person was developed into a song for the dedication of the Temple. That person had a near fatal illness that brought him to the very gates of death (Sheol, the pit).

He attributes his cure to God and invites all the people to praise God with him. If the illness was a divine punishment, then "divine anger lasts but a moment; divine favor lasts a lifetime."

Complacency was the key to the man's distance from God. It is only too true in the human condition that when things seem to go very well, people just take God for granted. In times of trial and trouble people naturally turn for divine assistance. Here we are warned about this, about letting a distance develop between ourselves and God.

The official theology of the time did not profess individual immortality, as opposed to the popular belief in some ghostly existence, such as the passage about Saul going to the witch of Endor to consult the dead Samuel (1 S 28:7). That accounts for the line, "Does dust give you thanks?"

However, when God does intervene, in a person's life or in the life of a nation, then mourning is changed into dancing, a very joyful aspect of Jewish community living. The psalm ends on this very joyous note.

For Christian usage, this psalm is a true paschal song. The tears of blood that Christ shed on Holy Thursday evening in Gethsemane are turned to a maximum of rejoicing at the Resurrection of Easter dawn. Never was God's power more clearly demonstrated.

That power is also evident in God the Creator's glorious power of giving life, but it is even more glorious in the restoration of life to the soul through the grace of Christ. But as St. Augustine points out, because God has given so freely he now demands that we cooperate with those graces. "God who created us without our cooperation will not save us without our cooperation."

God is everywhere, the theologians tell us, by his essence, his presence and his power. In praying this psalm we say, "Do not turn away from us or we return to dust." Or, as St. Paul remarked to the Athenians in the Areopagus, "For 'In him we live and move and have our being,' as even some of your poets have said" (Ac 17:28).

PSALM 31: *"In you, Lord, I take refuge..."*

The three sections of Psalm 31 are so distinctive that some have speculated that they were originally three separate poems. The lamentations in this psalm are reminiscent of Jeremiah's lament and some think that one has a real dependence on the other. It would depend on which one was chronologically first.

Section one is a typical lament which deplores the existing evils contemporary to the writer. This theme has been popular throughout the history of preaching. The author's references to God as a rock and refuge strongly suggest that the place is Jerusalem.

Verse 6 is familiar since it was used by Christ on the Cross, "Into your hands I commend my spirit" (Lk 23:46). It occurs again at the martyrdom of St. Stephen (Ac 7:59). It is also used repeatedly in the Office of Night Prayer (Compline) in *The Liturgy of the Hours*.

In the second section the psalmist is quite outspoken about his own personal pain — his friends scorn him, he is the object of conspiracy and beset by illness. He has become like a useless, fractured dish, as unimportant as the unremembered dead. He challenges God to be true to his promises to help Israel and the Israelites.

Verse 16, "My times are in your hands," is also familiar. Robert Browning, using the imagery of Jeremiah and Isaiah of the potter and the clay, wrote this verse:

> Our times are in your hand,
> Protect the cup as planned.
> Let age approve of youth
> And death complete the same.

The third section is a beautiful tribute to God who does fulfill his promises more generously and more powerfully than man could possibly imagine. The psalm ends with the simple injunction, "Love the Lord, all you faithful..." the only time this is expressed so directly in the Psalter.

For the Christian, besides its dramatic use in the Passion and Death of Christ, the psalm expresses confidence in God during times of need and the assurance that the love Christ brought to us will make us triumph over fear. "Perfect love casts out all fear" (1 Jn 4:18).

St. Gregory of Nyssa tells us:

"When love has entirely cast out fear, and fear has been transformed into love, then the unity brought by our Savior will be fully realized, for all men will be united with one another through their union with the one Supreme Good" (*On the Song of Songs*, #15).

PSALM 32: *"Happy the sinner whose fault is removed..."*

Classified by the scholars as a "thanksgiving" psalm, Psalm 32 is nevertheless the second of the traditional seven "Penitential Psalms." Forgiveness is certainly cause for thanksgiving for the sinner who has been spared.

The sinner finds himself mired in grief. The images are graphic: the debilitating heat of a desert summer, the threat of flood waters, the senselessness of brute animals who, though powerful, can be tamed with bit and bridle. When looked at calmly and logically, sin is irrational and stupid.

To receive the merciful forgiveness of God, the sinner must first turn to God and confess, acknowledge, his sins. Then he can touch the mercy of God and exult when the Lord no longer imputes sin to him. For the Christian, of course, the merciful Savior provided the Sacrament of Reconciliation for a sure and certain forgiveness. "Receive the Holy Spirit. Whose sins you forgive are forgiven them, and whose sins you retain are retained" (Jn 20:22-23).

When St. Paul describes the faith that is necessary for salvation, he discusses Abraham and quotes this psalm. "Blessed are they whose iniquities are forgiven and whose sins are covered. Blessed is the man whose sin the Lord does not record" (Rm 4:7-8). Note that St. Paul never speaks of "faith alone" and this psalm does not comment on any theories of justification, such as those debated during the Reformation and the Counter-Reformation of the sixteenth century. It is a statement of the reality of sin, repentance and forgiveness.

The relationship between faith and good works (charity) is a subject of Christian writings from the beginning. In the first century of the Christian era, Pope St. Clement I wrote:

"We are not justified by our wisdom, intelligence, piety or any action of ours, however holy, but by faith, the one means by which God has justified man from the beginning.

"But then must we give up good works? Stop practicing Christian love? God forbid! We must be eager and ready for every opportunity to do good and to put our whole heart into it. Even the Creator and Lord of the Universe rejoices in his good works" (*Letter to the Corinthians* #34).

Perhaps only another poet could express the combination of contrition and joy in this psalm. Listen to Francis Thompson in his autobiographical poem:

> I fled Him, down the night and down the days;
> I fled Him, down the arches of the years;
> I fled Him, down the labyrinthine ways
> Of my own mind; and in the midst of tears
> I hid from Him, and under running laughter.
> Up vistaed hopes I sped;
> And shot, precipitated,
> Adown Titanic glooms of chasmèd fears,
> From those strong Feet that followed, followed after.
>
> *The Hound of Heaven*

Then, in this long poetic work, Thompson tells of the story of a pursuing Christ who will pour out his mercy when the sinner lies exhausted from his excesses and who then brings the sinner to the joys of grace.

PSALM 33: *"Rejoice, you just, in the Lord…"*

Considered an "orphan psalm," since it is the only psalm in Book I not attributed "of David," Psalm 33 is a beautiful hymn of praise in honor of the providence of God. In fact, "the Lord (Yahweh)" is addressed thirteen times.

The first section, vv. 1-5, is an outright invitation to praise God for his faithfulness to his creation. "For the Lord's word is true; all his works are trustworthy." Looking at creation from the divine side, God fills the world with goodness, justice and right. Divine providence governs all.

The next two sections are a simple affirmation of the fact that God is the Creator. All the myths of the ancient world proclaimed the trouble their gods had in bringing forth the world and ruling it. Not Yahweh! It takes but a word for him to create. The world as the poet sees it is a simple triple hierarchy: the heavens with their stars (hosts), the cosmic water that surrounds creation, and the firm earth, all established by God. The Lord is master of all this, by a mere word.

Nor is he satisfied with the mere creation of all this earthly beauty. God looks down from heaven, knowing the hearts and consciences of his human creatures. Kings and common people alike are saved by God when they put their complete trust in him.

As an aside, the mention of the horse as useless despite its strength, reflects the guerrilla nature of warfare as practiced in the Palestine of this era. The chariots favored by the Egyptians and other "world powers" of the time were relatively useless in mountainous terrain.

The psalm ends on a positive note with praise for the God who is so worthy of the complete confidence of the people he has chosen for his own. In fact, the last verse has been incorporated into the Christian classic devotion, the *Te Deum*.

For the Christian, the use of "the word" immediately brings to mind the first chapter of St. John's Gospel. "In the beginning was the Word, and the Word was with God, and the Word was

God. He was in the beginning with God. All things came to be through him, and without him nothing came to be. What came to be through him was life" (Jn 1:1-3).

The new hymn we are called to sing is, for the Christian, something far greater than a musical production. As Father C.C. Martindale remarked: "The Christian has become a new creation through the grace of Christ and so we sing a liturgical song in which the worship Christ gave to the Father he continues to give through us."

In praise of the power and providence of God, St. Paul tells us: "Oh, the depth of the riches and wisdom and knowledge of God! How inscrutable are his judgments and how unsearchable his ways! For who has known the mind of the Lord or who has been his counselor? Or has given him anything that he may be repaid? For from him and through him and for him are all things. To him be glory forever" (Rm 11:33-36).

For the ancient Jewish psalmist, it was enough to receive temporal goods and safeguards from God. As St. Augustine reminds us, we see beyond the visible horizon of this creation and look for a greater good:

"Seek what is better than you are so that you can be made better by it. If you desire gold you may or may not obtain it. But you can always turn to God whenever you wish.

"Desire God so that you may have him and then finally you will be really happy. This alone will make you truly happy. Love this; possess this; you can turn to God whenever you wish, without cost" (*On Psalm 32 [33]*).

Speaking of divine providence, St. Francis de Sales writes:

"Do not fear what may happen tomorrow. The same loving Father who cares for you today will care for you tomorrow and every day. Either he will shield you from suffering or he will give you the unfailing strength to bear it. Be at peace, then, and put aside all anxious thoughts and imaginings" (*Introduction to the Devout Life* #30).

PSALM 34: *"I will bless the Lord at all times..."*

In Hebrew, Psalm 34 is an acrostic poem, where each verse begins with the successive letter in the Hebrew alphabet, 22 letters in all. Since one letter is missing, the experts tell us that the last verse was added at a later date to make up the full alphabet.

The title, through a scribal error, attributes this "Of David when he feigned madness before Abimelech..." The Philistine king was actually Achish (1 S 21:11-16).

The first section is a hymn inviting all to praise God for his great mercy to the poor and lowly. The second section is a beautiful act of thanksgiving to God for showing his power to protect true believers. "Look to God that you may be radiant with joy." After suffering and misfortune, when God steps in the joy is complete.

St. Peter uses a variation of v. 9 to urge Christians to have a simple trust in God. "For you have tasted that the Lord is good" (1 P 2:3). Other commentators have used this verse in eucharistic prayers, for where better can we "taste that the Lord is good," or "learn to savor the Lord," as the newer translation states it?

The third section is called "wisdom literature," simple admonitions to students to serve God through good moral actions. In this context St. Peter uses vv. 13-17, one of the longer quotes from the Old Testament to be found in the New (1 P 3:10-12). This includes telling the truth, avoiding lies, guarding the tongue. Compare with "If anyone does not fall short in speech, he is a perfect man..." (Jm 3:2).

The psalmist presumes that even the just will suffer evil and misfortune in this life. What separates the just from the unjust is that the believer has God to turn to for sure and certain help amid the tribulations that go along naturally with the human condition.

St. John applies this even to Christ, certainly sinless, who yet in obedience to God's plan, suffered death on the cross. "For these things happened so that the scripture passage might be fulfilled: 'Not a bone of his shall be broken'" (Jn 19:36).

In many instances, the verb "to fear" can also be translated as "to serve." "I will teach you the fear of the Lord," can mean "I will teach you how to serve the Lord." "The many troubles of the just" are not usually punishment for sin, but may be discipline, a test of faith or an invitation to a higher spirituality by detachment from material things.

For the Christian it can also be a spur to perfection. "We must not overlook an aspect which is inherent in Jesus' whole message of salvation, and also underlies the demands of the Sermon on the Mount. It is: the new eschatological and primordially pure morality of Jesus' disciples, the undivided surrender to God, and the unlimited love of brother, became possible only by God's antici- patory love and by his present work of salvation. Perfection is not only a requirement, it is a gift as well: it is man's answer to God's work which makes man capable of perfection" (Rudolph Schnackenburg, *Christian Existence in the New Testament*, ch. 6).

Perhaps St. Augustine approaches this invitation to perfec- tion a little more realistically:

"Be assured that you can never be perfect in this world un- less you realize that it is impossible for you to be perfect here. Therefore this should be your aim in life: always try your best in doing what you have to do, so that you may reach perfection. Never get tired of trying because there is always room for improvement" (*Commentary on Psalm 33 [34]*).

PSALM 35: *"Oppose, Lord, those who oppose me..."*

The older translation of v. 1, "O Lord, plead my cause against my foes," is more familiar than the new rendition, but the newer expresses more than adequately the rambling and emotional na- ture of this lament.

What frustration the innocent man must feel when he is be- trayed, publicly, by friends. As the old adage has it, "With friends like this I don't need enemies!" The poet knows that he is inno- cent but offers no proof. After all, God is the all-seeing witness who knows his innocence.

The imagery is vivid, that of the hunt, military activity, acute mourning and the courts of law, such as they were. The image of the battle ax, such as used much later in the Qumran scroll on warfare, the pits dug for ambushes and the malicious witnesses who publicly disgrace the author are just a sample of the rage and frustration he feels.

The vindictive tone of the psalm, begging God to heap the same distress and disgrace on his enemies that they have caused the poet, could lead to a wrong conclusion. It is rather a case of a cry for the public vindication that the psalmist feels he deserves, in justice. It is the "eye for an eye" justice, the *lex talionis* (Ex 21:23), taught by the Old Testament.

The rueful way in which the writer describes his grief for his friends' misfortunes, his mourning, praying and fasting for them, is in great contrast to their glee in his apparent downfall. Fasting as a penance for sin and to beg for divine forgiveness and help became a part of Jewish popular religious practices during and after the Exile. Before that it was rare (David begging for his son's life in 2 S 12:16) or it was a reaction of awe and fear over the greatness of God (Moses in Ex 34:27-28).

By the time of the Christian era, it was a very popular devotional practice, encouraged or ordered by the Church. "There are three things by which faith stands firm, devotion remains constant and virtue endures," says St. Peter Chrysologus. "They are prayer, fasting and mercy... Fasting is the soul of prayer" (*Sermon 43*).

The psalm then begs God to go beyond his passive role of witness to an active role of vindicator. So certain is this aspect of God's justice that the writer can thank God in advance for his action.

The Christian connotation is certainly seen in the actions of Judas the betrayer (Mt 26:50) and the anguish this must have caused Christ in his Passion and Death. Some modern versions of the Way of the Cross include the betrayal as one of the "stations."

The trial of Jesus before the Sanhedrin (Mt 26:57-61) demonstrated the evil of false witnesses who couldn't even agree on their perjuries. Abbot Columba Marmion, O.S.B., remarks:

"[This is part of a] series of humiliations and sufferings which we can scarcely begin to describe... Betrayed by the kiss of one of his apostles, bound by the soldiery as a malefactor, He is led before the High Priest. There He holds his peace in the midst of the false accusations brought against him (Mt 26:63)" (*Christ in His Mysteries*, p. 254).

How thoroughly the saints understood the benefits of the Passion of Christ can be seen in this quotation from St. Thomas More:

"By the merits of his bitter Passion joined to mine and far surpassing in merits for me all that I can suffer, his bounteous goodness shall release me from the pains of purgatory and shall increase my reward in heaven beside" (*Prison Letter*).

PSALM 36: *"Sin directs the heart of the wicked..."*

The contrast between the malice of human wickedness and the mercy with which God's providence surrounds his people is the theme of this psalm.

The translators have great difficulty with the Hebrew text of the first five verses and so there are many different versions. However, the imagery is so telling that the intent of the poet is clear. The picture of the wicked man, falling asleep plotting evil deeds, is equaled by his pride in feeling that he will never be caught. It is a classic picture of the overwhelming arrogant pride of the dedicated, professional criminal.

Contrasted to this is the kindness or mercy of God towards those who serve him and the fidelity of God to his covenant promises. He will do anything necessary to protect his just followers. God's love reaches the heights of heaven, his justice tops the highest mountains and his judgments are as mysterious as the greatest depths.

"To take refuge in his wings," a frequent biblical figure, refers to the winged cherubim in the Holy of Holies in the Temple of Solomon. The fat of the sacrificial offerings which enrich the just, and water, so necessary to sustain life, will be bountiful. God will also enlighten the minds of his faithful ones.

The psalm ends with a plea for continued protection against the wicked and their just condemnation. It is expressed with typical Semitic vehemence.

St. John takes up this theme of water, light and life in his Gospel. To the Samaritan woman Jesus promises: "Whoever drinks the water I shall give will never thirst; the water I shall give will become in him a spring welling up to eternal life" (Jn 4:14).

After forgiving the woman taken in adultery, Jesus proclaims, "I am the light of the world. Whoever follows me will not walk in darkness, but will have the light of life" (Jn 8:12). Before curing the man born blind, Jesus teaches, "While I am in the world, I am the light of the world" (Jn 9:5).

When St. Paul begins his lengthy explanation of justification through faith in Christ as opposed to the works of the Old Testament "Law," he quotes from this psalm as part of his look at the universal bondage of sin. "There is no fear of God before their eyes" (Rm 3:18).

Not surprisingly, Christian writers throughout the centuries have highlighted the Johannine theme. Thus, St. Dionysius of Alexandria writes:

"There certainly was never a time when God was not the Father. The Son, being the brightness of eternal light, He himself is absolutely eternal... Since, therefore, the Father is eternal, the Son is also eternal, light of light" (*Elenchus* #1).

St. Cyril of Jerusalem weaves it into his praises of Christ: "The very Son of God, older than the ages, the invisible, the incomprehensible, the incorporeal, the beginning of the beginning, the light of light, the fountain of life and immortality..." And so with many of the saintly writers.

In pursuing the Christian use of this psalm, we may be tempted to pass over too quickly verses 2-5 which describe the maliciousness of the sinner and, of course, sin. However, all of the great spiritual masters insist that we must purge out the sin and pride in our lives before we can make any progress. St. Ignatius in his *Spiritual Exercises,* St. Francis de Sales in his *Introduction to the Devout Life,* and Abbot Columba Marmion in his famous four books of conferences (*Christ in His Mysteries, Christ the Life of the Soul, Christ the Ideal of the Monk, Christ the Ideal of the Priest*) are typical of the classic approach to Christian spiritual growth and maturity. St. Teresa of Avila and St. John of the Cross probably take this to the maximum.

PSALM 37: *"Do not be provoked by evildoers..."*

Another acrostic poem, each couplet begins with the succeeding letter of the Hebrew alphabet. It is deceptively simple in its meditation on the dire fate of sinners and the sure reward of the just and faithful person.

How human it is to be tempted by the successes, wealth and power of wicked people in high places. The grandfatherly observations of the writer (v. 25) attest to the fact that God always stands by the just and always punishes the wicked, eventually.

He is very close to teaching that this divine reward and punishment may not always be in this world but may extend to eternal justice. He just couldn't make the jump from the earthly to the spiritual. For the Christian, of course, this step is easy to make, based on the Resurrection with Christ the first-born from the dead (Rm 8:29).

The "forever" of this writer has the sense of "indefinitely," that God will certainly, if eventually, get around to righting wrongs and rewarding goodness in this life. When it comes to the troubles that the just have, little distinction is made between sufferings that are disciplinary and those which have cleansing value. For the Christian there are also those trials that unite the saints to the sufferings of Christ: "Now I rejoice in my sufferings for your sake, and in my flesh I am filling up what is lacking in the afflictions of Christ on behalf of his body which is the Church" (Col 1:24).

Psalm 37 is a kin to the wisdom literature that proposes maxims to guide the way of people of good will. Phrases like "delight in the Lord," "turn from evil and do good," and "wait eagerly for the Lord," set the tone for this spirituality. The motivation here is to do good "that you may dwell in the land and live secure," that "the poor will possess the land," and they will pass it on to their posterity, "that you may inhabit the land forever."

This psalm also shows up in the teaching of Christ in the Beatitudes. "Blessed are the meek for they shall inherit the land" (Mt 5:5) or its elevation to a spiritual level in "Blessed are you who are poor, for the kingdom of God is yours" (Lk 6:20, 24).

In the Office for the sanctoral cycle, v. 30 is often used, "The mouths of the just utter wisdom; their tongues speak what is right." It reflects such words of Christ's as "Whoever obeys and teaches these commandments will be called greatest in the kingdom of heaven" (Mt 5:19).

The poet's observations on the wicked are colorful. They may seem to be as flourishing as the powerful cedars of Lebanon, but how quickly they can be cut down. "When I passed by again they were gone." They may seem as beautiful and gracious as a hillside of flowers, but "they wither like the grass" in the harsh sun and dry winds of Palestine.

In his sermon on the "Dangers of Riches," Cardinal Newman says:

"I think we should be very much struck with the warnings [the New Testament] contains, not only against the love of riches, but the very possession of them; we should wonder with a portion of that astonishment which the Apostles at first felt, who had been brought up in the notion that they, riches, were a chief reward which God bestowed on those He loved" (O'Connell, ed., *Favorite Newman Sermons*, p. 366).

The references to lending in the Psalms are all noteworthy. Interest rates on loans were staggering, up to 50% or more, so the just man lending without interest was indeed a charitable, even heroic man. The wicked man who borrowed and didn't repay was indeed a scoundrel.

To "gloat" over the downfall of the wicked is not as vindictive as it sounds, since their downfall is the work of God, the Vindicator. It was a triumphant, even a joyful response, really, to the justice of God at work.

Commenting on v. 16 of this psalm, "Better the poverty of the just than the great wealth of the wicked," St. Augustine points out, "Undoubtedly the path of Christ seems hard, but it is the safe way. Another path may hold out pleasures, but it is also teeming with robbers" (*Commentary on Psalm 37*, v. 16).

The evangelical virtue of poverty as practiced by St. Francis of Assisi is not the calling of every person. Right from the beginning of Christianity the relationship of poverty and riches has been a matter of interest. Besides the avoidance of attachment to material riches, listen to an early statement on the subject:

"The rich man has great wealth, but, so far as the Lord is concerned, he is poor because he is distracted by his wealth. His confession, his prayer to the Lord, is very limited; that which he makes is insignificant and weak and has no power above.

"So, when a rich man goes up to a poor man and helps him in his needs, he has the assurance that what he does for the poor man can procure a reward from God, for the poor man is rich in his power of intercession with God and in his confession" (*Shepherd of Hermas*, 2nd Parable).

PSALM 38: *"Lord, punish me no more in your anger..."*

There was no doubt in the mind of the ancient Semites that sickness, poverty, loss of face and even death were punishments from God for sin. In this, the third of the seven penitential psalms, the sinner confesses his guilt as he laments his condition.

The description of the disease is strikingly similar to what Father Damien the Leper found on the Hawaiian Island of Molokai. Daggers of pain, festering sores, blindness, burning loins, numbness and constant grief were consistent with various stages of leprosy. Exclusion from the community and exile were the only then known defense for the people, and that only added to the leper's grief and despair.

Granting the psalmist his poetic license, whatever the disease, only God could cure the person and restore him to his loved ones. So, in the midst of this picture of almost total despair there is a conversion, a turning to God as the source of the last hope. It reminds us of the World War II axiom, "There are no atheists in foxholes!"

The simple, sincere and soul-wrenching plea of the sinner at the end of the psalm says it all: "Forsake me not, O Lord; my God be not far from me! Come quickly to help me, my Lord and my salvation." There is no one to save me but you. In that spirit, "O Lord, make haste to help me," has become the introductory acclamation to each of the Hours of the Liturgy.

Leprosy as a physical affliction was well known in the time of Christ and several of his miracles involved the cure of lepers. Luke 17:11-19 tells the touching story of the ten lepers who were cured and of the one, a Samaritan, who came back to say thank you.

Death by crucifixion was another symbol of public disgrace and it was this aspect of it that made the enemies of Christ demand such a death from Pilate. The picture of Our Lady and St. John standing at the foot of the cross is contrasted to the other people who knew Jesus well, "All his friends were standing at a distance" (Lk 23:49).

Another Christian application is made by many preachers who point out that leprosy, as a physical affliction, causes revulsion in many observers. Mortal sin, a much more tragic disaster, because it is a spiritual affliction not seen by others, seldom causes much aversion.

In our society where sex and violence are constantly in the media, both as news and entertainment, how many people take a stand regarding the morality of these media events? Our moral senses are being dulled to the fact that "the wages of sin is death" (Rm 6:23).

But this is not just a modern problem. "If anyone says, 'I love God,' but hates his brother, he is a liar; for whoever does not love a brother whom he has seen, cannot love God whom he has not seen" (1 Jn 4:20).

There is no doubt in my mind that sin causes much of the grief, destruction, poverty and pain in the world. Greed, pride, lust for power and the like cause individuals and nations to rise up against one another. The money barons of the financial centers of the world, with their lust for money, cause the poverty and hunger of millions.

It seems to me that God may use these conditions to try, purify or strengthen his friends. There is no doubt in biblical theology that these may also be used to punish sins and sinners, and to encourage repentance.

Yet, many people blame God for "allowing" this! Because God is true to the gift of free will with which he endowed mankind, he respects that precious gift. Without free will we could neither love nor hate, be heroic or sinful; we could neither earn reward nor punishment. We would be no more than the animals that the media depicts us to be.

"This is the definition of sin: the misuse of powers given us by God for doing good, a use contrary to God's commandments. Virtue is the use of the same powers based on a good conscience in accordance with God's commands" (St. Basil the Great, *Rules for Monks* #2).

PSALM 39: *"I said, 'I will watch my ways...'"*

"If anyone does not fall short in speech, he is a perfect man," says St. James (Jm 3:2). "The tongue is a small member and yet has great pretensions. Consider how a small fire can set a huge forest ablaze. The tongue is also a fire... With it we bless the Lord and Father, and with it we curse human beings who are made in the likeness of God" (Jm 3:5-10).

The psalmist has the same spirit as he starts this poem. Suffering perhaps a mortal illness, he resolves to maintain silence rather than risk offending God. But as so often happens, the more he resolves to keep silent the more the pressure builds up in him.

His human condition is so frail and death is such an absolute that the author finally cries out in anguish. Our days are numbered and even the years seem to go faster as the end approaches. Since the traditional Hebrew view of death was so final, the end seemed even more tragic. The Christian belief in life after death and heaven as a homeland to be desired changes deeply our way of looking at life here on earth.

Since God has planned this shortness of human life, to question him about it seems rash, indeed. All the psalmist can ask is that life on earth could be more pleasant, more fulfilling, that such things as enemies and plagues be kept far off.

"Turn your face from me, that I may find peace" is a very primitive religious theme, the idea being that if we can avoid the attention of the gods we will be spared their caprice. On the political level, through human history, citizens have avoided kings and governors and just want to be left in peace. Only the politically ambitious court attention from those in high places and the risks involved.

How different for the Christian! "I consider that the sufferings of this present time are as nothing compared with the glory to be revealed in us. For creation waits with eager expectation the revelation of the children of God; for creation was made subject to futility, not of its own accord but because of the one who subjected it, in hope that creation itself would be set free from slavery to corruption and share in the glorious freedom of the children of God... For in hope we are saved" (Rm 8:18-25).

St. Gregory of Nyssa expressed this hope over sixteen centuries ago:

"The reign of life has begun; the tyranny of death is ended. A new birth has taken place, a new life has come, a new order of existence has appeared, our very nature has been transformed...

"Faith is the womb that conceives this new life, baptism the rebirth by which it is brought forth. The Church is its nurse, her teachings are its milk, and the bread from heaven is its food.

"Faith is brought to maturity by the practice of virtue, it is wedded to wisdom, it gives birth to hope. Its home is the kingdom, its end not death but the blessed and everlasting life prepared for us" (*Sermon on the Resurrection*).

PSALM 40: *"I waited, waited for the Lord..."*

Gratitude for God's help is here a prelude to begging for his secure protection in present needs. In this sense, it is used in both an Old Testament and a New Testament setting.

The psalmist alludes to the terrible perils of the exile, with the pierced ears of slaves, the lowly position of captives (down in the pit, up from the swamp) and this "new song" of praise for deliverance, after a long, patient, hope-filled wait.

The good deeds with which God continually surrounds his people (vv. 5-6) inspired St. Augustine to write:

"Now may our God be our hope. He who made all things is better than all things. He who made all beautiful things is more beautiful than all of them. He who made all mighty things is mightier than all of them. He who made all good things is greater than all of them. Learn to love the Creator in his creature, and the Maker in what he has made" (*Commentary on Psalm 40*).

The next few verses point out the need for interior conviction and conversion of heart if one's sacrifices are to be acceptable to God. The mighty liturgical rites of the Temple of Solomon had become splendid, before the exile, but eventually lifeless — mere ritual to be performed for its own sake.

Sacrifices, oblations, sin-offerings and holocausts were not an end in themselves. Our Lord warned his followers of that (cf. Mt 6) and modern liturgists have to fight the temptation to turn worship into mere ritual. As we were warned in the seminary, "When the red print (rubrics) becomes more important than the black print (the liturgical prayers) you are in trouble."

Samuel pointed out to Saul that obedience to the will of God was a more praiseworthy thing than the offering of the sacrifices

Saul had made while waiting impatiently for Samuel (1 S 15:22).

For the Christian, the Epistle to the Hebrews incorporates verses 5-9 applying them to the perfect obedience of Christ to his Father's will and the perfect sacrifice that Christ offered on Calvary that put an end to all other sacrifices. Christ's saving sacrifice was all sufficient and all embracing. The Sacrifice of the Mass makes that one sacrifice by the one priest of the New Testament present to us (Heb 10:5-10 but see entire chapter).

Theologian Louis Bouyer wrote:

"Sacrifice, then, is to be understood as the actual sacrifice which the Church has always intended to offer when it is assembled to celebrate the Eucharist... It is a striking fact that in the most primitive and basic usages of all the ancient Christian liturgies, the terminology of sacrifice is directly applied to what the Church does when she meets for the Eucharist" (*Liturgical Piety*, ch. 6).

The Jews who returned from the exile were surrounded by vicious enemies, so the psalm returns to the theme of the continued need for God's protection. The Christian, surrounded by a world that has embraced materialism, practical atheism and a media-inspired moral bankruptcy can make this same plea.

The Church uses this psalm in the Office for the Dead since human nature, formed from the slime of the earth, is called to eternal heights of happiness and begs God's help in passing this supreme transition.

PSALM 41: *"Happy those concerned for the lowly and poor..."*

Psalm 41 is basically a look at sickness as a mixture of curse and punishment. While there is no doubt here of a thanksgiving for a physical cure of an almost mortal illness, there is also an emotional illness and a psychological attitude that the psalmist must face.

The betrayal of friends is one of the most difficult, as these people come to speak insincere words of comfort, convinced that

God is judging the illness of the man as a just punishment for his sins.

Christians recognize this in the Passion of Christ, where the betrayal by Judas is listed among the more sorrowful aspects of his suffering. The fact that Christ knew it before it happened is specifically mentioned. "One of you will betray me, one who is eating with me" (Mk 14:18). Our Lord uses one form of verse 10 in this psalm to point out his sorrow over the betrayal. "The one who ate my food has raised his heel against me" (Jn 13:18).

The Passion, Death and Resurrection of Christ are so central to the economy of salvation, the Paschal Mysteries so sublime a proof of Christ's sacrificial love, that the saints of every age can be called to witness.

St. Leo the Great writes:

"How marvelous the power of the cross, how great beyond all telling the glory of the Passion — here is the judgment seat of the Lord, the condemnation of the world, the supremacy of Christ crucified.

"The different sacrifices of animals are no more. The one offering of your body and blood is the fulfillment of all the different sacrificial offerings, for you are the true Lamb of God who takes away the sins of the world. In yourself, you bring to perfection all mysteries" (*Eighth Sermon on the Passion*).

The Fathers of the Second Vatican Council declared:

"The work of man's redemption of God's perfect glory was foreshadowed by God's mighty deeds among the people of the Old Covenant. It was brought to fulfillment by Christ the Lord, especially through the Paschal Mystery of his blessed Passion, Resurrection from the dead and Ascension into glory. By dying He destroyed our death, by rising He restored our life..." (*Sacrosanctum Concilium* #5).

The psalm may well have been used in Temple worship as a form of thanksgiving for a recovery. That recovery is seen as a vindication of the integrity, not the innocence, of the one restored to health.

Phrases such as "that I may repay them as they deserve" may strike us as a desire for vengeance, hardly a Christian virtue. "'Vengeance is mine; I will repay,' says the Lord" (Rm 12:19). However, it has more of a judicial meaning in the Psalter where it is the justice of God that will be vindicated. This is stated more as a fact than a desire and should be interpreted in this way throughout the Psalter wherever it occurs.

The first book of psalms, and each book, ends with a beautiful doxology. The praise of God, one in nature and triune in persons, comes easily to our lips as we pray the psalms as Christians.

BOOK TWO: PSALMS 42 - 72

PSALM 42: *"As the deer longs for streams of water…"*

Books Two and Three of the Psalter contain hymns which, for the most part, were the repertoire of two major guilds of Temple singers, Korah (2 Ch 20:19) and Asaph (1 Ch 16:5). As such, they show a very definite and professional touch with true poetic ingenuity.

Psalm 42 (and its conclusion in what we number as Psalm 43) is a beautiful lament of a man who has been separated from the Temple worship. It would seem that he was a liturgical leader who had moved to the far north of the Holy Land. Was it business, exile or the result of a power play that separated him from Jerusalem? We can only surmise.

The two psalms are divided into three stanzas or strophes, each ending with the haunting refrain "Why are you downcast, my soul?" The first section suggests a desert motif wherein water plays a most important role. The deer longing for water, the tears and the "pouring forth of self" are the ardent expressions of a soul that longs to be in the presence of God, worshipping in the Temple.

For the Christian, we immediately think of Jesus' words to the Samaritan woman: "Whoever drinks the water I shall give will never thirst; the water I shall give will become in him a spring of water welling up to eternal life" (Jn 4:14).

In the last chapter of the New Testament, we find the same theme. "Let the one who thirsts come forward, and the one who wants it receive the gift of life-giving water" (Rv 22:17).

The second section of the psalm takes us to the mountain regions of northern Palestine or southern Lebanon where water is now a powerful force as it courses down the mountains. It reminds the poet of the forces of the sea which were indeed fearsome, awesome, to a landlubber.

"Deep calls to deep" is a phrase that has intrigued spiritual writers for many generations. Is it, perhaps, the depths of the human soul longing to share in the depths of God's revelation, to penetrate it ever more deeply?

St. Augustine's oft-quoted remark that our hearts were created for God and that they are restless until they rest in him is applicable. He cries out:

"Late have I loved you, O Beauty ever ancient, ever new; late have I loved you.

"You were within me but I was outside and it was there that I searched for you. In my unloveliness I plunged into the lovely things which you created. You were with me but I was not with you. Created things kept me from you; yet if they had not been in you, they would not have been at all.

"You called, you shouted and you broke through my deafness. You flashed, you shone and you dispelled my blindness. You breathed your fragrance on me; I drew in breath and now I pant for you. I have tasted you and now I hunger and thirst for more" (*Confessions*, Bk. 10).

This ardent longing for God was expressed well by Richard of St. Victor:

"I am wounded by love. Love urges me to speak of love. Gladly do I give myself up to the service of love and it is sweet and altogether lovely to speak of love...

"Above all there is that ardent and burning love which penetrates the heart, inflames the affection and transfixes the soul itself to the very core so that it may truly say, 'I am wounded with love'" (*On the Four Stages of Love*).

The ardent longing for God expressed in this psalm makes this a very appropriate part of the Office for the Dead, for the longing that the Christian has to attain the everlasting realms of heaven.

PSALM 43: *"Grant me justice, God..."*

How many thousands and thousands of young acolytes memorized this psalm in Latin for the prayers at the foot of the altar in the Roman Rite Mass, before the renewal of Vatican II! It staggers the imagination.

This conclusion to Psalm 42 is a beautiful and upbeat prayer for the poet's return to the Temple worship in Jerusalem. It expresses joyful optimism that this will be accomplished.

In the midst of the trials and tribulations that beset a religious person, including the taunts of unbelievers, the light of faith points out the way of righteousness. As Christ exclaimed, "I came into the world as light, so that everyone who believes in me might not remain in darkness" (Jn 12:46).

It is almost possible to feel the intensity of the pilgrim's joy as he ascends the holy mountain, Mount Zion, and his delight as he approaches the altar of God. It is still possible to feel this intensity at the Wailing Wall in Jerusalem.

Christians also experience this faith-in-action as they make pilgrimages to many world-famous shrines. The most intense that I ever experienced was at the Shrine of Our Lady of Guadalupe in Mexico City. The faith and love of these devout pilgrims was so evident, so sincere!

It reminded me of those words attributed to Father Pierre Teilhard de Chardin, S.J.: "Some day, after we have mastered the winds, the waves, the tides and gravity, we will harness for God the energies of love; and then, for the second time in the history of the world, man will have discovered fire!"

But, just praying the words of this psalm should remind the Christian of the great joy and longing we should have as we approach the Mass. All that the Temple worship of the Old Testament symbolized is fulfilled in the Holy Sacrifice of the Mass, the reality before which all symbols fail. Our souls cannot be downcast at the fulfillment brought by Jesus Christ, "my Savior and my God."

PSALM 44: *"O God, we have heard with our own ears..."*

To the ancient Israelites, there was no question that victory and defeat came from God. Their tradition firmly embraced the notion that victory was a reward for keeping the Law faithfully, and defeat was punishment for not keeping to the Covenant strictly.

But Psalm 44 takes in an event that did not conform to this traditional theology. After recounting in capsule form all the wonders God had worked to bring the people to their land, the situation has come up in which the nation has suffered a catastrophic defeat.

If the people were unfaithful to the Covenant, then this defeat would have been justified. But, the psalmist claims that the Law was being kept faithfully, so why this disgrace?

The second section of the psalm reads like an abridged version of the Book of Job. Why do the just suffer? Why are they clothed with disgrace? Why are they treated like "sheep for the slaughter"? The ancient Israelites were not adept at philosophy and they never came up with a good answer to this question about the suffering of the innocent. They couldn't believe that their God was capricious, but life for them was a mysterious blend of suffering and happiness, at best.

St. Paul had this same difficulty when he tried to argue with the philosophers in Athens (Ac 17:16-22). Note also his warning, "See to it that no one captivates you with an empty, seductive philosophy based on human traditions which follow the elemental spirits of the world rather than Christ" (Col 2:8).

St. Paul sums up his thinking on the matter in this way:

"Oh, the depth of the riches and wisdom and knowledge of God! How inscrutable are his judgments and how unsearchable his ways! For who has known the mind of the Lord or who has been his counselor? Or who has given him anything that he may be repaid? For from him and through him and for him are all things. To him be glory forever. Amen" (Rm 11:33-36).

The Passion and Death of Christ is a perfect example of the just suffering for the unjust. And it is precisely because Christ is innocent and perfect that he could suffer for us and be acceptable to God the Father. "For Christ also suffered for sins once, the righteous for the sake of the unrighteous, that he might lead you to God" (1 P 3:18).

The Ethiopian eunuch, puzzling over the prophet Isaiah, quotes this passage to Philip: "Like a sheep he was led to the slaughter..." (Is 53:7). In his humiliation justice was denied him (cf. Ac 9:32-33). Then Philip the deacon explains this passage as referring to Christ's saving death.

The way of the martyrs is also along this path. St. Ignatius of Antioch who died before the first Christian century was complete, wrote, on his way to Rome and martyrdom: "Let me be the food of beasts that I may come to God. I am his wheat and I shall be ground by the teeth of beasts that I may become Christ's pure bread" (*Letter to the Romans* #3).

Psalm 44 ends on a note of patient hope. "Awake, Lord... Rise up. Redeem us as your love demands." However mysterious God's actions are in this matter of national calamity, his very love demands that he turn to his people again. Like Ash Wednesday and Lent in the Christian liturgical year, the theme of this psalm is of repentance for sin and an increase in real, mature fervor.

PSALM 45: *"My heart is stirred by a noble theme..."*

A royal wedding in ancient times, as described by this writer, probably a court poet, must have inspired awe in the guests. Despite the efforts of a Cecil B. DeMille and Hollywood's biblical extravaganzas, life in ancient times was completely drab for the vast majority of people.

So, the splendor of the regal bridegroom described in Psalm 45 was a magnificent combination of pomp and circumstance. Yet however secular this poem in its conception, it must be compared with the Song of Songs — the most beautiful tributes to human love in the Scriptures.

Underlying the lavish praise for the king are the attributes that the prophet Isaiah reserves for the Messiah: beauty, humility, a passionate love for justice and a true warrior spirit. When kings no longer ruled Israel, this psalm was accepted as a messianic psalm, a prophecy of the savior who would come to rule and save all mankind. Christians understood here a direct reference to Christ.

The idea of God and Israel and later God and the Church as having a nuptial relationship was commonly accepted. Father Carroll Stuhlmueller, C.P., writes, "The human situation, here of marriage, is not only found worthy of modeling the divine, but the human institution is also challenged anew to live up to a divine ideal" (*Harper's Bible Commentary*, p. 454).

St. Francis de Sales offers this thought:

"With St. Paul I say, 'Husbands, love your wives as Christ loves the Church' (Eph 5:25), and wives, love your husbands as the Church loves her Savior... It is God who in his own mysterious, loving ways, brought you together. Cherish each other with a completely holy, completely sacred and completely divine love" (*Introduction to the Devout Life*, Pt. 3, #38).

The prayer in *The Liturgy of the Hours* for this psalm reads:

"When you took on flesh, Lord Jesus, you made a marriage of mankind with God. Help us to be faithful to your word and endure our earthly exile bravely, until we are called to the heavenly marriage feast, to which the Virgin Mary, exemplar of your Church, has preceded us" (Vol. 3, p. 866).

Turning to the bride, the poet advises her to forget the noble, but pagan, house from which she came and give herself loyally to her husband and his regal and religious duties. There is also an allusion to the queen-mother who alone of all the king's harem had free access to him. The gold of Ophir (probably in southwest Arabia), the gold-threaded garments and the ivory in the palaces all point out the splendor in store for the bride.

In the Office for both Virgins and Holy Women this psalm is used. The idea is that for the first, the virgins have given up all earthly ambition to join themselves to their savior and king. The holy women are brought into the king's presence adorned with good works, more precious by far than the "gold of Ophir."

The final two verses express the fulfillment of the promises made to the patriarchs that their descendants would be more numerous than the stars or the sands of the seashore (Gn 22:17). The promise made to David, that his sons would reign forever (2

S 7:8-16; 2 Ch 7:18), was fulfilled in Christ far more fully than anyone in the Old Testament could possibly have imagined.

PSALM 46: *"God is our refuge and our strength..."*

In the few centuries that Israel flourished as a kingdom, before the destruction of Jerusalem and the Temple in 586 B.C., its history was triumphant and turbulent, glorious and rebellious. How well that is mirrored in Psalm 46.

Whether the elements or the human enemies threatened Jerusalem, the poet expresses supreme confidence in Yahweh who controls the destinies of all and favors Israel. God was in its midst so it was to be firm forever.

This thought has made the psalm part of the Office for the Dedication of a Church. In the wider meaning, after the fall of the kingdom of Israel as a worldly power, the messianic plan became more evident — the kingdom of the Messiah would last forever.

However, in Christian devotion, this psalm has a definite Marian meaning. The refrain in the psalm, repeated three times, is "The Lord of hosts is with us; our stronghold is the God of Jacob." "The Lord with us" is the Emmanuel of Isaiah 7:14, which St. Matthew sees as fulfilled in the Incarnation: "All this took place to fulfill what the Lord had said through the prophet: 'Behold, the virgin shall be with child and bear a son, and they shall name him Emmanuel,' which means 'God is with us'" (Mt 1:22-23).

In commenting on this passage, St. Justin Martyr writes: "For what man has deemed incredible and impossible, God foretold through the prophetic spirit... The power of God descending upon the Virgin overshadowed her and caused her, while still a virgin, to conceive" (*First Apology* #33).

St. Alphonsus Liguori adds: "In the Incarnation of the Eternal Word, Mary could not have humbled herself more than she did. God, on the other hand, could not have exalted her more than he did exalt her" ("The Annunciation" in *The Glories of Mary*).

If the psalm expresses serene confidence in the presence of Yahweh with Israel, in the messianic sense it expresses the creative presence of the Son of God in Mary and through her, his entrance into the world to found his Church. Psalm 46 has an honored place in the Office of the Blessed Virgin Mary.

Among the beautiful O Antiphons, composed in the seventh century and used in the liturgy during Advent, we pray, "O Emmanuel, our King and Lawgiver, the expectation of all the nations and their Savior: come and save us, O Lord our God."

As a footnote, we might add that Martin Luther based his famous hymn, "A Mighty Fortress Is Our God" (*Ein' feste Burg ist unser Gott*) on this psalm.

PSALM 47: *"All you peoples, clap your hands..."*

In the 1960's, when a few of us young priests were introducing the Folk Masses into the Liturgy, there was consternation among some of the clergy that we were demystifying the Mass, making it "common." In defense, we mentioned the many instances in the Psalter when the music of various instruments and the clapping of hands was acclaimed.

Psalm 47 is one of these triumphant psalms. "Clap your hands with shouts of joy" is a long way from Gregorian chant, but each has its place. If the acclamation of an earthly king is an affair of great joy, then to acclaim the eternal majesty of God, who "was and is and will be" deserves a doxology of unrestrained joy. No wonder David was moved to dance before the ark (2 S 6:14-15)!

God is praised for his historical action in giving the people the Holy Land. The princes who were conquered and those who might ally themselves with Israel were also his people. It is possible that during the heights of Solomon's reign, there might have been hopes of a great empire. When that died with the defection of the ten northern tribes, the future of God's reign was seen to be messianic. Christ's reign through his Church would be universal and last until the end of time (Mt 28:19-20).

Jacob, the patriarch and father of the twelve tribal leaders, was held in popular esteem and so his name appears often in the Psalter. Isaac had a special place in the spiritual meaning of sacrifice, but Abraham was a distant and powerful figure reserved for most solemn mention. One of the few times he appears in the psalms is in this one.

In Christian devotion, verses 6 and 7 are applied particularly to the Ascension of the Lord into heaven where "he is seated at the right hand of the Father, and his kingdom will have no end" (*Nicene Creed*). "God mounts the throne amid shouts of joy, the Lord amid the trumpet blasts. Sing praise to God, sing praise."

Jesuit James Quinn's text for the hymn sung at Morning Prayer of the Office of the Ascension is a beautiful paraphrase and extension of Psalm 47:

> Praise him as he mounts the skies,
> Christ, the Lord of Paradise!
> Cry hosanna in the height,
> As he rises out of sight!
> Now at last he takes his throne,
> From all ages his alone!
> With his praise creation rings:
> "Lord of lords and King of kings!"

Abbot Columba Marmion, O.S.B., tells us:

"Jesus came forth from the Father and He has returned to the Father after having fulfilled his mission here below. He has rejoiced as a giant to run the course; He came forth from the highest heaven, from the sanctuary of the Divinity; and He now reascends to the summit of all things, there to enjoy divine glory, beatitude and power...

"If we may thus lisp about such mysteries, what joy for the heavenly Father, to crown his Son after the victory gained! What divine gladness to call the sacred humanity of Jesus to the enjoyment of the splendor, the beatitude and power of an eternal exaltation!" (*Christ in His Mysteries,* pp. 307-309).

PSALM 48: *"Great is the Lord and highly praised..."*

For those who love Rome, the title "the eternal city" is a mark of their devotion. For the psalmist, Jerusalem in all its splendor, because it was the city chosen by Yahweh, was considered an invincible, eternal city. Mt. Zion, the site of the Temple in Jerusalem, although actually little more than a hill, was so special that no praise was considered too extravagant.

The poet boldly uses the pagan mythology of the Canaanites to praise Yahweh and his citadel. "The heights of Zaphon" or, in another translation, "the true pole of the earth" draws on the imagery of the abode of the gods to express the idea that the home of the true God was Mt. Zion. Later Christian writers would appropriate the idea of Mt. Olympus, the abode of Zeus, as a type of heaven, the abode of the living God.

The psalm points back to a miraculous delivery by God of Jerusalem besieged and rejoices in the power of God. The enemies of Israel were the enemies of Israel's God so they are thrown into confusion by his intervention. They tremble before his power; their suffering is like a woman's anguish in labor; they are sunk like powerful sea-going ships before God's power as exhibited in a dread east wind. (Tarshish was probable Tartessa in Spain so the ships from there were much larger than coastal vessels.)

Pilgrims coming to Jerusalem for the first time would marvel, "What we have heard of its splendor we now see." The poet invites them to go around the city and rejoice in its beauty and its strength, all there to praise the name of God.

For the Christian, the truly indestructible city is the city of God, his Church. After the destruction of Jerusalem and its eclipse for many centuries, the psalm took on the messianic direction of the kingdom of God, in this world but not of this world (Jn 18:36).

In the temptation of Christ after his forty-day fast, the devil took him up to the parapet of the Temple for the second test (Mt 4:5). In his teaching about oaths and vows, Our Lord taught: "Do not swear at all, not by heaven for it is God's throne, nor by the earth, for it is his footstool, nor by Jerusalem for it is the city of the great King... Let your 'Yes' mean 'Yes' and your 'No' mean 'No'" (Mt 5:34-37).

In the Book of Revelation, the description of God's eternal kingdom in heaven is proclaimed under the symbol of the New Jerusalem (Rv 21).

As St. Hilary of Poitiers wrote:

"If we follow Christ closely, we shall be allowed, even on this earth, to stand as it were on the threshold of the heavenly Jerusalem and enjoy the contemplation of the everlasting feast, like the blessed Apostles, who in following the Savior as their leader, showed, and still show, the way to obtain the same gift from God" (*Letter* 14).

The liturgical prayer for this psalm is most meaningful:

"Father, the body of your risen Son is the temple not made by human hands and the defending wall of the new Jerusalem. May this holy city, built of living stones, shine with spiritual radiance and witness to your greatness in the sight of all nations" (*The Liturgy of the Hours*, Vol. 3, p. 772).

PSALM 49: *"Hear this, all you peoples..."*

One of the staples of science fiction is the notion that man will some day be able to live for centuries on this earth or some other planet. It is an awesome thought, since prolonging our life in this vale of tears does not seem desirable at all — if one believes in a happy life after death.

That's the problem posed in Psalm 49. What happens to us after we die? The psalmist is struggling with the then traditional Jewish thought that death is final. "They perish like the beasts."

Death is inevitable and there is no way that a man can redeem himself. It doesn't matter how wealthy, wise or powerful he is, death comes to the good and the bad, the rich and the poor inevitably.

Or does it? In contrast to the statement that no man can redeem himself, the poet says that God can redeem us. The verb used suggests the "taking up into heaven" as reported about Enoch (Gn 5:24) and Elijah (2 K 2:9-12). This is more than a prayer for avoiding a premature death. There is a hint that God will send a Redeemer and that there is a possibility of life after death.

Verse 16, "God will redeem my life, will take me from the power of Sheol or will take me to himself" is a very liberal notion thrown into the middle of a psalm that is extraordinarily conservative in its context. The theologians of the time did not question what happened after death for fear of being accused of witchcraft, sorcery or fortune-telling.

For the Christian, of course, this is a very hopeful prayer. After the trials of this earthly pilgrimage we look forward to a welcome in heaven. The Resurrection of Christ is the pledge of future glory. He, our Redeemer, is the first-born of the dead (Col 1:18). The inevitability of death "gives way to the bright promise of immortality" (*Preface for the Dead*).

When Christ told the rich young man that it is difficult for a rich man to enter heaven (Mt 19:23) the disciples were amazed, since it was thought that riches were a sign of divine favor. Instead, Christ told them to store up treasures for themselves in heaven (Mt 6:19) and, since one cannot serve both God and riches (Mt 6:24) it was important that they give service to God top priority.

The Church understood this from the beginning. In the early second century, Hermas wrote:

"The rich man has great wealth, but, so far as the Lord is concerned, he is poor, because he is distracted by his wealth. His confession, his prayer to the Lord, is very limited; that which he makes is insignificant and weak and has no power above.

"So, when a rich man goes up to a poor man and helps him in his needs, he has the assurance that what he does for the poor man can procure a reward from God, for the poor man is rich in his power of intercession with God and in his confession" (*Shepherd*, 2nd Parable).

St. Athanasius reminds us that Christ took a body to redeem us and therefore, "he utterly destroyed the power death had against mankind, as fire consumes chaff, by means of the body he had taken and the grace of the Resurrection" (*Sermon on the Incarnation* #8).

PSALM 50: *"The Lord, the God of gods, has spoken..."*

The biblical experts like the word "theophany" which means a show of God's power. The first verses of Psalm 50 describe this, with God summoning all the faithful to a court hearing. God, the judge of the whole earth, has something powerful to put before those who are his by the covenant of sacrifice.

The poet intends to invoke the great theophany at Mt. Sinai (Ex 19-24) where amid awesome heavenly signs, the covenant was given and ratified. St. John would later draw on this in describing his vision of the heavenly court (Rv 4).

In the second part of the psalm God speaks directly to the faithful and it is a remarkable passage. Considering the tremendous emphasis placed on animal sacrifice in the Temple worship, God tells them that those sacrifices must be made with sincerity of heart. The mere multiplication of sacrifices does not honor God if they do not express the inner "sacrifice of praise."

With striking irony God asks them: Do I need sacrifices? Do holocausts and blood sacrifices fulfill some need in God? Ridiculous! All the birds and beasts belong to him to begin with.

In the third strophe, God turns his attention to the wicked. It is a scathing attack on religious hypocrisy. You profess my commandments in words, he accuses, but in your deeds you profane that creed. You recite the commandments but you don't keep them. Thieves and the sexually immoral, calumniators and liars are tolerated, even welcomed. God will not be silent in the face of such contempt from those who should know better.

The psalm ends with a vigorous statement. The hypocrites will be punished and the obedient and sincere can be assured of God's special help.

How often Our Lord also called for sincerity in worship. Right after the Beatitudes, he taught his disciples: "You are the salt of the earth"; "You are the light of the world"; "Do not think I have come to abolish the law or the prophets. I have come not to abolish but to fulfill" (Mt 5:13-19). The disciples admired the Pharisees for their strict interpretation of the Law. However, Christ admonished them by saying: "Unless your righteousness surpasses that of the scribes and Pharisees you will not enter the kingdom of heaven" (Mt 5:20); "Beware of the leaven — that is, the hypocrisy — of the Pharisees" (Lk 12:1).

In the beautiful passage of the Samaritan woman, Christ tells her, "The hour is coming, and is now here, when the true worshipers will worship the Father in Spirit and truth; and indeed, the Father seeks such people to worship him. God is Spirit and those who worship him must worship in Spirit and truth" (Jn 4:23-24).

For the Christian, of course, the sacrifice of Christ on Calvary was the fulfillment of all sacrifice and his one offering of that supreme act of love was all-sufficient. As it is applied to us in each Mass, the sacrifice of the Altar becomes our sharing of Calvary in our own time and space.

St. Irenaeus taught this:

"Our Lord instructed his disciples to offer to God the firstfruits of creation, not because God has any needs, but so that they themselves should not be unproductive and ungrateful. That is why he took bread, a part of his creation, gave thanks and said, 'This is my body.' In the same way he declared that the cup, an element of the same creation as ourselves, was his blood. He taught them that this was the new sacrifice of the new covenant. The Church has received this sacrifice from the apostles" (*Against Heresies*, Bk. 4, #17).

St. Thomas Aquinas is equally explicit:

"Christ offered his body to God the Father on the altar of the cross as a sacrifice for our reconciliation. He shed his blood for our ransom and purification, so that we might be redeemed from our wretched state of bondage and cleansed from all sin. He left his body as food and his blood as drink for the faithful to consume in the form of bread and wine... It is offered in the Church for the living and the dead so that what was instituted for the salvation of all may be for the benefit of all" (*On the Feast of Corpus Christi*).

PSALM 51: *"Have mercy on me, God, in your goodness…"*
          (*Miserere*)

"You are the man!" the prophet Nathan thundered at King David, after David had pronounced a death sentence against a hypothetical sinner (2 S 12:7). It is high drama at its best and the title of Psalm 51 refers to Nathan who reproached David after his affair with Bathsheba.

Every sinner, that is Everyman, must turn to God with sincerity and promise a complete interior conversion to have God blot out offenses, wash away guilt and cleanse the soul. Sin has many consequences — spiritual, moral, physical, psychological and social — but essentially it is an offense against God. In justice, these other effects which occur flow from sin.

While v. 7 does not refer to the doctrine of Original Sin (which was only later revealed), "True I was born guilty, a sinner, even as my mother conceived me," it certainly implies that condition. It absolutely does not imply that intercourse is sinful, as some older commentators inferred. Human sexuality has to be one of the greatest gifts God has given us on the natural level.

The cleansing with hyssop, a native bushy plant used as a sprinkler, was a ritual sign of cleanliness that must reflect the sincere interior conversion.

The second part of the psalm turns to God's saving action following the sinner's conversion. After God has given one the grace to turn back to his Creator, the clean heart sought is the willingness to serve God with steadfast joy. This will naturally cause the forgiven person to want to share that joy with others.

"Lord open my lips; my mouth will proclaim your praise" has become the opening phrase for all the liturgical days' prayers.

The psalm quickly concludes with the idea of the importance of an interior sacrifice before a "proper sacrifice" can be accepted in the Temple.

The Christian uses of Psalm 51 are many and varied. Besides being one of the seven Penitential Psalms, it sets the theme for Ash Wednesday and the season of Lent. It is used almost every week in the Liturgy of the Hours, and it is prominent in the Office for the Dead.

The theme of true repentance, of truly turning back to God, is common to spiritual writers, starting with Jesus' parable of the prodigal son who goes back to his father to say "I have sinned against heaven and against you" (Lk 15:18).

St. Paul tells his converts to "put away the old self of your former way of life, corrupted through deceitful desires and be renewed in the spirit of your minds and put on the new self, created in God's way in righteousness and holiness of truth" (Eph 4:22-24).

In telling them that they must become a whole new creation in Christ, Paul makes bold to say, "For our sake he made him to be sin who did not know sin, so that we might become the righteousness of God in him" (2 Cor 5:21).

On the theme of repentance, St. Jerome writes:

"Return to the Lord your God from whom you have been alienated by your sins. Do not despair of his great mercy, no matter how great your sins, for great mercy will take away great sins.

"The Lord is gracious and merciful and prefers the conversion of the sinner rather than his death. Patient and generous is his mercy. He does not give in to human impatience, but is willing to wait a long time for our repentance...

"However, do not let the magnitude of his clemency make us lax in repentance" (*On Joel*).

Benedictine Abbot Columba Marmion's book *Christ the Life of the Soul* was the basis for courses in ascetical theology in many American seminaries. Almost two-thirds of the volume is devoted to the foundation and double aspect of the Christian life: (A) Death to sin, and (B) Life for God. It is not enough to cleanse the soul from sin. That would leave a void. The next and more important step is the interior renewal that builds a real Christian edifice.

The concluding reference to a true or "proper sacrifice" reminds the Christian of the Sacrifice of Calvary and it is continually being made present in the Mass, the Sacrament of the Altar.

St. Alphonsus Liguori writes:

"Jesus Christ has, then, paid the price of our redemption in the Sacrifice of the Cross. But he wishes that the fruit of the ransom given should be applied to us in the Sacrifice of the Altar, being himself in both the chief sacrificer, who offers the same victim, namely his own body and blood — with this difference only, that on the Cross his blood was shed, while it is not shed at the altar" ("The Sacrifice of Jesus Christ" in *The Holy Eucharist*).

PSALM 52: *"Why do you glory in evil…"*

The inscription of Psalm 52, verses 1-2, relates this psalm to Saul's chief shepherd, Doeg, who reported to Saul the priests of the sanctuary of Nob for helping David, and then killed the priests at Saul's command (1 S 21-22). With this in mind, Father Carroll Stuhmueller, in *Harper's Bible Commentary* (p. 458), relates this psalm to a bitter dispute between priestly factions in the Temple.

The priests who are at the head of the plot are seen as powerful and arrogant. "All day long" they scheme with lies and deceit and their "tongue is like a sharpened razor." They do not trust in God but in their own wealth and power to deceive. It's not a pretty picture of corrupt politicians in any setting or age.

The other priests can only draw back in horror and they rely on God to see justice done to the scoundrels. The virtuous priests are "like olive trees in the house of the Lord." They will lead the people in praise of God who always makes justice prevail.

The psalm can also be read as a simple denunciation of any powerful and arrogant person who trusts to his own devious ways to gain personal power and wealth. When God's justice prevails the righteous will look on with approval and will show their disdain for the one who loves "lies rather than honest speech."

The Christian will be reminded of the powerful discourse on the use of the tongue by St. James:

"If anyone does not fall short in speech, he is a perfect man, able to bridle his whole body also. If we put bits into the mouths of horses to make them obey us, we also guide their whole bodies. It is the same with ships: even though they are so large and driven by fierce winds, they are steered by a very small rudder wherever the pilot's inclination wishes. In the same way, the tongue is a small member and yet has great pretensions.

"Consider how a small fire can set a huge forest ablaze. The tongue is also a fire. It exists among our members as a world of malice, defiling the whole body and setting the entire course of our lives on fire, itself set on fire by Gehenna. For every kind of beast and bird, of reptile and sea creature can be tamed and has been tamed by the human species, but no human being can tame the tongue. It is a restless evil, full of deadly poison.

"With it we bless the Lord and Father, and with it we curse human beings who are made in the likeness of God. From the same mouth come blessing and cursing. This need not be so, my brothers" (Jm 3:2-10).

Put more succinctly, "If anyone thinks he is religious and does not bridle his tongue, his religion is vain" (Jm 1:26).

It is amazing the amount of trouble a person with a malicious tongue can cause in a small community. A community can be destroyed by the mischief and jealousy that a loose tongue can cause. St. Paul faced this with his small communities, at times (1 Cor 3:3; 2 Cor 12:20; Gal 5:20, etc.).

It is not surprising to hear from St. Benedict of Nursia, "Keep one's mouth from evil and depraved talk; do not love much speaking" (*Rule*); or from St. Bernard of Clairvaux, "There are three ways for wisdom, or prudence, to abound in you: if you confess your sins, if you give thanks and praise, and if your speech is edifying" (*Misc. Sermons* #15).

Thomas à Kempis also emphasizes silence:

"I wonder why we are so eager to chatter and gossip with each other since we seldom return to the quiet of our own hearts without a damaged conscience... If it is proper to speak, speak of what will benefit others spiritually" (*The Imitation of Christ*, ch. 10: "On Avoiding Unnecessary Talk").

PSALM 53: *"Fools say in their hearts..."*

With the exception of one verse, Psalm 14 and Psalm 53 are identical. Here in verse 6 the psalm is much more strict in its judgment on the evildoer and the atheist. "They have good reason to fear... God will certainly scatter the bones of the godless."

In their foolishness, they have denied God, but what is far worse, God will reject them. For the Christian, of course, there is always hope for forgiveness and a welcomed return to God:

"But now the righteousness of God has been manifested apart from the law... through faith in Jesus Christ for all who believe. For there is no distinction, all have sinned and are deprived of the glory of God. They are justified freely by his grace through the redemption in Jesus Christ, whom God set forth as an expiation, through faith, by his blood, to prove his righteousness because of the forgiveness of sins previously committed" (Rm 3:21-25).

And what about those who do not believe in Christ, or even in God? The Second Vatican Council turned its attention to this problem:

"Eternal salvation is open to those who, through no fault of their own, do not know Christ and his Church but seek God with a sincere heart, and under the inspiration of grace try in their lives to do his will, made known to them by the dictates of their conscience.

"Nor does Divine Providence deny the aids necessary for salvation to those who, without blame on their part, have not yet reached an explicit belief in God, but strive to lead a good life, under the influence of God's grace" (*Lumen Gentium* #16).

PSALM 54: *"O God, by your name save me..."*

Hollywood, in its heyday, valued the names of the movie stars, and actors and actresses battled for top billing on theater marquees. The axiom was: "It doesn't matter what the critics say, as long as they spell your name right!"

The name stands for the person and so the appeal in this psalm is directly to God himself. St. Gregory Nazianzen explains:

"As far then as we can reach, 'He who Is' and 'God' are the special name for his essence; and of those especially, 'He who Is,' not only because when he spoke to Moses on the mount, and Moses asked him what his name was, this was what he called himself, bidding him to say to the people, 'The I AM has sent me' (Ex 3:14) but also because we find this name is the more strictly appropriate... God always was and always is and always will be; or rather, God always IS, for was and will be are fragments of our time and of our changeable nature" (*Oration* #30).

St. Thomas Aquinas offers us another look at the name of God:

"Now from the divine effects we cannot know the divine nature in itself, so as to know what it is, but only by way of eminence, and by way of causality and of negation. Thus the name God signifies the divine nature, for this name was imposed to signify something existing above all things, the principle of all things, and removed from all things; for those who name God intend to signify all this" (*Summa Theol.* I:13:8 ad 2).

In Psalm 54 the poet prays a typical lament. There is a troubled supplicant who is set upon by an enemy or an evil person and he appeals directly to God for help. The title refers to the betrayal of David to Saul by the inhabitants of Ziph, a town southeast of Hebron. The enemies would be traitors and their just reward would be to grovel on the ground at the feet of the just. In a loose sense, any sinner would be a "traitor" before God. Therefore the lament has a universal usage.

The prayer concludes with an assurance of the presence and help of God. The poet shows his thanks by a generous, free will sacrifice, something joyfully offered over and above a ritual sacrifice or one offered as a result of a personal vow.

Psalm 54 can certainly be prayed with Christian depth. In times of trial we turn to Jesus Christ for help, knowing that he has the power to save, here and hereafter. At the Last Supper Christ said, "Whatever you ask in my name I will do so that the Father may be glorified in the Son" (Jn 14:13).

When Peter and John cured the cripple at the Temple's "Beautiful" Gate, Peter said, "Silver and gold I do not have but what I have I give you: in the name of Jesus Christ of Nazareth, rise and walk" (Ac 3:6). When they were hauled before the Sanhedrin, they said, in their defense, of Jesus, "There is no salvation through anyone else, nor is there any other name under heaven given to the human race by which we are to be saved" (Ac 4:12).

When President John F. Kennedy was assassinated I was the librarian at the University of San Diego. The news came over the radio shortly after 11:00 a.m. By noon, our University chapel was filled to overflowing for the noon Mass. It is second nature for the Christian to turn to God in times of trouble. It should also be second nature to return thanks promptly and fervently for favors received. We should remind ourselves that the word "Eucharist" means thanksgiving.

PSALM 55: *"Listen, God, to my prayer..."*

Is there any pain as bitter as betrayal by a close personal friend? Civil wars are usually the most bitter, and traitors, like Judas Iscariot or Benedict Arnold are most scorned, but on the personal level betrayal is the cause of the greatest anguish.

It is impossible to read or pray Psalm 55 without realizing the anguish of the poet. The setting is a city, no doubt Jerusalem, torn by inner strife and, possibly, invading enemies as well. "My heart pounds." "Deadly terror falls on me... fear and trembling." He longs to fly away like a dove, to get away from it all.

In the midst of all this upheaval, a trusted, intimate friend betrays him. "If an enemy had reviled me... if my foe had viewed me with contempt... But it was you, my other self, my comrade and my friend" who turned against me. Even their religious ties have been betrayed. This is stark drama, high tragedy.

But the poet turns to God in prayer, "at dusk, at dawn and at noon." Note, this is because the day began at sunset for them, not at midnight as for us. He prays for the death of his foes, not so much for personal vengeance as for the vindication of God's justice. These people have no fear of God and with speech softer than butter and smoother than oil, they turn against God's friends.

The confidence with which the psalm ends is magnificent. "Cast your care upon the Lord who will give you support." He will surely punish the evildoers so the poet can end with the simple declaration, "I put my trust in you."

The most obvious Christian reading of this psalm centers around the Passion and Death of Christ. Rejected by his people, Christ was betrayed with a kiss from a trusted Apostle, Judas Iscariot (Mk 14:43-52), and deserted by ten of the Twelve Apostles on Calvary (Jn 19:26).

Christ taught his disciples to have confidence in the Father who takes care of his people. He tells them that not even Solomon in all his glory was as splendid as the lilies of the field (Mt 6:25-34). He reminds them that God knows our needs; therefore, we are but to seek first the kingdom of God and "all these things will be given [us] besides" (Lk 12:22-31). St. Peter quotes this psalm in his closing advice to the younger members of the Church, "Cast all your worries upon him because he cares for you" (1 P 5:7).

Christians have also another dimension to their prayers of intercession in all the times of need and trial. The Blessed Virgin Mary is certainly the most powerful of advocates before the throne of her Son, Jesus Christ. Saints of every age and locality, Fathers, Doctors and spiritual writers have all praised her for her place in the economy of salvation and her power to intercede for us with her Son.

St. Bernard, who has been called "The Troubadour of Mary,"

was a prolific writer in the twelfth century. In his tribute to Mary as "The Star of the Sea," *Stella Maris,* he relates her intercession during trials and troubles such as those described in Psalm 55:

"When you find yourself tossed by the raging storms on this great sea of life, far from land, keep your eyes fixed on this star to avoid disaster. When the winds of temptation or the rocks of tribulation threaten, look up to the star, call upon Mary!

"When the waves of pride or ambition sweep over you, when the tides of detraction or jealousy run against you, look up to the star, call upon Mary! When the shipwreck of avarice, anger or lust seems imminent, call upon Mary!

"If the horror of sin overwhelms you and the voice of conscience terrifies you, if the fear of judgment, the abyss of sadness and the depths of despair clutch at your heart, think of Mary. In danger, difficulties and sins, think about Mary, call upon Mary!" (*Missus Est Homilies* #2).

PSALM 56: *"Have mercy on me, God..."*

The inscription to this psalm relates it to David's flight to Gath (1 S 21:10-15) where his reputation as a hero put his life in dire peril. God's care for David was a prophetic sign of the care that God has for his faithful people individually.

Thus the psalmist can take as his theme, "God, I praise your promise; in you I trust, I do not fear. What can mere flesh do to me?" There is more than simple trust in God here, for the poet can praise the promise God has made. The promises of protection made to the Patriarchs were firmly imbedded in the Jewish psyche. Those who fought either the nation or the righteous individual actually had God as a foe, so, "What can mere mortals do to me?"

There is a remarkable tenderness expressed in v. 9: "My wanderings are noted, my tears are stored up and recorded in your book." Nomadic life was a reality for many in ancient biblical times and exile was also a constant threat. God noted even the tears of the poor and the insignificant (*anawim*) and treasured them like water in a canteen in the desert. It is a tenderness that reminds us of Our Lord's: "The very hairs of your head are numbered" (Lk 12:7).

That the troubles should be recorded in a book is a custom that prevailed throughout the Old Testament culture. The Israelites were unique in the fact that all the men were expected to know how to read. The emphasis on the Law made "books" a precious sign. The "Book of Life" meant that the person so inscribed had a confirmed relationship with God.

St. Jerome in commenting on this psalm relates it to the Passion of Christ. He was the victim for our sins and when he was attacked on all sides he kept silent and obediently suffered. But his confidence in God was rewarded by the Resurrection, when God's justice was completely vindicated. We are to unite with that confidence and become a sacrifice of praise in the sight of God.

St. Paul also commends us to exult in this confidence:

"If God is for us, who can be against us? He who did not spare his own Son but handed him over for us all, how will he not also give us everything along with him?... What will separate us from the love of Christ? Will anguish or distress or persecution or famine or nakedness or peril of the sword?... In all these things we conquer overwhelmingly through him who loved us. For I am convinced that neither death, nor life, nor angels, nor principalities, nor present things, nor future things, nor powers, nor height, nor depth, nor any other creature will be able to separate us from the love of God in Christ Jesus our Lord" (Rm 8:31-39).

PSALM 57: *"Have mercy on me, God..."*

"I will wake the dawn," the poet cries in a vivid image about the end of an all-night vigil. The lyre and the harp accompany the chant which will coincide with the conclusion of the nightlong prayer.

The whole psalm is filled with these brilliant images, both

those that describe the trouble caused by evil men and the confidence the supplicant has in God.

The sinner is one who tramples down the just man. In this the sinner is like a hungry lion waiting for human blood. "Their teeth are spears and arrows, their tongue a sharpened sword!" They have set traps and dug pits and it would be poetic justice, indeed, if they fell into their own devices.

However, the just man finds refuge in the shadow of God's wing. The commentators all insist that this imagery is that of the two golden cherubim who spread their wings over the Ark in the Temple. In ancient Near-East mythology a cherub is a great flying animal but it seems evident that in biblical symbolism they are angels.

It is an interesting aside to note that Moses, in the Book of Exodus, is so completely strict about the divine prohibition of statues (Ex 20:2-5) and yet in that same book (Ex 25:18-20) he receives a divine command to place these two statues in the Holy of Holies. Although they came to signify the divine throne from which God ruled invisibly, they were never the object of a cult or figured in the worship itself.

The poet has supreme trust in God who will certainly send his help from heaven. This "steadfast heart" is secure in the knowledge that God always rights wrongs. The very covenant between Yahweh and Israel was founded on the kindness and fidelity of God (cf. Ex 34:6).

For St. Augustine this psalm referred to Christ's Passion, Death and Resurrection. He certainly is the Just One against whom evil men devised all sorts of plots up to and including his crucifixion. But God stepped in and vindicated him completely in the triumph of the Resurrection.

We Christians use the psalm as a prayer for mercy and truth to rescue us from the snares of the devil. We proclaim the Good News to all the nations, wanting to be known as the companions of God's Son.

St. Bernard of Clairvaux saluted the cause of Christian hope and trust in his hymn, *Jesu Dulcis Memoria* (vv. 1, 3, 4):

Jesus, the very thought of you
With sweetness fills my heart,
But sweeter far your face to see
And in your presence rest.
O hope of every contrite heart,
O joy of all the meek.
To those who fall, how kind you are,
How good to those who seek.
But what to those who find? Ah! This
Nor tongue nor pen can show
The love of Jesus, what it is
None but his loved ones know.

PSALM 58: *"Do you indeed pronounce justice, o gods..."*

The commentators agree that this is one of the most difficult psalms to translate, that parts of the text are hopelessly obscure and that some of the Hebrew vocabulary occurs only in this
psalm. It is one of the few psalms that is not used in *The Liturgy of
the Hours.*

The direct address to "gods" may refer to ancient myths that
certain spiritual powers, subject of course to God, ruled over various parts of the world. More than likely, it refers to judges, as in
Psalm 82 and in John 10:34, since they acted in a god-like way in
dispensing justice to the people. In this case, it may well be an
ancient example of "lawyer-bashing."

Therefore we can read the psalm as a denunciation of corrupt judges. The imprecations against them liken them to invet-
erate liars, to the poison of a rebellious snake, to voracious lions,
to a snail that oozes away in the sunlight, to an aborted fetus, to
water that vanishes in the desert sand and to a campfire that is swept
away by the wind.

Psalm 58 certainly contains some of the most violent images
in the Psalter. The seven curses hurled against false judges inten-
sify their vigor — seven, of course, also signifying a completeness,
a fullness, here, of evil.

God's justice will be fully vindicated when these corrupt officials are trampled or stoned to death. Then all will know, "Truly there is a reward for the just; there is a God who is (the just) judge on earth."

Chapter 13, in the Appendix to the Book of Daniel, comes to mind immediately. It is the story of the two wicked elders, judges, who bring false accusation against Susanna. It is a dramatic account of judgment gone astray, of lust overcoming men who should have been models of good example, and the climax when the young man, Daniel, catches them in their lies and denounces them.

The most obvious Christian application is to see ourselves, as sinners, betraying God's trust in us. We may put on a good face to the world and simulate virtue but God is never deceived by our hypocrisy. How often Christ hurled that epithet "O hypocrite!" at the insincere critics who surrounded him during his public life. How earnestly he warned his disciples against "the yeast of the Pharisees which is hypocrisy" (Lk 12:1).

We might well recall frequently the words of Pope St. Leo the Great: "Christian, remember your dignity and now that you share in God's own nature (by Baptism) do not return by sin to your former base condition. Bear in mind who is your Head and of whose body you are a member" (*First Sermon on Christmas*).

PSALM 59: *"Rescue me from my enemies, my God..."*

The inscription in verse one relates this lament to the time when David's house was put under surveillance by King Saul (1 S 19:11) who intended to kill David the next day. In this way, the poet describes his persecution by powerful men.

He protests his innocence but his enemies, like wild dogs roaming the streets of the city at night, are out for blood and will listen to no reason. Indeed, they plot without reason saying, "Who is there to hear us?"

But God, the lover of the innocent and the protector and

defender of the just, does hear and he comes to their aid. The psalmist has no doubt about this. The God who rules the nations is also the God the psalmist worships and he is confident of his help. The lies, the false oaths and the pride of the evildoers will certainly not go unpunished.

The psalm is certainly a reminder of the Passion and Death of Christ. The lies and the false testimonies of those who rose up to accuse him (Mt 26:60) speak eloquently of a psalm-prophecy fulfilled. Through it all, Christ preserved his confidence in the Father who would raise him up and let him triumph completely over his enemies (Eusebius of Caesarea). In such a way we learn to have confidence in God.

"I shall sing of your strength at dawn," suggests the morning sacrifice of praise, and thanksgiving at dawn promises the blessings of a new day. The refrain, vv. 10 and 18, is especially expressive, "O my strength! Your praise I will sing; you, God, are my fortress, my loving God."

Venantius Fortunatus has us sing of the victorious Passion of Christ in the beautiful hymn *Pange Lingua Gloriosi* (vv. 1 & 6):

> Sing, my tongue, the glorious battle,
> Sing the last, the dread affray;
> O'er the cross the victor's trophy,
> Sing the high triumphal lay:
> Tell how Christ, the world's Redeemer,
> As a victim won the day.
> Thirty years among us dwelling,
> His appointed time fulfilled,
> Born for this he meets his passion
> For that this he freely willed:
> On the cross the Lamb is lifted
> Where his life-blood shall be filled.

PSALM 60: *"O God, you rejected us, broke our defenses..."*

1942 began as a disastrous year in American history. After the attack on Pearl Harbor at the end of 1941, the news came of disasters at Corregidor and Bataan, and the loss of the Philippines. Yet these very defeats hardened the morale of the people as they tooled up for a long, bitter war.

This is the case with Psalm 60. The inscription refers to David's victories in taking over the Holy Land, in the light of some crushing defeat that the country had just suffered. The news was earth-shaking and the army, in rout, had to find a safe haven to regroup. As so often happens in times of disaster, people turn to God in desperation, for help.

They remind God of his promise to give them all of Canaan (Gn 12:1-2; Dt 34:1-4), mentioning geographical places that symbolize the fulfillment of that promise. The military might of the northern tribe of Ephraim, the royal splendor of the ruling tribe, Judah, and the subjugated races that were to serve the people are all mentioned. So that there will be no doubt, places to the north, south, east and west are named.

Then, recognizing that God is supreme in the Promised Land, they confidently ask him to lead them again to victory. Humiliated for a time, by turning back to God they can be sure of future triumphs.

A Christian praying this psalm will look to Christ for help in overcoming trials and temptations. One who has been defeated by sin in the spiritual battle of life can, through repentance, be lifted up again by the grace of God. "In the world you will have trouble," says the Lord, "But take courage, I have overcome the world" (Jn 16:33).

How gracefully St. Jerome comments on this:

"When the angel cried 'Hail, full of grace, the Lord is with you; you are blessed among women,' he told us by divine command how tremendous was the dignity and beauty of the ever-virgin Mary.

"How well we can understand that she would be 'full of

grace,' this virgin who glorified God and gave Our Lord to mankind, who poured out peace upon the earth by giving hope to the gentiles, protection against temptation, purpose of life and reason for sacrifice" (*On the Assumption*).

And St. Augustine reminds us:

"Your first task is to be dissatisfied with yourself, fight sin and transform yourself into something better. Your second task is to put up with the trials and temptations of this world that will be brought on by the change in your life and to persevere to the end in the midst of these things...

"Our pilgrimage on earth cannot be exempt from trial. We make progress by means of trial. No one knows himself except through trial, or receives a cross except after a victory, or strives except against an enemy or temptations" (*Commentary on Psalm 60*).

PSALM 61: *"Hear my cry, O God..."*

On one level, this is a prayer by the king, possibly David himself. On another level, it is the "shrill cry" of an exile, longing to return home, to Jerusalem.

"From the brink of Sheol" can mean either a prayer from one who is at death's door, or someone praying from the farthest edge of the earth. "To dwell in your tent," and find refuge "in the shelter of your wings," is a direct reference to the Temple in Jerusalem, God's tent or abode and his throne under the wings of the cherubim. On the lips of a Christian, this is a longing for eternal life in the heavenly Jerusalem.

"Add to the days of the king's life; may his years be many generations." In other words, "Long live the king!" In kingdoms where the monarch both reigns and rules, dynastic changes can be drastic, so the prayer for the long life of the king has deep-felt meaning.

Psalm 61 is used on the Feast of the Sacred Heart of Jesus since he does rule with truth and reign with mercy, eternally. His "exile" on earth was to ease the pains of our exile and to identify with our condition and help us change and improve it. His triumph in heaven gives hope to our efforts to reign with him after death.

Dietrich von Hildebrand wrote:

"The readiness to change is an essential aspect of the Christian's basic relation with God; it forms the core of our response to the merciful love of God which bends down upon us: 'With eternal charity has God loved us; so he has drawn us, lifted from the earth, to his merciful heart' (Antiphon, Feast of the Sacred Heart)" (*Transformation in Christ*, ch. 3).

That we Christians have a king who has identified with us, perhaps only another poet could express appropriately. Here is how Joseph Mary Plunkett reacted:

> I see His blood upon the rose,
> And in the stars the glory of His eyes,
> His body gleams amid eternal snows,
> His tears fall from the skies.
> I see His face in every flower;
> The thunder and the singing of the birds
> Are but His voice — and carven by His power
> Rocks are His written words.
> All pathways by His feet are worn,
> His strong heart stirs the ever-beating sea,
> His crown of thorns is twined with every thorn,
> His cross is every tree.   (*I See His Blood Upon the Rose*).

PSALM 62: *"My soul rests in God alone..."*

Scripture scholars tell us that in the Hebrew original of Psalm 62, the word "alone" appears six times at the beginning of six verses and the word "indeed" concludes at least two. In God alone can the soul find rest, peace and security. Even the word "soul" is too weak since the ancient Hebrews did not divide man into body-soul as did the Scholastics. Try something like "my very being can find rest in God alone."

St. Augustine testifies to this near the beginning of his *Confessions*: "Great are you, O Lord, and greatly to be praised. You have made us for yourself and our hearts are restless until they rest in you."

The praises of God as the basis of security are used often in the Psalter: a rock, a secure height, a fortified high place, etc. The enemies of the just never seem to take pause in battling the man who tries to be just in the sight of God. The just may seem to be like a weakened fence or wall, but their strength is from God so it cannot be overturned. Hypocrites delight in lies, and "they bless with their mouths but inwardly they curse."

The last stanza resembles Old Testament wisdom literature, a calm look at the human condition. So many people put their trust in great wealth or powerful friends, but all of these are but a passing breath in the divine plan for creation. The wise man puts his trust in the power of God, alone, and that power is tempered by kindness and mercy, indeed.

The poetic device, "One thing God has said," and "Two things I have heard" leads to three ideas, but it is simply a device to get attention.

The last line, "You render to each of us according to our deeds," has great theological significance. The thought is repeated in Psalms 28 and 31; it occurs in Job 34, and in the words of King David mourning for the General, Abner (2 S 3:39).

St. John writes, "I heard a voice from heaven say, 'Write this: Blessed are the dead who die in the Lord from now on.' 'Yes,' said the Spirit, 'let them find rest from their labors, for their works accompany them'" (Rv 14:13). St. Paul tells us that if we have faith great enough to move mountains but don't have charity, we are nothing (1 Cor 13:2). He also quotes from this psalm, "God, who will repay everyone according to his works" (Rm 2:6). And St. James reminds us that "faith of itself, if it does not have works, is dead" (Jm 2:17).

The great monastic traditions of Christianity were founded on the philosophy of prayer and work, *ora et labora*. St. Benedict writes:

"Girded with faith and the performance of good works, let us follow the path of Christ by the guidance of the Holy Gospel. Then we shall deserve to see him who has called us into his own kingdom. If we wish to obtain a dwelling place in his kingdom, we shall not reach it unless we hasten there by our good deeds" (*Rule*, Prologue).

PSALM 63: *"O God, you are my God…"*

Those who pray the liturgical hours regularly have used Psalm 63 hundreds of times through the years. It leads off Morning Prayer for the first Sunday and it is used on solemnities and feasts. It expresses the ardor of a soul thirsting for God whose love is more precious than life.

Linked to David's exile in the title, the poet prays from afar to be restored to the Temple worship in Jerusalem. He is in a desert, aptly described as a parched land, "lifeless and without water." Anyone who has flown over the Arabian peninsula or driven through the deserts in the U.S. Southwest knows what desolation the psalmist envisions.

In his longing for God, he considers love of God a greater good than life itself. This is an unique expression in the Old Testament where human life was considered the supreme God-given gift.

Confident of his return to Jerusalem, the poet calls upon God with uplifted hands, savoring the praises of God as a rich banquet. Safe under "the shadow of his wings," a Temple phrase, he will praise God day and night. Those who have unjustly tried to prevent his return will get their just deserts, death by the sword, their bodies unburied to be eaten by scavengers.

The final mention of the king may simply recall the title, or may refer to the king as the first in line at the head of the worshippers.

For the Christian, the love of God should be our first priority. St. Paul directly expresses this: "For me to live is Christ, and death is gain" (Ph 1:21). And he continues:

"Whatever I had gained from all this, I have come to consider a loss because of Christ. In fact, I consider everything as a loss because of the supreme good of knowing Christ Jesus my Lord. For his sake I have cast everything aside and regard it as so much rubbish, so that I may gain Christ and be found in him, having no righteousness of my own based on observance of the law but only that righteousness which comes through faith in Christ, the righteousness that comes from God and which is based on faith. My goal is to know him and the power of his resurrection, to understand the fellowship of his sufferings and to be conformed to his death in the hope of somehow attaining resurrection from the dead" (Ph 3:7-11).

St. John Chrysostom helps us appreciate St. Paul:

"Paul, more than anyone else, has shown us what man really is, and in what our nobility consists, and of what virtue this particular animal is capable. Each day he aimed ever higher; each day he rose up with great ardor and faced with new eagerness the dangers that threatened him. The most important thing of all to him, however, was that he knew that he was loved by Christ. Enjoying this love, he considered himself happier than anyone else" (*In Praise of St. Paul*, #2).

The motivation of the monks and mystics throughout the history of the Church was caught stirringly by Thomas Merton:

"Love is the key to the meaning of life. It is at the same time transformation in Christ and the discovery of Christ. As we grow in love and in unity with those who are loved by Christ, that is to say, everyone, we become more and more capable of apprehending and obscurely grasping something of the tremendous reality of Christ in the world, Christ in ourselves, and Christ in our fellow man" (*Disputed Questions:* "The Power of Love").

PSALM 64: *"O God, hear my anguished voice..."*

The harm that a sharp tongue can do is at the heart of many classic novels, tragedies and epics. One malicious gossip in a small village or a closed community can do irreparable harm.

The psalmist in Psalm 64 raises an "anguished cry" to be delivered from such enemies. Tongues sharpened like swords and arrows of poisoned words give a dramatic picture of the calumniator who hides his malice under friendly, even religious, guise and strikes in secret.

But God, the just judge who sees the secret deeds, will exact sure vengeance on the evildoers by turning their words back against them. This is Old Testament justice, an eye for an eye, a tooth for a tooth (Ex 21:24). Christ exercised his right as the Divine Lawgiver to urge his followers to rise above that in charity (Mt 5:38-48).

The psalm ends with a touching proclamation of the justice of God being a refuge for those of good will and a cause for joy. St. Thérèse of Lisieux, in pondering on the justice of God remarked that we can put even more trust in the justice of God than we can in his mercy.

The Liturgy of the Hours uses Psalm 64 in the Common of Apostles because of v. 10, "They will understand God's deeds." It was their mission to proclaim the Good News after being thoroughly instructed. After the Resurrection Christ "opened their minds to understand the Scriptures" (Lk 24:45).

St. Peter, in advising us on Christian conduct, includes the admonition, "Keep your tongue from evil and your lips from speaking deceit" (1 P 3:10). When St. Paul speaks of the condition of fallen human nature, he includes this: "Their throats are open graves; they deceive with their tongues; the venom of asps is on their lips; their mouths are full of bitter cursing" (Rm 3:13-14).

St. Augustine, in commenting on this psalm, links it to the Passion of Christ when the chief priests and elders plotted in secret to hand Jesus over to death (Mt 26:1-5).

In thinking about sins committed by speech, one cannot help but call to mind the gift of tongues, the charismatic outpouring described so often in the New Testament (cf. 1 Cor 12:10). From time to time throughout Church history, some of these charismatic gifts have been manifested but never with such richness as in the apostolic era of the Church.

St. Anthony of Padua alluded to this in one of his sermons: "One who is filled with the Holy Spirit speaks in different languages. These different languages are different ways of witnessing to Christ, such as humility, poverty, patience and obedience. We speak in these languages when we reveal, in ourselves, these virtues to others. Actions speak louder than words; let your words teach and your actions speak."

PSALM 65: *"To you we owe our hymn of praise..."*

The record-breaking weather in the United States in recent years will long be remembered. Unprecedented floods in the Mississippi watershed and the great drought in the Southeast caused immense damage and economic hardship.

In Palestine during ancient times, the people lived so close to the land that a tragedy of like proportions would have meant widespread starvation and caused countless people to emigrate. It was to escape such a famine that the family of Jacob migrated to Egypt (Gn 46:1-47:12).

Psalm 65 is basically an agricultural psalm, one that could be used to pray for rain and good growing weather, or one that could be used as a thanksgiving at harvest time.

The expressive opening stanza, directed to God from the Temple on Mt. Zion, starts with praise and thanksgiving. It is the same sentiment used in the Preface of the Mass in the Latin Rite of the Church: "Let us give thanks to the Lord our God. It is right to give him thanks and praise."

In the Temple the people fulfill their vows to God, and they confess their sins and failings, beg for mercy and forgiveness, and praise God for his blessings. This is a universal obligation: "To you all flesh must come."

The second stanza is a tribute to Yahweh, the God of nature, first to the God who created with such power, then to the same God who re-creates, refreshes and holds his creation in being. It is impressive in concept and in the finished poem.

God is praised as the universal Creator who set up the mountains and designed the oceans and rivers. To the Hebrew mind, this was plain and simply raw power beyond comprehension. It was an attribute unique to God.

But just as merciful and wonderful is the power that sustains creation in being. Without the rains to soften the ground for plowing and the later rains to nourish the grain, without moisture for the pasture lands, there would be no sustaining of life.

This was both a source of wonder and a cause of happiness. The last line probably led to a communal celebration: "They cheer and sing for joy."

This psalm with its poetic license is easy for the Christian to pray, as is. Sophisticated as we may think ourselves to be, it takes but a little of nature's wrath to bring us to a halt. "Through nature to nature's God" is just as true today as when the axiom was first coined.

But the Christian sees an even higher meaning. The fruits of the earth are important to sustain life, but the fruits of the Holy Spirit are given to bring us to the true Zion, heaven.

Of the Holy Spirit, Christ said, "I will ask the Father and he will give you another Advocate to be with you always, the Spirit of Truth" (Jn 14:16). When Our Lord warned the apostles of his imminent departure and they showed their sorrow, he told them it was "expedient" to them for him to go so he could send them the Advocate (Jn 16:7).

St. Paul would spend his whole life as an apostle to further the work of the Holy Spirit in forming Christ in Christians and in forming the Church, the mystical Body of Christ.

St. Mary Magdalen dei Pazzi wrote:

"Come, Holy Spirit. Let the precious pearl of the Father and

the Word's delight, come. Spirit of Truth, You are the reward of
the saints, the comforter of souls, light in darkness, riches to the
poor, treasure to lovers, food for the hungry, comfort to the wan-
derer: You are the one in whom all treasures are contained"
(*Prayer*).

We also make our own the words of St. Ambrose:

> Come Holy Spirit, who ever one
> Art with the Father and the Son,
> It is the hour our soul possess
> With your full flood of holiness.
> Let heart and flesh and lips and mind
> Sound forth our witness to mankind
> And love light up our mortal frame
> Till others catch the living flame.
>
> (*Nunc Sancte Nobis Spiritus*, vv. 1, 2)

PSALM 66: *"Shout joyfully to God, all you on earth…"*

All the commentators agree that Psalm 66 was at one time
two, or maybe even three separate poems. It is united in its thanksgiving (eucharistic) theme.

After a stirring opening, a sort of Invitatory that might be
accompanied by trumpet blasts, the whole community is called
upon to praise God and fall down in worship. His awesome deeds
and tremendous strength make all recognize his almighty power.

As evidence of that power, the second stanza or poem takes
the worshippers back into sacred history. The references are to the
guidance of Israel through the Red Sea to safety from the Pharaoh (Ex 14:10-31) and to the crossing over the Jordan River into
the Holy Land (Jos 3:14-17).

After these historic references, the poet refers to some more
recent deliverance, more than likely the return from the Babylonian
Exile (Ezr 1:1-11). The description of the absolute humiliation
suffered by the people seems to indicate something of that cata-
clysmic range.

The final stanza refers to the holocausts offered in thanksgiving for the great historic deliverances and the thanks due for individual survival from personal trials. As a part of the thanksgiving ritual the individual usually gave public testimony to exactly what God had done for him.

Because of the theme of deliverance and the quality of life restored, it is easy to find a Christian dimension to this psalm. Early Christian versions of the Psalter usually titled this a Resurrection Prayer because the Easter liturgy is a tribute to the life and love of Christ actually restored and then shared.

St. Paul proclaims it:

"The love of God has been poured out into our hearts through the Holy Spirit that has been given to us. For Christ, while we were still helpless, yet died at the appointed time for the ungodly. Indeed, only with difficulty does one die for a just person, though perhaps for a good person one might even find courage to die. But God proves his love for us that while we were still sinners Christ died for us" (Rm 5:5-8).

"For God so loved the world that he gave his only Son" (Jn 3:16) and the Son so loved us that he gave his life for our salvation (Gal 2:20). There is "no greater love than this, to lay down one's life for one's friends" (Jn 15:13).

But Christ not only died for us, in his Resurrection he was the pledge of resurrection for all mankind:

"But now Christ has been raised from the dead, the firstfruits of those who have fallen asleep. For since death came through a human being, the resurrection of the dead came also through a human being. For just as in Adam all die, so too in Christ shall all be brought to life" (1 Cor 15:20-22).

The thanksgiving theme was also easy to adopt for the Holy Eucharist, since there are few gifts from God for which we should be more grateful. Pope St. Alexander I, who was martyred about 115 A.D. wrote, "Among sacrifices there can be none greater than the body and blood of Christ, nor any more powerful oblation."

St. Thomas Aquinas wrote some of the classic Christian eucharistic hymns. Listen to a small sample:

Word made Flesh, the bread of nature
By his word to Flesh he turns.
Wine into his Blood he changes,
What though sense no change discerns?
Only be the heart in earnest,
Faith her lesson quickly learns.
Down in adoration falling,
Lo the Sacred Host we hail!
Lo o'er ancient forms departing,
Newer rites of grace prevail!
Faith for all defects supplying
Where the feeble senses fail.

(*Pange Lingua*, vv. 4, 5)

PSALM 67: *"May God be gracious to us and bless us..."*

The Lord told Moses that Aaron and his descendants should bless the people with these words,

The Lord bless you and keep you!
The Lord let his face shine upon you and be gracious to you!
The Lord look upon you kindly and give you peace!

(Nb 6:24-26)

These words are incorporated into this psalm of blessing and thanksgiving. Graciousness and kindness go hand in hand and are the glue that cements friendships. That God would let his "face shine upon us" is the poetic way of asking God to smile on us — certainly a friendly gesture.

Aaron, the brother of Moses and Miriam, was the first high priest of the Israelite nation by the direct choice of Yahweh. It is interesting to note that from the very beginning, the leadership role and the priestly role were separated.

Then there is the invitation for all the gentiles, "the nations," to praise the God who rules over all. This was hardly an invitation for them to be converts to the worship of Yahweh, since that particular worship was principally a prize of physical descent from the

Patriarchs, Abraham, Isaac and Jacob. Nevertheless, when the neighboring nations witnessed what generous blessings God showered on Israel, they should acknowledge that fact. And converts were accepted, known as "God-fearing men."

The true universality of the call to salvation would come much later. After the Resurrection, Christ commanded his apostles, "Go, therefore, and make disciples of all nations, baptizing them in the name of the Father, and of the Son, and of the Holy Spirit" (Mt 28:19). "Let it be known to you," said St. Paul, "that this salvation of God has been sent to the Gentiles; they will listen" (Ac 28:28).

The fact that God had just given the people a generous harvest is seen as a direct blessing from God. Therefore, the psalm can be used as a general song of thanksgiving or as a part of the harvest festival.

It is easy for the Christian to adopt this psalm as a prayer of thanksgiving and praise. It is also easy to raise the notion of graciousness to the gift of sanctifying grace, that grace of adoption that makes us sons and daughters of God through a share in the Christ-life. What Christ is by nature, we become by the grace of adoption. In the words of St. Paul:

"In his love he destined us beforehand to be his adopted sons through Jesus Christ, according to the purpose and desire of his will, to the praise of the glorious grace he bestowed upon us in his beloved.

"In Christ's blood we are redeemed and our sins are forgiven — such is the wealth of his grace which he poured out upon us! With every manner of wisdom and understanding he made known to us the mystery of his will, according to the purpose he displayed in Christ as a plan for the fullness of time — to bring all things together in Christ, things in the heavens and things on earth" (Eph 1:5-10).

St. Cyril of Jerusalem comments on this:

"When we were baptized into Christ and clothed ourselves in him, we were transformed into the likeness of the Son of God. Having destined us to be his adopted sons and daughters, God gave us a likeness to Christ in his glory, and living as we do in communion with Christ, God's anointed, we ourselves are rightly called 'the anointed ones'" (*Catechesis* #21).

Abbot Marmion based his whole spiritual doctrine on this great grace of adoption of the faithful:

"According to the designs of the Father, it is by faith that the children of adoption must enter into contact with the supernatural world: with Christ, the Church, the sacraments and above all the Eucharist. It is by faith that they must hope in God, love him and serve him" (*Christ the Ideal of the Priest*, ch. 16, #1).

If the psalm is used with the harvest theme, the Psalm-Prayer for Psalm 67 invites us "to make God known with reverence and to bring forth a harvest of justice" (*The Liturgy of the Hours*). It is axiomatic that the magnet of good works is one of the most attractive ways to bring people to the knowledge of Christ and his Church. That is truly a "harvest of justice."

PSALM 68: *"God will arise for battle…"*

The philosophy of history in today's academic world has shifted from an emphasis on names and dates to a more lofty look at the whole society being studied, in its context. Psalm 68 interprets history from a theological viewpoint, from Exodus to the time of the kings.

The psalm as we have it is a collection of nine poems or stanzas that reflect older hymns and texts. God is the principal actor in each segment, sometimes called Elohim (God), sometimes called Adonai (Lord) and once Yahweh.

The action starts with God's charge to Moses to lead his people from the captivity of Egypt and the journey to and the occupation of the Holy Land. Then God acts directly through the judges with allusions to Deborah's song taken from chapter five of the Book of Judges.

David's conquest of Jerusalem and the enthronement of the Ark of the Covenant on Mt. Zion is the next historical section commemorated. The other mighty mountains in the land are told not to be jealous of Mt. Zion which God has chosen.

The psalm then goes on to record military adventures, triumphant celebrations and various military and political problems. It ends with the prophetic hope for the future of the people, still led by God.

Psalm 68 is a truly dramatic view of the God of history acting in history. It proceeds from the austerity of Moses and the Exodus, through the charismatic role of judges and prophets to the glory and triumph of Solomon.

The psalm as it has been handed down to us probably reflects use in the great liturgical processions in Temple worship when the Ark itself was carried in the procession. It would also have been used as an extraordinary hymn of national thanksgiving.

The imagery is varied and impressive. Enemies will be dispersed like smoke or like wax being melted. God is the father of the fatherless and defender of the widow. St. James took up this point: "Religion that is pure and undefiled before God the Father is this: to care for orphans and widows in their affliction and to keep oneself unstained from the world" (Jm 1:27).

After the rigors of the desert of Sinai, God leads his people into a land with abundant rain, "a land flowing with milk and honey" (Ex 3:8). Egypt, and all oppressors, are described as "the wild beast of the reeds," no doubt a crocodile.

The Church follows the direction of the psalm in regarding God as the ultimate source of all blessings and glorifying him in the salvation history commemorated. Indeed, we can only marvel at the hand of God working through and in human history. When Christ came in the fullness of time, the old order was completed, only to go forward now as Church history, the history of the Kingdom of God. "The law and the prophets lasted until John (the Baptizer); but from then on the kingdom of God is proclaimed" (Lk 16:17).

The liturgy of the Church follows St. Paul's example in using this psalm as part of the Feast of the Ascension of the Lord.

"Therefore it says: 'He ascended on high and took prisoners

captive; he gave gifts to men.' What does 'he ascended' mean except that he also descended into the lower regions of the earth? The one who descended is also the one who ascended far above all the heavens that he might fill all things" (Eph 4:7-10).

Abbot Columba Marmion writes:

"After his Resurrection, Christ Jesus only remains forty days with his disciples. St. Leo says these days did not pass in inaction but by many apparitions to the Apostles, by his conversations with them, he talked to them about the Kingdom of God. In his *First Sermon on the Ascension of the Lord*, he says that Jesus filled their hearts with joy, strengthened their faith in his triumph, in his Person, in his mission. He also gave them his last instructions for the establishing and organizing of the Church (Ac 1:3)" (*Christ in His Mysteries*, p. 302).

PSALM 69: *"Save me, God…"*

Psalm 69 is one of the psalms most quoted in the New Testament, particularly in the Passion of Christ and on Holy Thursday. The anguish of the psalmist is obvious from the very first verses. The image of overwhelming floods and mire is taken from the chaos God worked out from in the creation of the world (Gn 1:1-2). The psalmist is besieged by treacherous enemies "more numerous than the hairs" of his head.

Admitting that he is not perfect, he still identifies himself with the friends of God and pleads for help against relatives and neighbors who have made him a despised outcast. In his zeal, they turn on him as a religious zealot, even ridiculing him for his religious practices. His only and his last resort is to turn to God for help and strength to overcome his enemies.

The "curse section" of this psalm causes some Christians pain when they read it, or they deliberately omit it. The fact is that the Semitic people were very expressive and emotional in their terms of endearment and anger.

Given the fact that the psalmist did not believe in life after death, the only way God's justice could be vindicated was here and now, in this life. The variety of evils that the poet wishes on his enemies is rather breathtaking and certainly is evidence of his grief and sense of the personal injustice that he has suffered. The stress he has suffered at their hands has caused him pain and sickness, even death-threatening illness. His imprecations are colorful, to say the least! His final curse is, "Strike them from the book of life." This concept is used by St. Paul (Ph 4:3) and St. John (Rv 3:5).

The psalmist returns to his plea for help and his promise to offer a song of thanksgiving which is recorded in verses 33-35. The final verses are a prophetic plea for the whole nation, possibly added after the destruction of the Temple in Jerusalem.

As used in the Passion narrative in the Gospels, part of Psalm 69 is very well known to Christians. "They gave Jesus wine to drink mixed with gall" (Mt 27:34). "One of them ran to get a sponge, he soaked it in wine and putting it on a reed gave it to him to drink" (Mt 27:48; Mk 15:23; Jn 19:29).

Our Lord uses the psalm to explain the hatred of the world for him and his message: "They hated me without cause" (Jn 15:25). St. Paul also uses part of the cursing section of the psalm as a prophecy fulfilled for the remnant of Israel. "Let their table become a snare and a trap, a stumbling block and a retribution for them; let their eyes grow dim so that they may not see, and keep their backs bent forever" (Rm 11:9-10). Again, in the context of being patient, Christ suffered patiently so that "the insults of those who insult you fall upon me" (Rm 15:3).

The Passion of Christ inspired many of the saints since it was such a complete sacrifice of love.

St. Francis of Paola wrote:

"Fix your minds on the passion of our Lord Jesus Christ. Consumed with love for us, he descended from heaven to redeem us. For our sake he endured every torment of body and soul and he shrank from no bodily pain. He himself gave us the perfect example of patience and love. Therefore, we are to be patient in adversity" (*Letters*).

St. Thomas More sought comfort in the Passion just before his martyrdom:

"By the merits of his bitter Passion joined to mine and far surpassing in merit for me all that I can suffer myself, his bounteous goodness shall release me from the pains of purgatory and shall increase my rewards in heaven besides" (*Prison Letter*).

Paul Claudel wrote, "Jesus did not come to explain away suffering or remove it. He came to fill it with his presence."

An anonymous poet from the fourteenth century gives us even more insight in his prayer-poem *Anima Christi*:

> Soul of Christ, sanctify me.
> Body of Christ, save me.
> Blood of Christ, inebriate me.
> Water from the side of Christ, wash me.
> Passion of Christ, comfort me.
> O good Jesus, hear me.
> Within your wounds, hide me.
> Never permit me to be separated from you.
> From the wicked enemy, defend me.
> In the hour of my death, call me
> And bid me come to you,
> That with your saints I may praise you
> Forever and ever. Amen.

PSALM 70: *"Graciously rescue me, God…"*

> O God, come to my assistance!
> O Lord, make haste to help me.

This older translation of Psalm 70 is familiar to anyone who prays the Divine Office, *The Liturgy of the Hours*, since every "hour" still begins with this petition. There is sort of a divine impatience here since we know that God can and will help, but we want it right now.

The troubles imposed by "those who seek my life" are really rather vague, so it must be supposed that this is a general lament for the everyday problems in life. When God does intervene, the petitioner will gratefully proclaim, "Glory be to God!"

The psalmist identifies himself with the afflicted and the poor, those who traditionally have an especial claim on the mercy of God. The "poor" are often not those in dire poverty but those who are the unsophisticated, the plain and ordinary citizens who depend on God in simplicity of heart.

St. Matthew gives us an instance of this in the story of the calming of the stormy sea. Christ was asleep in the boat when the storm suddenly swept down on them. They woke him with the simple, direct plea, "Save us Lord! We are perishing!" and his response was immediate (Mt 8:23-27).

Dorothy Day is an example of this living, simple faith:

"I try to practice the presence of God after the manner of Blessed Lawrence, and pray without ceasing, as St. Paul advised. He might even have had women in mind. But he himself was active enough, weaving goat's hair into tents and sailcloth to earn a living, and preaching nights and Sundays.

"So I am trying to learn to recall my soul like the straying creature it is as it wanders off over and over again during the day, and lift my heart to the Blessed Mother and the saints, since my occupations are the lowly and humble ones, as were theirs" (*On Pilgrimage*, Mar. 18, 1948).

When it comes to actual poverty St. Caesarius of Arles sends us some good advice from the late fifth century:

"What sort of people are we? When God gives we wish to receive, but when he begs we refuse to give. Remember, it was Christ who said, 'I was hungry and you did not feed me.' When the poor are starving, Christ also hungers.

"Do not neglect to improve the condition of the poor if you wish to be sure that your own sins are forgiven. Christ hungers now, my brethren; it is he who deigns to hunger and thirst in the person of the poor. What he will return in heaven tomorrow is what he receives here on earth today" (*Sermon 25*).

Since priests and religious are the ones who pray the psalms most regularly on a daily basis, St. Polycarp's advice is timely:

"Priests should be sympathetic and merciful to everyone, bringing back those who have wandered, visiting the sick and the poor. Deacons, in the same way, must be blameless in the sight of God.

"Be steadfast, then, and follow the Lord's example, strong and unshaken in faith, loving the community as you love one another. United in the truth, show the Lord's own gentleness in your dealing with one another, and look down on no one. If you can do good, do not put it off because almsgiving frees one from death" (*Letter to the Philippians* #5).

Psalm 70 is used in the Office for the Dead, since theirs is certainly an urgent plea for mercy. Most of us can remember the Sisters in grade school explaining to us the plight of the "Poor Souls in Purgatory." All Souls Day, Nov. 2, is still a major devotional Feast Day.

Psalm 70 is a repeat of several verses in Psalm 40, with minor textual differences such as the name for God here being Yahweh instead of Elohim.

PSALM 71: *"In you, Lord, I take refuge…"*

"Grow old along with me, the best is yet to be," wrote the poet Robert Browning. "Our times are in your hand, perfect the cup as planned. Let age approve of youth and death complete the same" ("Rabbi Ben Ezra").

It would be hard to sum up this psalm more succinctly or more beautifully. Briefly, it is the prayer of an old man who was raised with fervent religious training and who has been as faithful to that background as possible. Now, sick and aged, his enemies look at his afflictions as proof that God is punishing him.

He knows this is not the case and he asks that God's way be vindicated on the false judgment of these "enemies." Then he settles down to a serene and sure appreciation of God's power at work among mankind.

The fact that this poet is a religious man can be demonstrated by his extensive use of other psalm verses, almost twenty in number. However, it is not merely a collection of such verses. It shows a way of using the whole Psalter as the basis of a prayer life.

His faith is shown with the verse, "On you I depend since birth; from my mother's womb you are my strength." His plea is powerful: "Do not cast me aside in my old age," and "Now that I am old and gray, do not forsake me, God." So is his confidence in God, "You have done great things; O God, who is your equal?"

But without the confidence in life after death, there is precious little consolation in growing old. Our American devotion to the "youth culture" and the shameful way we treat our senior citizens cast our civilization in that same light.

Christ told St. Martha, "I am the resurrection and the life: whoever believes in me, though he should die, will come to life, and whoever is alive and believes in me will never die" (Jn 11:25-26). He promised that he would go to the Father to prepare a place for his faithful ones (Jn 14:1-6).

The Resurrection of Christ is the pledge of our own immortality. In chapter 15 of the First Letter to the Corinthians, St. Paul goes on at great length about the resurrection of the dead. So important is this that he could write, "If Christ has not been raised, your faith is vain" (1 Cor 15:17). If we believe in Christ only for this world, then we are the most pitiable people of all (1 Cor 15:19).

He returns to this theme frequently, as when he writes, "For we know that if our earthly dwelling, a tent, should be destroyed, we have a building from God, a dwelling not made with hands, eternal in heaven" (2 Cor 5:1). With complete confidence, then, Paul can advise, "Rejoice in hope, endure in affliction, persevere in prayer" (Rm 12:12).

Reborn in Baptism and with souls refreshed by the Holy Eucharist, we are actually called to eternal youth, a life in which we shall never grow old or feel infirmities. St. Thomas Aquinas was of the firm opinion that in the resurrection of the body, we will be given a mature body at the height of our human potential.

Aristides, a second century writer says, "Christians have the commandments of the Lord Jesus Christ himself engraved on their hearts, and these they observe, looking for the resurrection of the dead and the life of the world to come" (*Apology*, ch. 15).

St. Irenaeus, writing shortly after that, declared:

"Our bodies, which have been nourished by the Eucharist, will be buried in the earth and will decay, but they will rise again at the appointed time, for the Word of God will raise them up to the glory of God the Father. Then the Father will clothe our mortal nature in immortality and freely endow our corruptible nature in incorruptibility, for God's power is shown most perfectly in weakness" (*Against Heresies*, Bk. 5, #2).

How much the Christian dimension adds to this important psalm! Death becomes a *natalitia*, a birthday to eternal life and the "golden years" become a special opportunity to prepare for eternal life and love.

PSALM 72: *"O God, give your judgment to the king..."*

The biblical epics of the Cecil B. DeMille era in Hollywood's heyday loved to film court scenes as rich and opulent as that described in Psalm 72. How historical they were is open to question, but they were splendid.

The royal psalms depict the King of Israel as God's vicar, dispensing justice and enforcing peace. In this psalm, some part of the verb "to judge" is used 25 times. It is used in the sense of vigorously upholding the Law of God and forthrightly defending the oppressed.

The reward for such a reign was wealth, power and fertility. The prayer for the king, since he was human, was that he be endowed with wisdom for many years, while the "sun endures and like the moon" through all generations.

His kingdom would stretch from sea to sea, and the geographical places mentioned signify north, south, east and west. He would be a king of kings, receiving tribute from lands not ruled directly.

Solomon, of course, was the truly "grand ruler" and the kingdom never stretched beyond the boundaries he ruled. The dynasty established by God for King David (2 S 7:8-17) was to endure for centuries in an ever-diminishing role. With the Babylonian Captivity, the messianic role of the royal psalms became more pronounced.

By the time of Christ, after the seventy weeks of years, announced by the archangel Gabriel to the prophet Daniel (Dn 9:24-27), the messianic expectations were rampant in Palestine. Over and over again Christ had to raise the expectations of his followers from a political messiah to a spiritual one (cf. Jn 18:36).

The parables in the Synoptic Gospels, Matthew, Mark and Luke, begin so often with phrases such as "the Kingdom of God is like..." Over and over Christ had to emphasize the spiritual nature of his kingdom and the spiritual conversion of his followers. A revolutionary Christ wasn't, but he was a radical if we mean that he went to the root, or the heart, of spiritual matters.

The Blessed Mother (Lk 1:46-55) accepted the Incarnation as a fulfillment of the promises made to Abraham (Gn 12:1-3) and Zechariah, the father of St. John the Baptizer, saw the child's role as a step in restoring the glory of the house of David (Lk 1:69). The first verse of his prayer, the *Benedictus*, is from Psalm 72:18.

From the beginning of the Church, Christians have recognized the royal psalms as being fulfilled in the Incarnation, recognizing that the line of King David had finally triumphed with a King who is eternal. His reign, quite literally, will last forever. He was like the dew coming down from heaven to refresh and renew the whole world. He will rule with absolute justice, temper it with mercy and give life that will go on forever.

Jesus fulfilled the royal idea in a transcendental manner far beyond anything the prophets could have imagined.

As the liturgy for the Feast of the Epiphany developed, the

Christian imagination associated this psalm with the magi (Mt 2:11) and used verses 10 and 11: "May the kings of Tarshish and the islands bring tribute, the kings of Arabia and Seba offer gifts. May all kings bow before him, all nations serve him."

Novatian, writing in the early third century, described the common belief of Christians:

"Therefore, let those who read in the Scriptures that the man, Christ Jesus, is the Son of Man also read there that this same Jesus is called both God and the Son of God.

"In the same manner that he, as man, is of Abraham, even so, as God, is he also before Abraham himself.

"In the same manner that he, as man, is the Son of David, so is he also, as God, called the Lord of David" (*The Trinity*, ch. 11).

During the Dark Ages, Jonas of Orleans wrote a description of what Christian kings should be and his work was definitely influenced by the royal psalms:

"It is the king's chief duty to govern the people of God and rule them with equity and justice, and to work for them to have peace and concord. First of all he must be a defender of the Church and the servants of God... The needs of widows, orphans, the poor, and indeed all the needy, should be attended" (*On the Institution of Kings*).

St. Peter Canisius adds a very homey touch to his reflection on the fulfillment of David's dynasty:

"Why did the Fathers of the Church call the Virgin Mary by the title 'Queen'? They recognized the tremendous praise heaped on her in the Scriptures. She is singled out as having a king for her father, noble David, and the King of Kings and Lord of Lords for her Son, whose reign will never end...

"There is not one who excels her in dignity, beauty or holiness. Only the Holy Trinity is above her; all others are below her in dignity and beauty" (*On the Virgin Mother of God*).

BOOK THREE: Psalms 73 - 89

PSALM 73: *"How good God is to the upright..."*

The Hebrews never excelled in philosophy which must start out by answering from reason alone, such basic questions as "Why do the good suffer?" The Greeks answered it in one way and the Romans codified the answers. Eastern philosophies sought answers along different paths.

But for the Hebrews, faith was absolutely necessary to make any sense whatsoever of human affairs, and at that, only dimly. The Book of Job was the closest thing to a Hebrew philosophy, but the questions are answered by saying that we don't really know and that all that is necessary is to put your faith and trust in God. That's good theology but very poor philosophy.

Psalm 73 starts out with a conclusion: How good God is to the upright and clean of heart! The rest of the psalm is an expansion of that emphatic statement.

The poet looks around him and sees the unjust growing rich and fat on ill-gotten goods, treachery and cunning. The justice of God demands that the good prosper and the wicked suffer. However, that doesn't always seem to happen in the real world.

The psalm paints a bright picture of the worldly pursuing their seemingly happy ways, a picture not unlike that described by Francis Thompson in *The Hound of Heaven*. The writer almost loses his faith in God when he sees this all around him. "Is it vain," he asks, "that I have kept my hands clean and washed my hands in innocence?"

Then he enters the Temple and experiences God. It is not reason that gives him the answer but faith. It is not an unreasonable faith, of course, but it is one that involves the "leap of faith." No matter how prosperous the wicked become, their bitter end can come at any time, without warning. Their doubts and pains can be hidden, for the rich have the luxury of privacy, but they do suffer from the human condition and their end is certain. Wealth does not guarantee happiness and you can't take your wealth with you in death.

The Christian recognizes Christ's parable of the rich man who hoarded his wealth. When his treasuries were full, he relaxed to eat, drink and be merry, "You fool!" cries God, "This night your life will be demanded of you; and the things you have prepared, to whom will they belong?" (Lk 12:20).

In v. 24, the certainty of God's friendship is a lasting reward. It gives a deep inner joy that cannot be taken away. Is there a hint, here, of the belief in a personal life after death? Possibly, but most scholars do not think so. They think it refers to such mysteries as the translation of Enoch from this world (Gn 5:24) and the ascension of Elijah (2 K 2:1-12).

The Christian, of course, secure in the knowledge of a personal immortality, reads this part of the psalm with both love and thanksgiving. After this earthly pilgrimage, "at the end you receive me with honor." The belief in the doctrine of the Communion of Saints means that we all live in Christ whether on earth, in purgatory or in heaven.

The wicked will, indeed, receive their just punishment from God, but for the faithful, "To be near God is my good." Just to be in his presence, especially before the Blessed Sacrament, is the inspiration of the spiritual life of most of the saints.

St. Richard of Chichester wrote:

"Thanks be to you, my Lord Jesus Christ, for all the blessings and benefits which you have given me, for all the pains and insults you have borne for me.

"O most merciful Friend, my Brother and Redeemer, may I know you more clearly, love you more dearly, and follow you more nearly, day by day, day by day" (*Day by Day*).

St. Alphonsus Liguori wrote many pamphlets on the Blessed Sacrament that have been published in English under the title *The Holy Eucharist*. He declares:

"It is impossible to find on earth a more precious gem, or a treasure more worthy of all our love, than Jesus in the Most Holy Sacrament. Certainly, among all devotions, after that of receiving the sacraments, that of adoring Jesus in the Blessed Sacrament holds the first place, is the most pleasing to God and the most useful to ourselves" ("Visits to the Blessed Sacrament and to the Blessed Virgin" #1).

And again he writes:

"The principal effect of love is to tend to union. For this very purpose Christ instituted Holy Communion that he might unite himself entirely to our souls. He had given himself to us as our master, our example and our victim; it only remained for him to give himself to us as our food; that he might become one with us as food becomes one with the person who eats it.

"This he did by instituting the Sacrament of Love: 'The last degree of love,' says St. Bernardine of Siena, 'is when he gave himself to us to be our food'" ("Meditations for the Octave of Corpus Christi," V).

Biblical scholar Father Roland E. Murphy, O. Carm., says that Psalm 73 is one of the most sublime and beautiful prayers in the Old Testament.

PSALM 74: *"Why, God, have you cast us off forever?"*

The Temple in Jerusalem was the center of the sacrificial and liturgical life of the Jewish nation. It was much more than a mere symbol of the identity of that nation. Its destruction by the Babylonians in 587-586 B.C. was a catastrophe so great that it numbed them completely.

Psalm 74 is a lament of national proportions, of faith wounded by agony. The agony is so great that the people can't even blame themselves for their guilt, unlike the prophets who always assigned the reasons of sin and therefore punishment.

Just as the Jews today rightly keep alive the horror of the Nazi Holocaust in Europe, so this psalm keeps alive the calamity of the overthrow of the Temple. The first section reads like the script for a newsreel.

The walls are breached; the sanctuary is devastated; foreign flags are raised over Mt. Zion; axes tear apart the wood; the engravings are pounded to dust. It was then put to the torch. Fi-

nally, the plunderers go about the land trying to destroy all re-
membrances of Yahweh. Barbarians seem to like to destroy beauty
just for the sake of destruction.

In the first few centuries of the Christian era, the Roman
Empire tried to stamp out Christianity. The law was enacted,
"*Christiani non sint*" — Christians may not exist! How precious
are the martyrs of that era and how triumphantly the Church treasures their memory! St. Polycarp wrote, "We worship Christ as the
Son of God, while we love the martyrs as disciples and imitators
of the Lord" (*Letter to the Philippians* #17).

The psalm goes on in the second half to recall the tremendous creative power of God. Drawing colorful images from the
myths of the peoples around them, Leviathan (a coiled serpent),
dragons, chaos, etc., it proclaims that all those images of creation
were actually performed by Yahweh as an almost casual use of his
power. It was hardly an extraordinary use of power for Yahweh to
"set the sun and moon in place." "Yours is the day and yours is
the night."

Certainly this God of such power would not forget the Mosaic covenant (Ex 34:6-7) and he could exercise his power again
to restore his people. The silence of God in the midst of this calamity was almost as painful as the destruction. Even prophetic
guidance was silent.

As a matter of fact, the implied hope underlying this psalm
was fulfilled when at the end of the Babylonian Captivity, Cyrus,
King of Persia, sent the remnant of the house of Israel back to
Jerusalem (Ezr 1:1-11). I am not sure how unique an event this is
historically, but for a people to retain their identity for seventy years
in a foreign land and not be absorbed there, is proof to me of God's
providential care and his faithfulness to his covenanted promises.
No doubt the same could be said about the modern state of Israel
after almost two millennia of exile.

Jesus warned his followers to expect persecution for his name
(Mt 10:16-33) but urged them to be faithful in patient perseverance. "Do not be afraid of those who can kill the body but cannot

kill the soul. Be afraid of the one who can destroy soul and body in Gehenna" (Mt 10:28).

The New Covenant which superseded and fulfilled the Mosaic covenant has been sealed in the blood of Christ (Mk 14:24). The Church is a spiritual temple (1 Cor 3:16-17) made up of living stones (1 P 2:5-6) built upon Christ, one that will last until the end of time (Mt 28:20).

In the sixth century, St. Fulgentius of Ruspe proclaimed:

"Christ is the priest through whom we have been reconciled, the sacrifice by which we have been reconciled, the temple in which we have been reconciled, the God with whom we have been reconciled.

"Now in the time of the New Testament, the holy Catholic Church throughout the world never ceases to offer the sacrifice of bread and wine, in faith and love, to him and to the Father and the Holy Spirit, with whom he shares the one godhead" (*Treatise on Faith* #22).

PSALM 75: *"We thank you, God, we give thanks..."*

There are many reasons for giving thanks to God, liturgical, social and personal, but here the psalmist rejoices in the justice of God. Amidst the setting of all God's wonderful deeds, God the just judge of the world is the subject of this prayer.

The poet has God speaking directly, assuring the faithful that he will judge with justice when he sees that the time for judgment is proper. In the "flat world" understanding of the earth of the biblical writers, even something as terrifying as an earthquake is still in God's plan of judging and he will keep the world steady on its pillars.

And the God who can use nature in his judgments can certainly take care of the arrogant and the proud. The symbol of the horn, so frequently used in the Old Testament, is a symbol of power taken from strong animals, such as a ram, goat, ox or rhino.

The raised horns of vv. 5 and 6 are an arrogant sign of defiance of God himself.

God's judgment is universal, not coming from the east or west, the mountains (north) or the desert (south). It presides over the whole world simultaneously. The "cup of God's wrath," is a familiar Old Testament symbol and it means that the wicked will be punished right down to the dregs, with perfect, impartial justice.

It is indeed praiseworthy to know that God will break off the horns of the wicked, pare them down to size, and lift up the horns of the just in final victory. In this, the psalmist rejoices.

This complete assurance in the final triumph of the justice of God has certainly entered into Christian spirituality. The Lord's Prayer, taught as a direct result of his disciples' request about prayer, has us say, "Your kingdom come, your will be done on earth as it is in heaven" (Mt 6:10).

In the magnificent canticles in the first chapter of the Gospel according to St. Luke, we read: "He has shown might with his arm, dispersed the arrogant of mind and heart. He has thrown down the rulers from their thrones but lifted up the lowly" (Lk 1:51-52). And again, "He has raised up a horn of salvation within the house of David his servant" (Lk 1:69).

"That God would confuse the proud, that he would use his power to save the humble, was a theme that led St. Bernard to consider the humility that Christ exercised in the Incarnation. In his first *Missus Est* homily he writes, 'Christ was subject to them. Who? And to whom? God was subject to man! God, I repeat, to whom the angels are subject, whom Principalities and Powers obey, was subject to Mary, and not only to Mary, but to Joseph, too, because of Mary'" (Dollen: *Prophecies Fulfilled*).

Father Raymond E. Brown, S.S., is quoted in the same book, commenting on these two verses in the *Magnificat*:

"The Christian good news meant that the ultimately blessed were not the mighty and the rich. . . The *Magnificat* anticipates the Lucan Jesus in preaching that wealth and power are not real virtues since they have no standing in God's sight" (*The Birth of the Messiah*).

Humility is a much misunderstood virtue. It is not simply an "O Lord I am not worthy" approach. It is the truth of the relationship between God and humanity, the greatness of God and the joyful dependence that we have on him and with one another. And St. Ignatius of Antioch reminds us, "In humility be patient with one another, as God is with you" (*Letter to Polycarp* #6).

PSALM 76: *"Renowned in Judah is God..."*

Considered one of the oldest of the psalms, Psalm 76 is a song that glorifies God as the omnipotent protector, ruling from Mt. Zion in Salem, over a kingdom not yet divided into Judah and Israel.

Salem, the ancient name for Jerusalem as a place of adoration to the one true God, recalls directly the story of Melchizedek (Gn 14:18-22). Melchizedek blessed Abraham in the name of God Most High, offered sacrifices of bread and wine, and accepted a tithe from the Patriarch.

Note that the enemies of Israel are the enemies of God who fights for and protects his people. The barbaric warriors who assault Israel are stunned, dazed, and even slain by the divine power. "When you arose, O God for judgment" all the earth trembled in the face of such awe-inspiring deeds. This expectation is reflected in the Last Judgment scenes, "They will see the Son of Man coming upon the clouds of heaven with power and great glory" (Mt 24:30).

Verse 11 in the most recently revised translation reads, "Even wrathful Edom praises you; the remnant of Hamath keeps your feast." This refers to King David's victories against Moab, Edom, the Arameans, Hadadezar, Hamath, etc. (2 S 8:1-14). The older translation gives the sense of the psalm with "Men's anger will serve to praise you; its survivors surround you in joy." Much of the difficulty comes from the Hebrew alphabet which does not have vowels. Msgr. Ronald Knox wrote a delightful book titled *The Trials of a Translator*, but he only had to worry about translating the

Bible from Latin and Greek. Going from Hebrew to English is truly heroic at times.

The last two verses recommend making vows of praise and thanksgiving to God as well as bringing gifts to his Temple. St. Augustine comments on them:

"Do not make vows and then neglect to keep them. What vows are we all expected to make without distinction? The vow of believing in Christ, hoping for eternal life from him and living a good life in keeping with the ordinary norms of good conduct.

"As for any other vows, let each of us make any we wish. But let us also take care to observe the ones we have made!" (*Commentary on Psalm 76,* 16).

George Martin in *God's Word Today* (May 1993, p. 17) suggests that we can use this psalm as a petition for peace, asking God to shatter the weapons of war (v. 4), disarm armies (v. 6) and deliver those afflicted by war (v. 10). No doubt there will be wars and rumors of wars right up to the end of time (Mt 24:6) but that just means that Christians must work and pray for peace without tiring. The Popes of the twentieth century, from the eve of World War I until the present, have been apostles of peace.

The Fathers of the Second Vatican Council declared:

"Peace is not merely the absence of war or the simple maintenance of a balance of powers between forces, nor can it be imposed at the dictates of absolute power.

"Peace is called, quite rightly and properly, a work of justice. It is the product of order, the order implanted in human society by its divine founder. It is to be realized in practice as hunger and thirst for ever more complete and perfect justice" (*Gaudium et Spes* #78).

The gift of internal peace, however, is truly a Christian treasure. Pope St. Clement I wrote:

"Hasten toward the goal of peace, set before us from the very beginning. Keep your eyes firmly on the Father and Creator of the whole universe and hold fast to his splendid and transcendent gifts of peace and all his blessings."

St. John Chrysostom also commented on this:

"Prayer and conversation with God is a supreme good. It is a partnership and union with God. Prayer is the light of the spirit, true knowledge of God, mediating between God and man. Prayer stands before God as an honored ambassador; it gives joy to the spirit and peace to the heart" (*Sermon on Prayer* #6).

Or as we read in Dante's much-quoted axiom: "In his will is our peace."

PSALM 77: *"I cry aloud to God..."*

Three psalms — 39, 62 and 77 — are attributed to Jeduthun. He was a temple musician appointed by the High Priest Zadoc and his descendants were the gate-keepers there (1 Ch 16:37-42). His three songs are a masterful blend of the subtle and the gentle.

The immediate cause of Psalm 77 seems to be a national disaster, probably a major military defeat. The occasion was probably an all night vigil, a practice frequently mentioned in the Old Testament and a practice that still endures in the Christian liturgy on such occasions as the Easter Vigil or the vigil that follows the Mass on the night of Holy Thursday.

The question that Jeduthun raises is one that has always plagued the faithful in times of distress. "Will the Lord reject us forever, never again show his favor?" In good times it is easy to forget God; in bad times we fall prostrate before him, at least figuratively.

The questions the poet raises may be doubts. They may be dramatic, or even rhetorical, questions. Because the second half of this psalm is a psalm of praise, I tend to favor the last idea.

The anguished cry, "Has the right hand of the Lord deserted us?" is a transition to the hymn of praise which recounts the powerful deeds of the Lord in favor of Israel. Historically God has always helped his chosen ones so there is every right to hope for help in the present trouble.

The watery chaos reflects God the creator in Genesis 1:1-2 but the mention of the descendants of Jacob and Joseph also positions us in the Exodus story. The crossing of the Sea of Reeds under the guidance of Moses and Aaron is a high point in the catalogue of marvelous deeds performed by Yahweh for Israel. By God's direct power the people were led through the sea, though his footsteps were invisible.

For the Christian, these wonders of the Old Testament are only signs and figures pointing to the more wonderful work of redemption in Christ. The sacrifice of Christ on Calvary, a supreme act of love, saved the Church once and for all. The waters of baptism join individuals to that sacrifice, to the Church, and there is every right to hope for the graces necessary for the successful pilgrimage through life to the true Promised Land, heaven.

For the Christian, there is a call to pray always, not just in time of trouble. In the parable of the persistent widow, Our Lord begins with "the necessity for them to pray always without becoming weary" (Lk 18:1).

St. Paul, too, had his dark moments but they simply pointed him to higher things:

"But we keep this treasure in earthen vessels so that this extraordinary power will be seen to be from God and not from us. We are afflicted in every way, but we are not crushed; perplexed, but not driven to despair; persecuted, but not abandoned; struck down, but not destroyed; always bearing the death of Jesus in our bodies so that the life of Jesus may also be manifested in our bodies. For in our lives we are constantly being given up to death for the sake of Jesus so that the life of Jesus may be manifested in our mortal flesh" (2 Cor 4:7-11).

St. Augustine in his commentary picks up verse 14, "Your way, O God, is holy; what god is as great as our God?" and tells us to rejoice in God:

"Joy — who can live without it? Do you think that those who reverence, worship and love God have no joys? Do you think that the arts and the theater, hunting and fowling and fishing all bring joy, but God's works do not? Do you think that meditation on God's works does not bring inner joy?" (*Commentary on Psalm 77*, 14).

To which Abbot Columba Marmion adds, "Joy is the echo of the God-life in us."

St. Bernard of Clairvaux applies this to our personal spiritual lives:

"The whole of the spiritual life consists of these two elements. When we think of ourselves, we are perturbed and filled with a salutary sadness. When we think of the Lord, we are revived to find consolation in the joy of the Holy Spirit. From the first we derive fear and humility and from the second hope and love" (*Miscellaneous Sermons* #5).

For a modern example of prayer, the Christian can look at the Jewish tradition celebrated in the musical *Fiddler on the Roof.* Tevye pours out his heart to God in a passionate song and he doesn't mind at all telling God it would be better to be rich! Would that we could all pray with such decisiveness!

PSALM 78: *"Attend, my people, to my teaching..."*

Psalm 119 is the longest psalm in the Psalter and Psalm 78 is the second longest. According to rabbinical count, there are 5896 verses in the Psalter. The middle verse is verse 38 of Psalm 78, "But God is merciful and forgave their sin; he did not utterly destroy them." The merciful forgiveness of God toward the sinner is a pivotal point in our relationship with God, as well as the pivotal verse in the Psalter. (Psalm 80:14, incidentally, contains the middle Hebrew letter in the Psalter.)

Psalm 78 is an epic poem retelling the events portrayed in Deuteronomy 32, the "Song of Moses." They are retold so that each succeeding generation may proclaim them to their children and so hand on the testimony of God at work in their history. This is tradition in the best sense of the word.

This is not a history lesson as such. It is a witness to the goodness of God to his people and their fidelity or infidelity. It is a witness to the covenant between God and Israel.

Two events highlight the recital, both of about equal length and structure: God's wonderful work — the rebellion of the people and God's punishment, but his final forgiveness.

The first account is the crossing of the wilderness and God's might and power in bringing them across it. He fed them with manna, "the bread from heaven," and quails, but still they rebelled against God, demanding the vegetables and the flesh-pots of Egypt. The divine anger was enkindled and the rebels lost their lives.

The second account is the deliverance from Egypt. The ten plagues were decreed by God against the Egyptians until even the obdurate Pharaoh let the Jewish people go. After the wilderness event, God brought them into Shiloh in northern Palestine where the Ark of the Covenant was enshrined.

But again the people were unfaithful to Yahweh. They worshipped the gods of the land and the fertility gods and goddesses, and Baal and Astarte. God therefore punished them and the Ark was captured by the Philistines (1 S 4:4-11).

"Then the Lord awoke as from sleep, like a warrior from the effects of wine." The final section shows God coming to the rescue to destroy the enemies of the people. However, he also rejects the leadership of the tribes of Ephraim and Joseph in the north and transfers his favor to Judah, King David and the Temple in Jerusalem.

The conclusion is a less than subtle appeal for the northern tribes to reunite with the Davidic kings in Jerusalem and return to a unified worship of God in the Temple. Ephraim was the largest and strongest of the tribes and, historically, it would have been the one to exercise leadership. However it was God's choice to take David from the flocks and make him the Shepherd and King of God's people. Therefore, come home to Jerusalem.

The Christian use of this psalm is old and varied. Perhaps the most obvious is that Jesus called himself the "Good Shepherd" (Jn 10-11) and is the final and eternal completion of the Davidic dynasty (Rm 1:3-4).

Verse 2 is used by Christ to explain why he taught in parables: "I will open my mouth in parables" announcing things hidden since the foundation of the world (Mt 13:35) to encourage his listeners to ponder his words.

St. Paul alludes to this psalm, verse 3, when he warns against overconfidence. What we learn from history shows us how easy it is to fall away from God, especially when things seem to be going so well (1 Cor 10:6-9).

St. John quotes verse 24 in his discourse on the Eucharist, the Bread of Life, the true Manna come down from heaven (Jn 6:31-33). St. Peter alludes to verse 37 in putting down Simon the Magician (Ac 8:21). In Revelation 16:4 we see the use of verse 44 in the third of the seven bowls of God's fury, the bowl whose water turns to blood.

So often when modern Christians ponder the covenant interplay between Yahweh and Israel we tend to put it alongside ancient history and distance ourselves from it. How wrong that is. The New Covenant in the blood of Christ has us right in the middle of the interplay.

Christ's mystical body is the Church; he the head, we the members (Eph 1:23). Christ is the true vine and we are the branches (Jn 15:1). Our bodies are temples of the Holy Spirit (1 Cor 6:19). The list could go on and on.

In the face of God's goodness to us, through Word and Sacrifice, through Baptism, the Blessed Sacrament and the other sacraments, through all the great richness of our Catholic faith, can we be anything but ungrateful and rebels when we sin, when we are unfaithful to his gracious and mighty works? Yet God is faithful to his New Covenant and he has left us the Sacrament of Reconciliation so we can seek his sure and certain forgiveness.

St. Augustine gives us food for thought:

"Although the lost sheep could lose itself while wandering, it could not find itself. It would not have been found if the mercy of the Shepherd had not sought it out.

"Similarly, the prodigal son was also sought out and raised up by the One who gives life to all things. And by whom was he found if not by the One who came to save and seek out what was lost?" (*Commentary on Psalm 78*, 24).

St. Catherine of Siena meditates on this new covenant relationship with God:

"Moved by love and wishing to reconcile the human race to yourself, you gave us your only-begotten Son. He became our mediator and our justice by taking on all our injustice and sin, out of obedience to your will, eternal Father, just as you willed that he take on our human nature. What an immeasurably profound love! Your Son came down from the heights of his divinity to the depths of our humanity. Can anyone's heart remain closed and hardened after this?" (*On Divine Providence* #4).

We, indeed, must count our blessings as living members of a living covenant:

"God sent his Son, the eternal Word, who enlightens all men, to dwell among men and make known to them the innermost things of God... The Christian dispensation, because it is the new and definitive covenant, will never pass away, and no new public revelation is any longer to be looked for before the manifestation in glory of Our Lord Jesus Christ" (Vatican II, *Dei Verbum*, #2, 3).

PSALM 79: *"O God, the nations have invaded your heritage..."*

The destruction of Jerusalem by Nebuchadnezzar (2 K 25:9-10) was a tragedy so unimaginable that when Jeremiah prophesied it, he was ridiculed and threatened with death. When he told the people that their confidence in the presence of the Temple was not sufficient to cover their sins he wasn't believed:

"Put not your trust in the deceitful words: 'This is the Temple of the Lord! The Temple of the Lord! The Temple of the Lord!' Only if you thoroughly reform your ways and your deeds" would they be allowed to stay in the land (Jr 7:4-7).

Psalm 78 looked at the past history of the people. Psalm 80 will consider the restoration of the people and Psalm 81 will rejoice in the liturgical restoration of Temple worship. However, in Psalm 79, the utter destruction of Jerusalem is an excruciatingly present agony. It is probably the most plaintive psalm in the Psalter.

The goyyim, the nations, the gentiles, have invaded the sacred heritage of Yahweh, defiled his holy Temple and left Jerusalem in ruins. It brings to mind the destruction of Washington, D.C. by the British, the Battle for Britain when the Luftwaffe rained bombs on London or the atomic bombing of Hiroshima and Nagasaki. For the ancient Israelite, it would be the equivalent, or worse. That God had turned his back on his heritage was devastating.

Bodies were left unburied, a physical horror and a psychological terror. The neighboring peoples show no compassion; instead they heaped scorn on the survivors. And the people themselves cried, "How long will your anger last?"

They knew why the destruction had come and been so thorough. Their sins, their iniquities, their infidelity (decried by all the pre-exilic prophets) were the cause. There is not a single protestation of innocence.

What the poet does do is beg God for help and compassion for the glory of his own name. If the pagans see that God does not defend his people, is it because he is a powerless God, unable to come to their aid? That is unthinkable!

And the rage, the unnecessary cruelty and fierce brutality of the invaders also must be avenged. The cry is for a sevenfold repayment of their inhumanity.

This song, a wail of agony, ends with a beautiful prayer. "Then we, your people, the sheep of your pasture, will give thanks to you forever; through all ages we will declare your praise." That's faith!

This psalm should remind us that St. Paul writes that our bodies are temples of the Holy Spirit: "Do you not know that you are the temple of God and that the Holy Spirit dwells in you?" (1 Cor 3:16).

The next step Paul makes is to remind us that the Church is the new Temple of God:

"So then you are no longer strangers and sojourners, but you are fellow citizens with the holy ones and members of the household of God, built upon the foundation of the apostles and prophets, with Christ Jesus himself as the capstone. Through him the whole structure is held together and grows into a temple sacred in the Lord; in him you are also being built together into a dwelling place of God in the Spirit" (Eph 2:19-22).

Therefore, as individual Christians and as members of the Catholic Church we must heed the admonition to grow in holiness. The Church is one, holy, catholic and apostolic so we ask ourselves if our ways and words are contributing to the growth and promotion of Christ's Church. Does our holiness attract people to his Church? Does our sinfulness keep people from God?

Blaise Pascal wrote, "The serene, silent beauty of a holy life is the most powerful influence in the world, next to the might of the Holy Spirit" (*Pensées*). St. Maximilian Kolbe adds, "Everyone cannot become a genius, but the path of holiness is open to all" (*First Editorial*).

The holiness of the Church and its members is closely allied to its unity. St. Cyprian teaches:

"He cannot have God as Father who does not have the Church as Mother. He who breaks the peace and concord of Christ acts against Christ; he who gathers somewhere outside the Church scatters the Church of Christ. He cannot possess the garment of Christ who tears and divides the Church of Christ" (*The Unity of the Church* #6).

Cardinal John Henry Newman, a man who struggled arduously for years over this issue of the unity of the Church wrote:

"In spite of my ingrained fears of Rome, and the decision of my reason and conscience against her usages, in spite of my affection for Oxford and Oriel, yet I had a secret longing love of Rome, the mother of English Christianity, and I had a true devotion to the Blessed Virgin, in whose college I lived, whose altar I served [he was Rector of St. Mary's Anglican Church] and whose immaculate purity I had in one of my earliest sermons made much of...

"When I was fully confident that the Church of Rome was the only, true Church, I joined her" (*Apologia pro Vita Sua*).

PSALM 80: *"Shepherd of Israel, listen…"*

The first time the word "shepherd" is used in the Bible is in the blessing which Jacob (Israel) gave to Ephraim and Manasseh, the sons of Joseph. "May the God in whose ways my fathers Abraham and Isaac walked, the God who has been my shepherd from the day of my birth to this day… bless these boys" (Gn 48:15).

The last time it is used is in the advice St. Peter gives to the first bishops:

"Tend the flock of God in your midst, overseeing it not by constraint but willingly, as God would have it, not for shameful profit but eagerly. Do not lord it over those assigned to you but be examples to the flock. And when the chief Shepherd is revealed, you will receive the unfading crown of glory" (1 P 5:2-4).

Therefore, when this prayer for the restoration of Israel begins with the title "Shepherd of Israel," the whole tone of loving supplication is set. The poem may have been written in the Northern Kingdom, Israel, since the tribes mentioned are Ephraim and Manasseh, the leaders in the north and there is no mention of Zion or the Temple.

Wherever it was written, its chief concern is the loss of the ten northern tribes. (Benjamin was disputed territory and the battleground many times between North and South.) There is evidence that the dangers this posed for the south, Judah, are also considered.

The refrain, repeated three times, is from the priestly blessing in Numbers 6:24-26. "O Lord of hosts, restore us; let your face shine on us, that we may be saved." The "Lord of Hosts" is a title for God who leads the hosts or hordes of militia taken from the general public in times of war, not professional soldiers.

The anger of God, caused by the people's sins, is so fierce that it brings forth barrels of tears. The derision shown by their neighbors is directed not only at them, but at God who has turned away from his people. God is asked to act to restore his own good name!

The next image of the vine and the vineyard is also very familiar, used from Genesis to Revelation, but especially in the prophets. It is the image of a precious vine transported from Egypt to Palestine where it flourished until it grew from the Mediterranean to the Euphrates. Since in ancient thought, water circled the land, it is equivalent to our "from sea to shining sea."

The vine was so powerful that it overshadowed the giant cedars of Lebanon. The walls around it, erected by God, were like a fortified vineyard that could withstand all assault. Now the wall is gone and the enemies of God and his people are like wild boars whipping through the vineyard.

The psalm ends with a fervent prayer that God will turn again and restore the people, even the northern tribes. It is also a plea to them to return in unity to the man at God's right hand, that is, David and his descendant kings.

As it turned out, the political downfall of Israel and Judah was a necessary prelude to a restoration in which spiritual "new life" was more important than political power. This resurgence would lead to a belief in personal immortality as described by the prophet Daniel: at a time of great distress, Michael the great prince will arise and "Many of those who sleep in the dust shall awake; some shall live forever, others shall be an everlasting horror" (Dn 12:1-3).

For the Christian, Christ as the Good Shepherd sums up all that divine providence can offer a striving and repentant mankind (Jn 10:2-16). Christ used the parable of the vineyard to describe his own mission (Mt 21:33-46). He also said, "I am the true vine and my Father is the vinegrower… I am the vine, you are the branches" (Jn 15:1-5).

Mother Katherine Drexel wrote:

"The Eucharist is the continuation of the Incarnation. In it Jesus communicates himself to me and to every human heart and becomes in very truth the Vine that bears God's plants, sending the sap of his divine life into all their branches and shoots, causing them to blossom and bear fruit into eternal life" (*Reflections on Life on the Vine*, p. 10).

The importance of the Eucharist was understood from the earliest days of the Church. St. Ignatius of Antioch, who was martyred about the year 110 A.D., teaches:

"Be careful, therefore, to take part in the one Eucharist, for there is only one flesh of our Lord Jesus Christ and one cup to unite us with his blood, one altar and one bishop with the priests and deacons who are his fellow servants. Then, whatever you do you will do according to God... As sons of the light of truth, flee divisions and evil doctrines" (*Letter to the Philadelphians*, #3).

(Editorial note: In the Hebrew Psalter, the middle verse for the whole book is Ps 78:38. The middle Hebrew letter is in Ps 80:14, in the word we translate as "forest" and the Hebrew letter is *ayin* which means "eye" — the eye of God is upon his chosen people, as a special spiritual mercy.)

PSALM 81: *"Sing joyfully to God our strength..."*

When we pray the psalms, we tend to see them as a unified prayer. However, in the Temple, they may well have been the setting for a lengthy liturgy. There are indications in many of the psalms for a place to pause and meditate and at other times pause for a prophetic sermon.

This festival psalm, used most often at the final harvest festival (Feast of Booths or Tabernacles), starts out with thanksgiving for the present harvest, but this gift reminds the people of other gifts: liberation from the slavery of Egypt, God's voice at Sinai, the feeding with manna.

Linking the "God of Jacob" with the tribe of Joseph indicates that this psalm is of northern origin, although it has come down to us preserved in the southern, the Jerusalem, canon.

That it was a gala festival is evident from the orchestra that is mentioned. When Folk Masses were introduced into the United States after Vatican II, many people were upset to see guitars and other musical instruments introduced into the sanctuary or choir. This psalm presumes that the New Year's Feast, opened with trumpet blasts, and the Harvest Feast were joyous occasions, a time for singing and, no doubt, dancing. This was a pilgrimage feast and the people lived for the week in a "tent city," the booths or tabernacles.

The second, and longer, section of Psalm 81 alternates between God addressing Israel in the third person, and then in the second person. God spoke to them from Sinai and the first commandment is repeated, "There must be no foreign gods among you; you must not worship an alien god. I the Lord am your God."

Mention is made of Meribah, the Place of Contention, in the desert during the exodus when Israel "contended with God" (Ex 17:7). Whenever Israel rebelled against God there was sure and swift punishment. Whenever Israel really turned back to God with sincere repentance, God forgave them. He will continue to do that.

The psalm ends on the triumphant note of God feeding his people with manna (Ex 6:4-15) and giving them Canaan, a country overflowing with milk and honey (Ex 3:8).

Psalm 81 has many Christian applications. Thanksgiving to God for material goods should lead to greater thanksgiving for the spiritual goods God gave through Christ and the Church. Fidelity to God is just as important in the New Testament era as it was in the old. "See that no one among you has a faithless heart" (Heb 3:12). Our journey through life as Christians is a pilgrimage to the eternal Promised Land.

As St. Augustine remarks:

"Earthly life is a pilgrimage and as such it is full of temptations. But our spiritual growth is worked out in temptation. By experiencing temptations we know ourselves. By fighting them we have the chance to become winners. By overcoming them we are crowned victors" (*Commentary on Psalm 81*, 3).

The last verse is used as one of the themes of the Feast of Corpus Christi. The manna in the desert was considered a figure of the true bread which comes down from heaven. In the Bread of Life discourse in the sixth chapter of St. John's Gospel, Christ applies the manna event to himself, the true bread come down from God. Verses 51-59 of that chapter are eucharistic in theme.

St. Alphonsus Liguori comments extensively on this passage of St. John's Gospel:

"This is the principal effect of the Most Holy Sacrament of the Altar, to nourish the soul that receives it with this food of life and to give it great strength to advance to perfection and to resist those enemies who desire our (spiritual) death. Therefore Jesus calls himself in this Sacrament, heavenly bread. 'I am the living bread that came down from heaven; whoever eats this bread will live forever; and the bread that I give is my flesh for the life of the world' (Jn 6:51)" ("Octave of Corpus Christi, Meditation 7" in *The Holy Eucharist*).

St. Ambrose teaches us:

"The Lord Jesus himself declares, 'This is my body.' Before the blessing of the heavenly words, another species is mentioned (bread); after the consecration the body is signified. He himself speaks of his blood. Before the consecration it is mentioned as something else (wine); after the consecration it is called blood. And you say 'Amen,' that is 'It is true.' What the mouth speaks let the mind within confess. What words utter let the heart feel" (*The Mysteries*, ch. 9).

Pope St. Alexander I put it this way: "Among sacrifices there can be none greater than the body and blood of Christ, nor any more powerful oblation."

The Board of Governors of the International Eucharistic Congress that was held in Philadelphia in 1976 sponsored a competition for a new eucharistic hymn. The winner, by Robert E. Kreutz, begins: "You satisfy the hungry heart with gift of finest wheat. Come, give to us, O saving Lord, the Bread of Life to eat" (*Gift of Finest Wheat*).

PSALM 82: *"God rises in the divine council..."*

The religious world of the ancient Israelites was a time of continuing revelation. Abraham, Isaac and Jacob may well have considered Yahweh the territorial god of Canaan and gradually the revelation showed him to be not just a god, but the one and only God.

Just as Christians in the First World today have to try to christen a world riddled with materialism, skepticism and eroticism, so the Israelites had to deal with the overwhelmingly pagan culture of their neighbors.

In Psalm 82, we are introduced to a heavenly assembly in which Yahweh condemns the pagan gods for their indifference to the needs of the poor and the lowly, the afflicted and the needy, the fatherless and the widow. At all times and in all societies, these are notably among the oppressed.

Yahweh's judgment is sure on these incorrigible gods and they are destined to fall, to die, to be exposed. The very foundations of the world are shaken (earthquakes) at God's judgment. There is here a very strong teaching that the moral order and the physical order affect each other intimately. The ecological movement in our times has finally discovered this.

Our Lord's use of this psalm gives us the thinking of his contemporaries. When he was accused of blasphemy for calling himself the Son of God, he says to them:

"Is it not written in your law 'I have said that you are gods'? If it calls them gods to whom the word of God came, and scripture cannot be set aside, can you say that the one whom the Father has consecrated and sent into the world blasphemes when he says 'I am the Son of God'?" (Jn 10:34-35).

Those who receive the word of God should act in a godly manner. Those who judge the people of God must judge them with the impartial justice of God. In either case, whether the psalm is to be considered Yahweh's judgment against false gods, or his condemnation against judges who acted unjustly, the psalm is a strong call for just judgment.

The charitable action that Christ demands of his followers means a merciful acceptance of one another. "Judge not and you will not be judged" he told them (Lk 6:37). St. Paul adds, "Do not attempt to judge another now; the Lord's coming will reveal all" (1 Cor 4:5).

The Last Judgment, which was expected imminently by the first Christians, a view that had to be corrected vigorously in 2 Peter 3, is always a consideration in the final triumph of justice. The teaching of Christ is that when he returns to judge it will be based on justice and charity. "I was hungry and you gave me food, I was thirsty and you gave me drink... Whatever you did for the least of my brothers you did for me... I was hungry and you gave me no food..." (Mt 26:31-46). Those most easily oppressed will be the focal point of judgment.

The Abbot St. Smaragdus wrote during the Dark Ages a treatise of advice to the petty kings of Europe:

"Therefore, O King, love justice and judgment, the royal road, which has been trodden by former kings from of old... But temper justice (with mercy) and diligently guard against sinister cruelty... If you wish your throne to be firmly established by the Lord, O King, do not cease to do justice to the poor and the orphaned" (*The Royal Way*, #8, 9).

The medieval poet, Thomas of Celano gives us another view of the justice to be expected on the Last Day:

> Day of wrath that dreadful day,
> When heaven and earth shall pass away,
> Both David and the Sibyl say.
> What terror than shall us befall
> When lo! the Judge's steps appal,
> About to sift the deeds of all.
> The mighty trumpet's marvelous tone
> Shall pierce through each sepulchral stone
> And summon all before the Throne.
> > (*Dies Irae, Dies Illa*. vv. 1-3)

PSALM 83: *"God, do not be silent..."*

If you consider the map of the modern state of Israel, you cannot help but be impressed by the huge territory and immense population of the enemies of that state. They have vowed that Israel must not exist. It is reminiscent, also, of the decree of the Roman Emperor, "*Christiani non sint.*" "Christians may not exist!" With a shudder, one may contemplate the Nazi plot, the Holocaust, which destroyed millions of Jews in the twentieth century.

Psalm 83, possibly the oldest in the collection of psalms, is a lament in time of trouble when powerful enemies are determined to exterminate the early Israelite confederacy. The classical inimical neighbors are listed: Ishmael, Edom, Moab, Gebal, Ammon, Amalek, Philistia, Tyre and the more distant Assyria which gives aid to the children of Lot, Moab and Edom.

But also listed are the some of the classical victories related in the Book of Judges, chapters 4-8, particularly against the Midianite leaders when the judge Gideon was the military hero. God intervened, sometimes spectacularly, to put down the foe. It was easy to make the judgment that the enemies of God were the enemies of Israel and vice versa.

The psalm begins with the traditional entreaty that God stir himself up against "his enemies." The enemies listed were never in actual league with each other in the same historical period, but the poet uses their names to symbolize all the forces of evil which war against the forces of good.

He calls down typical Semitic curses on the evil alliances, from pursuit by fire to other natural and physical disasters. Since in the end God will ultimately and certainly triumph, these may also be viewed as prophetic utterances.

God's triumph will be his ultimate vindication since he, alone, is Lord and Master of all the earth.

Even though this psalm is not used in the weekly psaltery in *The Liturgy of the Hours*, it can be read from a Christian perspective. In a positive sense, we pray, in the Lord's Prayer, "Your kingdom come, your will be done, on earth as it is in heaven" (Mt 6:9-13; Lk 11:2-4).

The heavenly kingdom is already present on earth in the Church, working its pilgrim way to heaven. Church history is as fascinating an adventure and account of successes and failures as is the story of Israel in the time of the Judges.

The Fathers of the Second Vatican Council wrote:

"The Church believes that Christ died and rose for all and can give man light and strength through his Spirit to fulfill his highest calling; his is the only name under heaven by which man can be saved.

"The Church believes that the center and the goal of all human history is found in her Lord and Master. Underlying all changes there are many things that do not change; they have their ultimate foundation in Christ who is 'the same yesterday, today and for ever' (Heb 13:8)" (*Gaudium et Spes* #10).

This also brings to mind Hilaire Belloc's admonition:

"Now the most difficult thing in the world in connection with history, and the rarest of achievement, is the seeing of events as contemporaries saw them, instead of seeing them through the distorting medium of later knowledge" (*The Great Heresies*).

The Church as the New Israel is also beset by its enemies. Some are historical, some contemporary. The examples will vary as much as the preachers and teachers who use this notion.

Take, for example, the three times when the Church has seen the ranks of the clergy decimated: the time of the Black Plague, the Protestant Reformation and the exodus of priests after Vatican II. Yet, in all of this, we are confident that God will protect and build up his Church.

"Sin," says Abbot Columba Marmion, "is the enemy of God" (*Christ the Life of the Soul*, p. 170). Sin is an interior cancer which attacks the vigor of the Church by weakening the basic cell of the Church, the individual, and blunting the proclamation of the Good News and silencing the social message of the Gospel in the world around us.

The individual must be at peace with God in the soul, but the poet José Antonio Esquivel has caught the need for the individual Christian to build on that inner peace and strength and reach out to the Third World where social justice is denied:

"Hail Mary of the Third World, full of grace, you who know pain, know the anxieties and subhuman conditions of your people.

The Lord is with you, with all who suffer, who know neither letters nor figures, who hunger and thirst for justice.

"Blessed are you among all the women of our footpaths and pueblos, women of furrowed, sunburned faces, of brawny muscles, of calloused hands, of forlorn eyes, but with hope...

"Pray for us sinners, for it is our fault in one way or another by our egoism, selfishness and greed that you joined with the men and women of the Third World to suffer disastrous poverty, totalitarian governments, blood, hatred and early death" (*Mary of the Third World*).

PSALM 84: *"How lovely is your dwelling place..."*

Modern pilgrims flock to Jerusalem and the Holy Land and it is, indeed, a soul-satisfying journey. The Holy Sepulchre, Calvary, the Via Dolorosa, Bethlehem, Nazareth and so many other places excite the Christian imagination. But Jews, Moslems and Christians all gather at Mt. Zion and the Wailing Wall to acknowledge a common spiritual treasure.

Psalm 84 captures the spirit of an ancient pilgrimage as zealous men and women made the journey. Three times in the year all Jews were expected to go to Mt. Zion to worship the Lord: Passover, Weeks (Pentecost) and Booths (Tabernacles) (Dt 16:1-17).

The first stanza salutes the "dearest of dwellings," the Temple, as the longed-for goal as the journey begins. It is the spiritual home of the Israelite and he expresses the joys that must fill the hearts of those who can worship there daily.

It is a place so secure and strong that even the birds of the air can nest there safely. Where we might be annoyed at the dirt and mess of the pigeons, the poet sees in the birds' safe haven a symbol of loving security for all the faithful. It is a gentle, even sentimental, gesture.

The journey was long and difficult, especially for those who came from the northern tribes. There was the matter of finding water, for one thing, and safety for their numbers. "The Valley of Baca" may have been the last difficult passage, and it has been translated as "the Valley of Tears."

Finally, they pass through the walls of the city and the walls of the Temple and can "see the God of gods on Zion."

Two short verses sum up the time spent in worship and include a prayer for the king who was the shield provided by Yahweh to keep his people safe.

As the pilgrims prepare to return home, their thoughts and hearts are still on the Temple. "Better one day in your courts than a thousand elsewhere!" God himself is the sun who enlightens all his faithful and the shield to go before them. Those who live with an upright conscience and trust in God can hope for all the good things they need.

The Christian dimensions for this psalm are varied. In the Fifth Joyful Mystery of the Rosary we meditate on the Finding of the Child Jesus in the Temple. It was on one of these feasts, the Passover, that Joseph and Mary introduced the Christ Child to his adult obligation to make the pilgrimage (Lk 2:41-52).

"Once again the Holy Family is just an inconspicuous part of a devout Jewish throng who appear before the Lord on a Passover feast. They are fulfilling the law of the Lord with commendable piety. This was probably Our Lord's first return to the Temple since the Presentation, and as might be expected of a young Jew, he was impressed, even overwhelmed by the glories of the Temple and all that it signified. That he would be tempted to stay and give his whole life to God could be expected" (Dollen, *My Rosary: Its Power and Mystery*, p. 60).

This is the same Jesus who wept over the city of Jerusalem even as he predicted its destruction (Lk 19:41-44). Yet whatever love is had for the city, the Christians realized that it was part of the passing beauty of this world. "Here we have no lasting city, but we seek the one that is to come" (Heb 13:14).

This psalm is used on the Feast of the Transfiguration when Our Lord showed his glory to Peter, James and John as he conversed with Moses and Elijah (Mt 17:2; Mk 9:2). It is also used for the Dedication of Churches, the local temple for Christians, the sacred place where we worship through the Mass, the central act of Catholic worship.

The phrase sometimes translated "the Valley of Tears," has been enshrined in one of the most venerable hymns to the Blessed Mother, the *Salve Regina*. St. Alphonsus devotes half of his book, *The Glories of Mary* to an explanation of and meditation on this powerful hymn:

"Someone may object that we cannot ask Mary to save us (in this vale of tears) since this belongs to God alone. But since a culprit condemned to death can beg a royal favorite to save him by interceding with the king that his life may be spared, why cannot we ask the Mother of God to save us by obtaining eternal life for us?" (*The Glories of Mary*, ch. 5).

Pope John Paul II writes:

"The Church knows and teaches that all the saving influences of the Blessed Virgin on mankind originate... from the divine pleasure. They flow forth from the superabundance of the merits of Christ, rest on his mediation, depend entirely on it, and draw their power from it. In no way do they impede the immediate union of the faithful with Christ. Rather, they foster this union" (*Redemptoris Mater* #38; he also quotes the Vatican II document, *Lumen Gentium* #60).

PSALM 85: *"You once favored, Lord, your land..."*

A case can be made for the notion that African American music is our own native American psaltery. From slave camps to slave festivals, from camp meetings to revivals, their plaintive prayers reached out, and up, "Moans, chants, shouts, psalms, hymns and jubilees, first African songs, then African American songs. In the crucible of separation and suffering, African American sacred song was formed" ("Cepree," Sister Thea Bowman: *Shooting Star*, p. 60).

Sister Thea points out that "each spiritual is in its own way a prayer — of yearning or celebration, of praise, petition or contemplation, a simple lifting of heart, mind, voice and life, to God" (*Ibid.*, p. 49).

That is what I hear in Psalm 85. It was probably written either during the Exile or in the immediate post-exilic times, and it is the plaintive cry to God to restore his favor. The Jews at that time had no doubt that the Babylonian Captivity was a direct punishment from God because of their sins. God had pleaded with them through powerful prophets but they had spurned the call. Now they would listen (v.9).

"O Lord, you once favored your land" is as plaintive a statement as that made by the two disciples going to Emmaus: "But we were hoping that he would be the one to redeem Israel" (Lk 24:21). It is not a cry of despair but it is the call from an anguished heart of a now seemingly forlorn hope. O what could have been!

In the past, God had worked marvels and forgiven his people time and time again. Now, "restore us once more" — give us one more chance. How human the aspiration!

Also human is the idea that "the good old days" were always better than now. Looking back to the former days made the poet think that the Kingdom of Israel, in the days of David and Solomon, was the ideal kingdom. Unfortunately that wasn't historically true. The kingdom described in vv. 10-14 is messianic and will be fulfilled only with the Incarnation of Christ.

Then "love and truth will meet, justice and peace will kiss." Spiritual abundance and prosperity will be the blessings of the Kingdom of Christ. While the Jews never defected from Yahweh as a nation after the Exile, they never attained the political greatness of the times of David and Solomon. The fulfillment of the promise is spiritual, begun in the Church and fulfilled perfectly in heaven. An anonymous second century author writes:

"God the Lord and Creator of all, who made all things and set them in order, was not merely a lover of mankind, but was full of compassion. Mild and good, calm and true, he always was and is and will be; he alone is good.

"The great and ineffable Idea which he conceived he communicated to his Son alone... When, through his beloved Son he removed the veil and revealed what he had prepared from the beginning, he gave us all at once, participation in his gifts, the graces of being able to see and understand things beyond all our expectations" (*Letter to Diognetus* #8).

But once again we turn to a poet, Dante Alighieri, for some further illumination on the Incarnation:

"When the immeasurable goodness of the divine nature willed to restore human nature to the image and likeness of God which had been lost by the sin of Adam, it was decreed in the high and united consistory of the Trinity that the Son of God should come to earth to bring about this concord.

"And because at his coming it was fitting that the earth should be in the most perfect disposition, and because the world is at its best when there is a world community, that is, when all are subject to a single law, it was ordained by divine providence that the people and the glorious city of Rome should be the means of bringing this to pass.

"And because it was proper that the inn where the heavenly king was to rest should be immaculate, a holy race was chosen in which, after the lapse of years, a woman above all other women should be born to serve as the resting place for the Son of God. The race was the race of David, and from it sprang the boast and the glory of the human race, that is, Mary" (*Convivio*, 4, v. 3).

PSALM 86: *"Hear me, Lord, and answer me..."*

Many of the psalms are characterized as "laments," because they exclaim with great Semitic passion the terrors that come with defeat, illness, betrayal, sin, etc. They demand, as it were, God's help for his chosen people and that he back up with deeds the words of his covenant with them (Dt 26:16-19).

Psalm 86 has these characteristics but it seems to be an act of meditative repentance and a plea for mercy by an individual. The danger envisioned does not seem to be immediate. The psalm is somewhat retrospective and composed of bits and pieces of many other psalms.

Just looking at the human condition, the poet can speak of being poor and oppressed and in danger, but he can regularly turn to God for forgiveness and help, especially if he can claim loving loyalty to God. Father Carroll Stuhlmueller quotes Voltaire as saying God has a penchant to forgive and that is his metier or normal life-style (*Harper's Bible Commentary*, Ps. 86).

The monotheistic hymn in vv. 8-10 is remarkable for its forthright proclamation of the uniqueness of the one and only true God. No one can equal you; "You alone are God."

The psalmist then continues his ruminations, asking to be shown the ways of God in truth and given the strength to run in those ways. Reminding God that he is slow to anger and most loving and gracious, the worshiper can be assured of God's kind help and reassured by his protection. He asks for a sign of God's protection, but this may just be the general petition for a good and peaceful life which would refute his enemies.

For the Christian, there is a grand general application of the whole psalm, and several individual verses are revealing. The reference to the single-hearted observance of God's law (v. 11) brings to mind Our Lord's Beatitude, "Blessed are the single-hearted, for they shall see God" (Mt 5:8).

The heart that praises God (v. 12) makes us think of Christ's gentle invitation to his disciples, "Come to me all you who labor and are burdened, and I will give you rest. Take my yoke upon you and learn from me for I am meek and humble of heart and you will find rest for yourselves. For my yoke is easy and my burden light" (Mt 11:28-30).

The urgent plea to "save this child of your handmaid," reflects the fact that children born to slave women, handmaidens, belonged entirely to the master. The idea of total devotion and total submission is meant. It was in this sense that the Blessed Virgin Mary replied to St. Gabriel at the Annunciation. Mary said, "Behold, I am the handmaid of the Lord. Be it done unto me according to your word" (Lk 1:38).

St. Ambrose has this to say:

"See the humility! Note well the devotion. She who has been chosen to be the mother of the Lord calls herself his little servant girl. She certainly does not become haughty over this promise of so exalted a position. By calling herself a handmaiden she does not take as a right what is freely given as a grace" (*On Luke* #2).

The medieval poet, Adam of St. Victor, reflects on the Annunciation this way:

> Gabriel from heaven descending,
> On the faithful Word attending,
> Is in holy converse blending
> With the Virgin full of grace.
> That good word and sweet he plights
> In the bosom where it lights,
> And for "Eva," "Ave" writes,
> Changing Eva's name and race.
>
> (*Missus Gabriel*)

The whole psalm, however, reminds St. Augustine of the Passion and Death of Christ, especially his prayer in the Garden of Gethsemane. Christ called out to God his Father and was ultimately to triumph over all God's enemies. This leads St. Augustine to comment on prayer:

"We pray to Christ as God, and he prays for us as a servant. In the first case he is the Creator, in the second a creature. Himself unchanged, he took to himself our created nature in order to change it, and he made us one man with himself, Head and Body. We pray then to him, through him, and in him. We speak along with him and he speaks along with us...

"God could give no greater gift to us than to make his Word, through whom he created all things, our Head and to join us to him as his members. Thus when we speak to God in prayer we do not separate the Son from him, and when the Body of the Son prays it does not separate its Head from itself" (*Commentary on Psalm 86*).

PSALM 87: *"The Lord loves the city…"*

Rome is called the "Eternal City" and Genoa is called "La Superba." Boston is called "The Hub" and Nashville, TN is called "The Athens of the South." The citizens of New York, Chicago and Philadelphia, and many other places, all think of their hometowns as somewhere near, or at, the center of civilization.

The author of Psalm 87 had no doubt that Jerusalem, firmly established on Mt. Zion, was the real center of the universe. The psalm is as joyful and festive as a celebration at a kibbutz. The dancing and singing can almost be envisioned and heard. The psalm must have been used on great feast days such as Pentecost, and was probably used to welcome pilgrims from around the world.

"The gates of Zion" is a popular expression to designate the city itself and has great symbolism. Gates open were a sign of peace and of welcome. Gates fortified and defended were a sign of strength and security. Gates breached meant defeat and oppression. Thus Christ said to St. Peter, "You are Peter (Rock) and upon this rock I will build my Church, and the gates of hell shall not prevail against it" (Mt 16:18).

The glorious things that were said of Jerusalem were based on the fact that it was the center of worship of the one, true God. All flowed from that. Because of that, all nations were invited into the fold, an especially forthright understanding of the universality of the call to all the nations, even those who were formerly enemies — Babylon, Egypt (Rahab), Philistia, Ethiopia (Cush) and Tyre, to worship God.

For Christians, the Church, the New Jerusalem, has the universal mission to share the Good News with all people. "The heavenly Jerusalem is the mother of us all" (Gal 4:26). The Church is the City of God *par excellence*. St. Augustine writes:

"It clearly follows that the whole redeemed city, that is the assembly and fellowship of the saints, is offered to God as a universal sacrifice through the great High Priest, who, in the nature of a slave, offered himself for us in his Passion, in order that we might be the body of so great a Head" (*The City of God*, Bk. 10, #6).

All true believers are born of Zion and God places them on his register of natural citizens, not naturalized ones. For the Christian, this again applies especially to all those who are reborn in Baptism. "As you well know, we have our citizenship in heaven" (Ph 3:20).

The psalm ends on one of the happiest notes in the Psalter, "So all sing in their festive dance: within you is my true home." It was the same spirit of the ecstatic dancing of King David when the Ark was brought into Jerusalem (2 S 6:16). Our Lord used this same idea in the parable of the Prodigal Son, where there was dancing and singing at the young man's return (Lk 15:25-26).

As an expression of joy and triumph, the liturgy uses this psalm in the Office for the Dedication of Churches where the symbolism is obvious. Each new church makes the temple of God more accessible on the local level. For the Christian it is a sacred place and a spiritual home.

Perhaps the most joyful use of the psalm is in the Office of the Blessed Virgin Mary and the Feast of the Solemnity of the Mother of God, Jan. 1st. Since Mary is the Mother of the Head of the Church, she is truly the Mother of each one of us, his members.

St. Thomas Aquinas summed it up in this way:

"To be conceived and to be born are attributed to the person (*hypostasis*) according to the nature conceived and born. Since a human nature was taken by a Divine Person in the very instant of conception, it follows that it can be said in actual truth that God was conceived and born of the Virgin. From this, a woman is called a man's mother, namely that she conceived him and gave birth to him. Therefore, the Blessed Virgin Mary is truly called the Mother of God" (*Summa Theol.* 3:33:4).

A modern writer, Father James Alberione, tells us:

"Through the Gospel, devotion to Mary became widespread among Christians and we have the first manifestations of Marian devotion. After the Council of Ephesus, love and veneration for the Mother of God grew considerably by reason of the abundance of literature defending, explaining, illustrating the dogma of Mary's motherhood" (*Mary, Hope of the World*, conclusion).

PSALM 88: *"Lord, my God, I call out by day..."*

The absolute certainly of death oppresses many modern people, especially if they deny that there is life after death. "You only live once," they say. And not just our contemporaries are so despairing, for there is an ancient philosophy that says, "Eat, drink and be merry, for tomorrow you die."

It seems strange that a psalm as joyful as Psalm 87 should be followed by the most grim psalm in the whole Psalter. No modern editor or librarian would arrange a book like the Psalter. It's possible that Psalm 88 would have been rejected!

But let's look at it. The writer is a man who has been chronically ill with a disease that makes his friends shun him. It must have been something as disfiguring as leprosy. Father Damien of Molokai gave himself to these poor disintegrating persons until one morning he could begin his sermon with the words, "We lepers." That is the stuff of heroes!

Here the man's friends avoid him as if the sickness were a punishment from God. Where he could have and should have expected help and consolation, he is rejected and despised. He cries out to God day and night, lifting up his hands in prayer, but God doesn't even seem to listen, much less act.

He tries logic. In Sheol, the afterlife of shades and shadows, no one praises God, according to the current theory of his time. Therefore, God should restore him to health so he can continue to praise God. It's a nice try, but it doesn't work.

Many experts call this a "despairing lament," but is it really? Isn't it rather an anguished lament? In despair the man would have either been silent or cried out against God. Instead, in anguish he turns to God again and again. Whatever the case may be, the concluding line is unutterably sad, "My only friend is darkness."

The Liturgy of the Hours refers this psalm to the death of Christ. In the Garden of Gethsemane, he said to those who arrested him, "This is your hour, the time for the power of darkness" (Lk 22:53). The psalm-prayer takes it from there:

"Lord Jesus, Redeemer of all and author of our salvation, for us you went down to the realm of death and became free of death. Hear the prayers of your family and lift us from our slavery to evil, that we may be redeemed by you and see your Father's glory" (Week 4, Tues., Daytime; Night Prayer, Fri.).

What a tremendous difference our belief in life after death makes. In the Mass for the Dead we pray:

"Father, all-powerful and ever-living God, we do well always and everywhere to give you thanks through Our Lord Jesus Christ. In him who rose from the dead our hope of resurrection dawned. The sadness of death gives way to the bright promise of immortality. Lord, for your faithful people life is changed, not ended. When the body of our earthly dwelling lies in death, we gain an everlasting dwelling place in heaven..." (Preface of the Dead - I).

St. Polycarp called martyrdom a *natalitia*, a birthday to eternal life (*Martyrdom of Polycarp* #18) and Petrarch remarked, "A good death does honor to a whole life" (*Canzone* 16).

This psalm might also make us pause to say something about the "dark night of the soul," which all the great Christian mystics have experienced. It is a time when all of the happy, peaceful, joyful aspects of religion seem meaningless. It is a time when the soul must go forward on faith alone. St. Thérèse of Lisieux in her *Story of a Soul* tells of her bouts with this.

The classic, of course, is St. John of the Cross:

"It will happen that while an individual is being conducted by God along a sublime path of dark contemplation and aridity in which he feels lost, in the midst of his darknesses, trials, conflicts and temptations, someone will proclaim that all of this is due to melancholia, depression, temperament, or some hidden wickedness and that therefore God has forsaken him" (*The Ascent of Mt. Carmel*: "The Dark Night of the Soul," prologue).

Doesn't that sound like the poet's friends in this psalm? St. John's lengthy treatise on the dark night of the soul is almost a spiritual commentary on Psalm 88 in which the anguish of the ill man is now the trial, purification and strengthening of the soul seeking God.

Having passed through this dark night St. John provides a poet's song:

> O guiding night!
> O night more lovely than the dawn!
> O night that has united
> The Lover with his beloved,
> Transforming the beloved in her Lover...
> I abandoned and forgot myself,
> Laying my face on my Beloved;
> All things ceased; I went out from myself,
> Leaving my cares
> Forgotten among the lilies.
>
> (*One Dark Night*, v. 5, 8)

PSALM 89: *"The promises of the Lord I will sing forever..."*

If politics make strange bed-fellows, then victory and defeat define heroes and villains. If the forces of King George III had won, George Washington would have been branded a traitor.

Psalm 89, written after a disastrous military defeat, took on added significance with the overthrow of the last Davidic king. What began as a lament for a tragedy became a wail of anguish over a catastrophe.

The psalm begins with the recollection of the promises made to King David (2 S 7:8-16) that his dynasty would last forever. He was told that if his descendants were bad kings, they would be punished, but God would continue to love them. The covenant qualities of God's faithfulness and mercy unite all four strophes of this psalm.

This is followed by a cosmic hymn (vv. 6-19) praising the majesty of God. It is almost a separate psalm, but it fits in with the third and fourth sections of Psalm 89. Yahweh is the God of gods and King of kings. His power as Creator reined in the chaos and brought about the land, his power as Lord created the Chosen

People and their chosen King, David. "By your favor our horn is exalted," signifies the strength and power that God has given and guaranteed.

Section three now applies the same power, *mutatis mutandis*, to the King and his dynasty. God is sharing his power with his surrogate, his vicar, over the Israelites. This is almost a divine commentary on 2 Samuel 7:8-29. God actually had given power, strength, richness and wisdom to David and his seed, "forever."

That "forever" is what leads to the final section. The disastrous end to the political power of the Davidic dynasty is evidenced by the military, economic and social chaos visited upon the land. It is described vividly with great poetic power.

Has God broken the covenant? Has God forsaken his promise to David? "How long, O Lord?" is the cry. Show yourself faithful and merciful! The poet does not lose faith in God, but that faith is sorely tried. Jehoiachin was probably the last true ruling king of David's line, although Nebuchadnezzar had installed his brother, Zedekiah, as king. After that the dynasty disappears in history, but not the faith that God would raise up a successor. It was now a messianic promise — a Savior would come from the house of David.

For the Christian, that successor was Jesus Christ, born of the line of David. The Archangel Gabriel brought the Good News to Mary, that she was to be the mother of a son who would inherit "the throne of David his father" (Lk 1:32). In the *Magnificat* Mary rejoices in the fulfillment of the promise made to Abraham (Lk 1:46-55) and Zechariah sees the fulfillment of the promise made to David and his dynasty in the *Benedictus* (Lk 1:68-79). Faith in God's promises was still valid. The "forever" was literally fulfilled in the Son of God, the Son of Mary in the line of David.

On the first Christian Pentecost, St. Peter addresses the people with the good news that God has been faithful to his promises in sending Jesus as the Messiah, the one who would be the everlasting King of David's line (Ac 2:29-36). When St. Paul addressed the synagogue at Antioch in Pisidia, he, too, referred to the messianic promise made to David as proof of Christ's legitimate claim to the prophecy fulfilled (Ac 13:22-23).

St. Augustine in commenting on this psalm writes about the new covenant, so far superior to the former one, so firmly founded on the sacrifice of Christ. God is not only true to his promises, he has raised the new covenant to the greatest heights. The promises made to the Davidic dynasty are fulfilled in the new Christian dynasty, the Catholic Church:

"Unflaggingly let us love the Lord our God and let us love his Church. Let us love him as the Lord and the Church as his handmaid. No one can offend the one and still be pleasing to the other. What does it avail you if you do not directly offend the Father but do offend the mother?" (*Commentary on Psalm 89*).

Theodulf of Orleans, writing in the Dark Ages left us this classic poem:

> All glory, laud and honor,
> To Thee, Redeemer King,
> To whom all lips of children
> Made sweet Hosannas ring.
> Thou art the King of Israel,
> Thou, David's royal son,
> Who in the Lord's name cometh,
> The King and Blessed One.
>
> 　　　　(*Gloria, Laus et Honor*, v. 1, 3)

BOOK FOUR: Psalms 90 - 106

PSALM 90: *"Lord, you have been our refuge..."*

It is typical of stories in the science fiction genre that humans have conquered death and live hundreds or thousands of years. Great beings from alien galaxies frequently have some type of practical immortality. Yet these same authors usually deny, pointedly, the true promise of immortality offered by Christ.

The psalmist here looks at the human condition, and since he had the haziest of notions of life after death, he bemoans his fate. Death always comes too soon. And for many people, even today, death is considered a punishment for individual sin.

How often have you heard something like this, "Mother was such a good person. Why did God take her?" Is the implication there that God should have waited until she was living in sin and then punished her? How often have we heard it said, "Only the good die young"? Is a long life given so that people have time to repent? The human condition continues to confound us.

The psalmist gives glory to God as he starts his ruminations on this subject. God always exists: "From eternity to eternity you are God." And then the beautiful verse, "A thousand years in your eyes are merely a yesterday!" When discussing the delay in Christ's Second Coming, the Parousia, we read, "But do not ignore this fact, beloved, that with the Lord one day is like a thousand years" (2 P 3:8).

Contrasted to the eternal life of God man's days are short, like a watch that passes in the night, or a dream that vanishes at dawn, or like grass (weeds) that springs up quickly and just as quickly is dry and gone. Unfortunately, these short years are often filled with trials and troubles. There is no doubt in the poet's mind that these difficulties are the result of God's punishment for individual and collective sins. We bring God's wrath upon ourselves.

"Seventy is the sum of our years, or eighty if we are strong," is more a prayer than a fact. In biblical times the average lifespan was about forty-five, so the poet is hoping to be given extra years. The shorter lifespan was the basis for their profound respect for senior citizens, the elders. They had the wisdom and experience of two or more lifetimes and this was considered a gift from God.

As a special blessing the psalmist prays for at least as many trouble-free years as troubled ones. "Fill us at daybreak with your love, that all our days we may sing for joy." This would fulfill the heart's desire of someone who considered death the ultimate and final blow.

The concluding verse makes a beautiful prayer all by itself: "May the favor of the Lord our God be ours. Prosper the work of our hands! Prosper the work of our hands!"

The story of Original Sin (Gn 2:3) makes as much sense theologically as any other attempt to explain the "why" of death. Writing in the second century, St. Theophilus of Antioch said:

"So also for the first time, disobedience procured his expulsion from Paradise. It was not as if there were any evil in the tree of knowledge, but from his disobedience man drew, as from a fountain, labor, pain, grief, and at last fell a prey to death" (*To Autolycus* 2:25).

St. Irenaeus, also writing in the second century, hastens to add:

"That is why the Lord proclaims himself 'Son of Man,' the one who renews in himself that first man from whom the race born of woman was formed; as by a man's defeat our race fell into the bondage of death, so by a man's victory we were to rise to life again" (*Against Heresies* Bk. 5: #20).

True immortality is given us in Christ. That most precious truth gives us the hope that sustains us in our human condition and through all the days of our life, however long or short they may be. "Whoever wishes to come after me must deny himself, take up his cross and follow me. For whoever wishes to save his life will lose it, but whoever loses his life for my sake will find it" (Mt 16:24-25).

PSALM 91: *"You who dwell in the shelter of the Most High..."*

The same book in the Bible which strictly forbids the use of idols in worship (Ex 20:4-5) also contains the command to make an elaborate pair of statues of cherubim with wings that touch each other and orders that they be placed at each end of the propitiatory, or mercy-seat, that covered the Ark (Ex 25:10-12). When Solomon built the Temple, the cherubim receive the same prominence.

This is the significance of the phrase "to abide in the shadow of the Lord in the shelter (Temple) of the Most High." The supplicant has taken refuge in the Temple, or may be a simple worshipper there. As a mother bird spreads her wings over her little ones to guard them, so tender and sure is the protection God gives to his faithful (cf. Mt 23:37).

It is part of the human condition to have fears and anxieties and whether it was the simple fear of the unknown terrors that attacked primitive peoples — plagues, nightmares, sunstroke, leprosy, or the terrors of more sophisticated nations — psychological and psychiatric in nature, we all have need for security under God's protection.

Whether from pestilence or war, no matter what the disaster, if thousands or ten thousand fall to left and right, God's power can save and spare. He sends his angels to protect the faithful from all sorts of dangers, symbolized by "asps, vipers, lions and dragons." The older translations also included "the noon-day devil," a colorful but faulty translation that was impressive to a desert dweller. Christ used the same symbolism when he gave his disciples the "power to tread upon serpents and scorpions" (Lk 10:19).

The psalm closes with God's assurance that he will help, protect and deliver in times of distress. A satisfying length of days will demonstrate God's loving care.

Psalm 91 has been popular with Christians on several levels. The assurances it offers make it an excellent evening prayer at the close of the day. However, verse 10 seems to guarantee that no evil will befall those who trust in God. This is more of a hope than a promise. Christians suffer the same illnesses and misfortunes that others suffer. God cares enough for us to see us through these unfortunate afflictions in what is ultimately the best thing for us. Many times the final approval or relief comes in heaven.

When Satan tempted Christ, he used verses 11 and 12 to urge Christ to throw himself off the Temple tower (Mt 4:6). God has given his angels the command to guard us, and most Christian children grow up with the security of devotion to their Guardian Angels. "See that you do not despise one of these little ones, for I say to you that their angels in heaven always look upon the face of my heavenly Father" (Mt 18:10).

St. John Baptist de la Salle incorporated this belief into his oft-quoted prayer:

"You, O Lord, are my strength, my patience, my light and my counsel. It is you who make the children confided to my care attentive to me. Do not abandon me for one moment.

"For my own conduct and for that of my pupils, grant me the spirit of wisdom and understanding, the spirit of counsel and fortitude, the spirit of knowledge and piety, the spirit of the holy fear of the Lord and an ardent zeal to promote your glory.

"I unite my labors with those of Jesus Christ, and I beg the most Blessed Virgin Mary, St. Joseph, and the Guardian Angels to protect me in the exercise of my employment" (*Prayer for Teachers*).

"To cling" to God, "to know" his name and "to call upon" God are various ways of encouraging us to pray. Christians are called upon to be men and women of prayer. It is amazing the number of times Christ himself withdrew to pray, and both by word and example he encouraged his disciples to pray.

St. John Brebeuf and the Jesuit martyrs of North America were called "men who pray" by the Native Americans. St. Charles Lwanga and the martyrs of Uganda were called by their fellow Africans, "those who pray."

St. Isidore of Seville, writing near the end of the Patristic period advises:

"If a person wants to be continually in God's presence, he must pray regularly and read regularly. When we pray we talk to God. When we read God talks to us.

"All spiritual growth comes from reading and reflection. By reading we learn what we do not know. By reflection we retain what we have read" (*Book of Maxims* #3).

St. John Cassian is a little more succinct: "He prays too little who only prays while he is on his knees. But he never prays who, while on his knees, is roaming the fields in his heart" (*Conference* 10).

PSALM 92: *"It is good to give thanks to the Lord..."*

The inspired poems, canticles and hymns of the Old Testament, many of them more than 2,500 years old, are a rich treasure that can be savored over and over again, always with spiritual profit. But most people do not realize that there were highly developed musical settings for most of these prayers. Unfortunately, they have been lost.

The exuberant nature of Psalm 92, the outpouring of praise and adoration, calls for exciting melodic treatment. Indeed, the psalm mentions musical instruments to accompany this at morning and evening Temple services. It was eventually brought into the regular Sabbath services.

Whether this psalm was influenced by the wisdom literature of the Old Testament, or vice versa, there is the regular theme of the lack of understanding of the fool, the unbeliever. Ordinarily, if something seems too good to be true, it isn't true. Not so with the works of God. The tremendous deeds of God simply tell us something about God, who is infinitely greater than these marvelous deeds. "When we speak of God we can only lisp," is the phrase often attributed to Abbot Marmion.

The name of Yahweh is mentioned seven times in the psalm, a fitting tribute to the seven "days" of creation. The tone of the poem is much like the conclusion of the creation account in Genesis: "So God blessed the seventh day and made it holy, because on it he rested from all the work he had done in creation" (Gn 2:3). If God is satisfied with his work and gives it his blessing, then it is indeed a wonderful world, as God intended it.

God also has established the moral order. The just shall flourish like palm trees and fruit trees in the Temple precincts. The evil-doers, no matter what their temporary material success, are destined for oblivion.

God has also set Israel apart, his Chosen People, and given them the strength of the wild bull and joy in defeating their enemies, as well as material success: "They shall bear fruit even in old age, always vigorous and sturdy."

Christians have always loved this psalm for its more profound meaning. By the redeeming sacrifice of Christ on Calvary, God has not only restored human nature to friendship with God but has given a higher and deeper meaning to human life — life filled with the grace of Christ by which we become God's adopted sons and daughters (Eph 1:3-14). This is a much greater cause for jubilation. The wonderful work of creation pales in view of the more wonderful work of re-creation in Christ.

In the words of Abbot Marmion:

"And now God — not in order to add to his plenitude, but by it to enrich other human beings — extends as it were his paternity. God decrees to call creatures to share this divine life, so transcendent that God alone has the right to live it, the eternal life communicated by the Father to the Only Son and by them to the Holy Spirit.

"In a transport of love which has its source in the fullness of Being and Good that God is, this life overflows from the bosom of divinity to reach and beatify beings drawn out of nothingness, by lifting them above their nature. To these mere creatures God will give the condition and sweet name of children. By nature God has only one Son; by love, he wills to have an innumerable multitude: that is 'the grace of supernatural adoption'" (*Christ the Life of the Soul*, p. 6).

"As proof that you are children, God sent the spirit of his

Son into our hearts, crying out, 'Abba, Father!' So you are no longer a slave but a child, and if a child an heir, through God" (Gal 4:6-7; Rm 15:14-17). What we are destined to inherit is eternal life and love in Christ, in heaven, where there is the eternal Sabbath of praising God.

Edward Schillebeeckx writes:

"Even in his humanity Christ is the Son of God. The second person of the most holy Trinity is personally man; and this man is personally God. Therefore Christ is God in a human way, and man in a divine way.

"As a man, he acts out his divine life in and according to his human existence. Everything he does as man is an act of the Son of God, a divine act in human form; an interpretation and transportation of divine activity into a human activity. His human love is the human embodiment of the redeeming love of God" (*Christ the Sacrament of Encounter with God*, 2:1).

Psalm 92 is used in the Common Office of Confessors, Pastors and Holy Men in the Liturgy of the Word. The Church rejoices in the power of God's grace which can make saints who are heroic in faith, hope and charity. One more example of the wonderful works of God!

PSALM 93: *"The Lord is king, robed with majesty..."*

Psalms 47, 93 and 95-100 comprise the Enthronement cycle of psalms. They may have been used in a liturgical setting that acclaimed the rule of Yahweh, or they may have been used in coronation ceremonies when the King, God's vicar in Israel, took the throne. Their immediate theme is the omnipotent and eternal power of the reign of God.

When Balboa discovered the vast ocean to the west of the New World, it was so serene and beautiful that he called it the Pacific Ocean. How wrong he was! To this day, tourists stand on the land overlooking the Pacific Ocean with all its grandeur and mood changes, and marvel at its power and beauty.

This is the rolling power of Psalm 93. In the ancient Canaanite myths, Flood covered the earth with her waters, making it unfit for human life. The gods battled with Flood to make room for mankind on firm earth. Here, Yahweh conquers the chaos of Flood, ruling from his throne eternally established on high.

The staccato of rapidly repeated phrases make it sound like thunder as the battle for dry earth goes on. It is a very powerful poem in content and form. God's decrees are firmly established; therefore the world will stand firm, depending on God's will.

Christ the King now reigns with complete authority over the Church and all mankind. "All authority in heaven and on earth has been given to me. Go therefore and make disciples of all nations, baptizing them in the name of the Father, and of the Son and of the Holy Spirit, teaching them to observe all I have commanded you" (Mt 28:18).

If holiness belonged to the Temple worship, how much more does holiness belong in the service of Christ. "So be perfect as your heavenly Father is perfect," was Christ's invitation to his followers (Mt 5:48). St. Paul called his converts "saints" in many of the epistles.

If this is the general advice to all Christians, the call to holiness among priests is even stronger. St. John of Capistrano wrote:

"It is indeed a double task that worthy priests perform. That is to say, it is both exterior and interior, both temporal and spiritual and finally, both a passing task and an eternal one.

"So it must be with the glowing lives of upright and holy clerics. By the brightness of their holiness they must bring light and serenity to all who look at them. Their own lives must be an example to others" (*Mirror of the Clergy* #1).

For the Christian, there is an eschatological awareness that God who now rules supreme, from all eternity, in heaven and over earth, will come in glory and power to judge the living and the dead in the last days:

"Then I heard something like the sound of a great multitude or the sound of rushing water or mighty peals of thunder, as they said, 'Alleluia! The Lord has established his reign, our God, the almighty. Let us rejoice and be glad and give him glory'" (Rv 19:6-7).

Bernard of Morlas (Cluny) gives a poetic vision of the return of Christ in glory:

> The world is evil,
> the times are waxing late.
> Be sober and keep vigil,
> the Judge is at the gate.
> The Judge that comes in mercy,
> the Judge that comes with might
> To terminate the evil,
> to diadem the right.
> Arise, arise good Christian,
> let right to wrong succeed,
> Let penitential sorrow,
> to heavenly goodness lead.
> (*De Contemptu Mundi*, vv. 1-3)

PSALM 94: *"Lord, avenging God..."*

Psalm 94 starts out with a real attention-getter. The avenging God rises up and destroys the arrogant. It invokes all the terror that a raging, destroying God could cause. As a matter of fact, it is a beautiful psalm that asks God to restore justice as a matter of personal honor. The poet loves his countrymen too much to allow injustice to plague them.

Pride, arrogance, oppression and injustice torment the land and murder is tolerated, even among the most helpless, the widow, the orphan and the alien. Does God see all this? Indeed he does. Does he who "shaped the ear not hear... who formed the eye not see?" God "sees and hears" the plans, the thoughts of man, and knows how passing and trivial they are.

The central thought of the psalm is a supreme act of confidence that God will restore justice to the land. Even the punishment will show that God can use that for purifying and instructing the people.

The reason the psalmist is so sure and confident is that he has personally experienced God's protection from the wrath of the evildoers. Then there is a sublime personal testimony: "When I say, 'My foot is slipping,' your love, Lord, holds me up. When cares increase within me, your comfort gives me joy."

The psalm concludes with a warning to judges and lawyers who work within the law to subvert it and to create more burdens for the people. "Lawyer bashing" is not just a modern invention! Simply and bluntly stated, the final point is: The Lord God will certainly restore justice for the faithful.

The Christian dimension of Psalm 94 can be seen from its use in the Epistles of St. Paul. Speaking to the worldly wise, Paul quotes, "The Lord knows the thoughts of the wise, that they are vain" (1 Cor 3:20). In speaking of morality, he says, "The Lord is an avenger in all these things, as we told you before and solemnly affirm. For God did not call us to immorality but to holiness" (1 Th 4:6-7).

When Paul speaks of the mutual love and peace that should be found in the typical Christian community, he concludes:

"Do not repay anyone evil for evil; be concerned for what is noble in the sight of all. If possible, on your part, live at peace with all. Beloved, do not look for revenge; for it is written 'Vengeance is mine, I will repay, says the Lord'" (Rm 13:17-19).

This flows with certainty from the many times that Christ taught his disciples to love their neighbors, including their enemies (cf. Mt 5:43-48; Lk 6:27-36, etc.).

The psalmist has commented on the upright of heart who seek justice from the works of the proud. St. Augustine comments on these two terms:

"Who are the proud? Those who do not perform penance and confess their sins in order to be healed through humility. Who are the proud? Those who attribute to themselves the few good qualities they seem to possess and endeavor to diminish the mercy of God. Who are the proud? Those who, while attributing to God the good they accomplish, insult others for not performing such good works and raise themselves above them..."

"Do you know who the upright of heart are? They are those who wish what God wishes. Therefore do not try to twist God's will to your own but correct your will to that of God. The will of God is a rule of conduct. By it you have the means of being converted and of correcting your evil ways" (*Commentary on Psalm 93 (94)* 15, 18).

A medieval poet tells us what taking vengeance into our own hands can do to the soul:

> Three cruel vengeances pursue
> Those miserable wretches who
> Hoard up their worthless wealth; great toil
> Is theirs to win it; then their spoil
> They fear to lose; and lastly grieve
> Most bitterly that they must leave
> Their hoards behind them. Cursed they die
> Who living, lived but wretchedly;
> For no man, if he lack love,
> Has peace below or joy above...
> (*Romance of the Rose*)

PSALM 95: *"Come, let us sing joyfully to the Lord..."*

In the early fifth century, Etheria, a Christian noblewoman from western Europe spent a couple of years touring the Holy Land. She left a diary in which she detailed the magnificent liturgies that had already grown in Jerusalem. They went on for hours including such things as a "sermon from every priest present" and "suitable psalms and hymns [that] are said on every occasion" (*The Pilgrimages* II:2 quoted in Dollen et al., *The Catholic Tradition: Mass and the Sacraments*, v. 1).

It was fitting that the Jerusalem Christian liturgies should be as splendid as the great Jewish liturgies in the Temple. There was a tradition of excellence in worshipping God to be continued. Psalm 95 is a part of that tradition. It was used for the grand procession into the Temple for Sabbath worship. It is also the call to prayer, the Invitatory, for the Catholic *Liturgy of the Hours* and the Episcopalian *Book of Common Prayer.*

It begins with the invitation to worship God joyfully, he who is the rock foundation of our faith and the strong firm citadel which protects us. God created and continues in being "the depths of the earth... the tops of the mountains... the sea and the dry land."

Then, as the procession approaches the Temple gates, "Enter, rejoice and come in!" Acknowledge God who cares for his well-tended flock, his own people. This is ample cause and reason for loving adoration.

Then the psalm takes an abrupt turn. The ancestors of the Jews had even more cause to rejoice, witnessing the miracles of the Exodus, yet the generation that benefited most directly was not allowed to enter into his rest. They rebelled at Massah (place of testing) and Meriba (place of quarreling) demanding water in the desert from God through Moses (Ex 17:1-7).

With typical Semitic force, the poet writes, "Forty years I loathed that generation." Actually God protected them throughout the Exodus journey and chastised them when they needed it, but they were not allowed to enter the Holy Land. It's a sad warning, a sad lesson, but human nature is prone to forget God when things go too well. The last lines of Psalm 95 are a salutary warning at the beginning of the liturgical day.

Besides the daily use of Psalm 95, Christians read it in the Epistle to the Hebrews where it is quoted five times (3:7-11, 15; 4:3, 5, 7). There is the warning to remain faithful to God and to consider the Sabbath rest as leading to the eternal Sabbath rest in heaven.

Modern Christians also have cause to marvel at God the Creator as modern science has widened our view of the universe. The Jewish poet was in awe at the notion of God taming earth and sky and sea. Scientists today paint us a picture of a universe that has widened into the vast distances between stars and galaxies. Our God is the infinite Creator of all these immense, but finite creatures. Just yesterday, walking on the moon was a marvel. Will tomorrow bring us out into that vastness of space? God just be-

comes more wonderful the more we know of his creation!
In the words of Venantius Fortunatus:

> The God whom earth and sea and sky
> Adore and laud and magnify,
> Whose might they own, whose praise they tell
> In Mary's body deigned to dwell.
> O Mother blest! the chosen shrine,
> Wherein the Architect divine,
> Whose Hand contains the earth and sky
> Vouchsafed in human guise to lie.
>   (*Quem Terra, Pontus, Sidera* vv. 1-2)

PSALM 96: *"Sing to the Lord a new song..."*

When the Ark of the Covenant was brought into Jerusalem, King David danced before the Ark with great abandon, so great was his joy (2 S 6). He immediately set up a liturgical setting for continued worship in the tent before the Ark. Music was an integral part of that liturgy and the first song recorded is "Give thanks to the Lord, invoke his name; make known among the nations his deeds..." (1 Ch 16:8-36).

The words of that lengthy song are so similar to Psalm 96 that there can be no doubt about the dependence of one upon the other. Here we have the command to sing a "new song to the Lord," a song that proclaims the marvelous deeds of God. It is a song that is almost ecstatic in its passionate expression of exuberance and joy.

The God of Israel is the only God. All others who are so-called gods are nothing. They are zeros. Splendor, power and grandeur mark the works of God the Creator. All the peoples of the earth are invited to give worship to God and to bring him their tribute. God not only created the world, he keeps it in being and rules everyone on earth with fairness, faithfulness and justice.

This joyful psalm of adoration invites animate and inanimate creatures to praise God — the earth and the sea, the plains and the trees of the forest. Most of all, human beings adore God who governs all people, his creatures.

Christians pray this psalm with equal fervor. "There is no God but one" (1 Cor 8:4). The redeemed in heaven "sing a new hymn before the throne… they belong to the Lamb" (Rv 14:3). The justice of God's kingdom on earth is in a constantly growing state which is why we pray in the Lord's Prayer, "Your kingdom come, your will be done."

Christ, the King of kings, rules over the world, Head of his Body, the Church. He has won for us a share in his own divine life and when we sing in that state of sanctifying grace, when we cry out "Abba, that is, Father," it is Christ the Lord who praises the Father in us and through us (Rm 8:15; Gal 4:6).

"Your Church throughout the world sings you a new song, announcing your wonders to all. Through a Virgin, you have brought forth a new birth in our world; through your miracles, a new power; through your suffering, a new patience; in your Resurrection, a new hope; in your Ascension, new majesty" (Psalm 96 Prayer, *Liturgy of the Hours*).

Again we must let the poet, Venantius Fortunatus, shed light on this new and eternal truth:

> Abroad the regal banners fly,
> Now shines the cross's mystery;
> Upon it Life did death endure,
> And yet by death did life procure.
> That which the prophet-king of old
> Had in mysterious verse foretold,
> Is now accomplished, while we see
> God ruling nations from a tree.
>
> (*Vexilla Regis Prodeunt* vv. 1, 3)

PSALM 97: *"The Lord is king; let the earth rejoice..."*

"No more perfect effort at worthy worship of the Most High has ever been accomplished than is to be seen in the Gothic cathedrals in every country in Europe as they exist to the present day" (James J. Walsh, *The Thirteenth, Greatest of Centuries*, p. 12).

Religious art, architecture, literature and music are attempts to express in human form some notions of the transcendent power of God along with his immanent presence. Psalm 97 fits into that category.

The awesome power of lightning, the terror inspired by uncontrolled fire, the destruction caused by a volcano ("the mountains melt like wax") — all these image, just a little bit, the Omnipotent. Yet the call for (social) justice in this poem demonstrates that this same All-powerful One is lovingly concerned for the welfare of the individual.

The old axiom "through nature to nature's God" is really the theme of the first half of the psalm. The second half of Psalm 97 turns from the imagery of nature to the goodness of God toward Israel. There is a contrast set up between those who worship idols and those called by Yahweh to his service. That election is a cause for rejoicing in Jerusalem and all the cities of the land.

The Lord, the Most High, reigns supreme, yet protects the lives of the faithful. "He rescues them from the hand of the wicked." Events in the history of Israel show that God's radiant presence is known in the land and is another reason to rejoice.

Psalm 97 is a favorite in the Christian liturgy. Besides its regular use in the monthly psalm cycle, it is used for the Epiphany and the Transfiguration, the Feast of the three Archangels, the Feasts of the Apostles, and the Christmas octave.

Psalm 97 "touches on what theologians call the transcendence and the immanence of God; he is the awesome creator of the universe, hidden in unspeakable glory, yet he also has made himself known to us and is near us. His transcendence and immanence find ultimate expression in Jesus Christ: he through whom the world was made walked among the villages of Galilee, and is with us yet today" (George Martin, *God's Word Today*, May 1993, Psalm 97).

The theme of justice and righteousness that runs through this, and many other psalms, reminds us that true worship always includes social justice. "Religion that is pure and undefiled before God the Father is this: to care for orphans and widows in their affliction and to keep oneself unstained from the world" (Jm 1:27).

In his first public address, Pope Paul VI emphasized how important it is to work for "continued efforts for the establishment of greater justice in public affairs and social matters according to the social doctrine" set forth by earlier popes (Dollen, *Civil Rights: A Source Book*, p. 111).

Pope Pius XI had written eloquently in his encyclical *Quadragesimo Anno* on the absolute need for charity and justice to work together:

"Clearly charity cannot take the place of justice unjustly withheld, but even though a state of things be pictured in which everyone receives at least all that is his due, a wide field will nevertheless remain open for charity.

"For justice alone, even though most faithfully observed, can remove indeed the cause of social strife, but can never bring about a union of hearts and minds. Yet this union, binding people together, is the main principle of stability in all institutions, no matter how perfect they may seem, which aim at establishing social peace and promoting mutual aid" (*Ibid.*, p. 74).

The American bishops issued five Pastoral Letters on matters of social justice between 1919 and 1958, and much more frequently in recent years. Most of the modern popes since Pope Leo XIII have turned out major encyclicals on social justice.

PSALM 98: *"Sing a new song to the Lord..."*

Cardinal Cushing of Boston loved to tell the story of the grandmother who was reading the story of Creation from Genesis to her little granddaughter. The child grew more silent and listened more intently as the reading continued. When it was over she looked at her grandmother and said thoughtfully, "You never know what God will do next!"

It's in that spirit of awe and joy that the psalmist proclaims in a new song of the marvelous works of God. As a champion of justice, he goes to war to save the oppressed and the lowly. Once again, religion, charity and justice combine in God's plan for his chosen people and for all people. God's reign will be universal and "all the ends of the earth" will proclaim his triumph.

The third and final stanza returns to a frequent theme in the psalms, that nature itself will also proclaim the justice and the fairness of the God "who comes to judge the earth." How joyfully the poet puts it, "Let the rivers clap their hands" in joy and the "mountains shout with them for joy." All the creatures of land and sea will share the joy.

The series of psalms, 95-100, closely resemble in content the message of Isaiah 40-55, given as Babylon was about to fall to King Cyrus. The exiles would be liberated and the Liberator would suffer to lead them back home. After the long purification process, God's triumph would shine out for all to see. God was faithful to his covenant promise; his mercy and faithfulness would continue forever.

For us, Christ, of course, is the Liberator, the Messiah. His triumph was more than economic or political. His is the victory of goodness and truth and right. His rewards are not temporal, but eternal, and they are shared with us. "God is love" (1 Jn 4:16) and that love is to be shared by each one of us. What a transformation would occur in society if everyone really believed that "God loves me!"

Trying to transform society in our times has led to the Church's struggle for social justice and civil rights. Pope Leo XIII sounded a distinctive note in that battle over a hundred years ago with his defense of private property:

"Let it be regarded as established that in seeking help for the masses, this principle before all others is to be considered basic:

that private ownership must be preserved inviolate... Private possessions are clearly in accord with nature... To own goods privately is a right natural to man, and to exercise this right, especially in life in society, is not only lawful but clearly necessary" (*Rerum Novarum* ## 15, 26, 36).

The Christian liturgy also delights in this psalm, used during the Christmas octave, the Feasts of the Epiphany and the Sacred Heart of Jesus. The joyful Epiphany events — the Magi, the Baptism in the Jordan and the Wedding Feast at Cana — are the first manifestations of Christ to the world and a cause for great rejoicing.

The new song of sanctifying grace pours forth from the Sacred Heart of Jesus, as St. Bonaventure explains:

"It was a divine decree that permitted one of the soldiers to open the side of Jesus with a lance. The blood and water which poured out at that moment were the price of our salvation. Flowing from the secret abyss of our Lord's Heart as from a fountain, this stream gave the sacraments of the Church the power to confer the life of grace, while for those already living in Christ it becomes a spring of living water welling up unto life eternal" (*Minor Works* #3).

Writing at the end of the thirteenth century, St. Gertrude adds her comment:

"I salute you through the Sacred Heart of Jesus, all you holy angels and saints of God; I rejoice in your glory and I give thanks to Our Lord for all the benefits which he has showered on you. I praise him and glorify him and offer for you, for an increase of your joy and honor, the most gentle Heart of Jesus. Deign, therefore to pray for me so that I may become according to the Heart of God. Amen" (*Prayer*).

PSALM 99: *"The Lord is king, the peoples tremble..."*

The first time women were allowed to vote in presidential elections in the United States was in 1920. My mother, the former

Cecilia Pfeiffer, had just turned 18 but she boldly went out to vote on that historic occasion. The men in the precinct treated her very courteously and when they gently asked her age, she drew herself up to her full height (she was a large woman) and said decisively. "I am a married woman. I do not tell anyone my age!" So they gave her a ballot and said "Go right in, Mrs. Dollen, and vote." And to this day, she has never told anyone whom she voted for.

Now if such a patriotic event could so thrill a young American woman, think of the joy and exultation of the poet as he extols the kingship of Yahweh. He is ecstatic in his praise and adoration of his holy King. In fact, Psalm 99 is divided into three stanzas, each ending with "Holy is God!"

In this psalm, Yahweh is a holy king for three reasons.

First, he has really ruled his people in the theocratic days when they first entered the Holy Land. Then he shared his rule with the Judges and finally with King Saul and King David, a man after his own heart (1 S 13:14).

Second, Yahweh is a holy king because he governs directly or indirectly in fairness and justice. "You alone have established fairness; you have created just rule in Jacob." How different this reign is from the tyranny of ancient rulers in the biblical world. The arrogance and the dictatorial sway of human rulers is far different from that of the holy Yahweh.

Yet God, ruling with omnipotence from heaven deserves unswerving obedience and service. His throne upon the cherubim, the two figures surrounding the Ark of the Covenant, is merely a footstool for one whose throne is in the heavens. Though he punishes wrongdoers, he is a forgiving God, as well.

Third, the poet sings of God's holiness because he has revealed himself to Moses, Aaron and Samuel (and others). He has spoken to them and through them on Mount Sinai, Mount Zion and throughout his Holy Land.

Besides its regular use in the Office, Psalm 99 is used for the Feasts of the Solemnity of Mary, the Mother of God (Jan. 1), the Transfiguration of the Lord (Aug. 6) and that of St. John the Evangelist (Dec. 27).

Mary cries out in the *Magnificat*, "The Almighty has done great things for me, and holy is his name" (Lk 1:49). The holiness of Yahweh is reflected in his creation, but in Mary he surpassed himself. In the words of Archbishop Fulton Sheen:

"In the streets of the Roman world, of which Israel was but a conquered part, there stands an exultant woman proclaiming to all the world the tidings of her emancipation. 'He that is mighty has done great things for me.' It was a representative voice, not only of Israel, but of womanhood and the world. It was the clarion call of a long-repressed sex claiming its right and hailing its emancipation...

"Not in her times alone, but in her for all times, woman would find her glory and her honor. They could not call her Jew nor Greek nor Roman; not successful nor beautiful, but 'blessed,' that is holy. And blessed she is because by giving birth to the God-Man she broke down the trammels of nationality and race. Her Son was cosmopolitan, He was Man *par excellence*. And she is The Woman because she is the Mother of God" (*Wisdom for Welfare*, preface).

The Feast of the Transfiguration is an ancient and popular feast and commemorates the vision witnessed by Saints Peter, James and John on Mt. Tabor when Moses and Elijah appeared with Christ (Mt 17:3-4; Mk 9:4-5; Lk 9:30-33). The glory of Jesus appears as he is conversing with the two men who represent the Law and the Prophets, both of which prefigure Christ.

As for the Feast of St. John, of all the evangelists he most fully and deeply witnesses to the divinity of Christ: "And the Word was made flesh and dwelt among us, and we saw his glory, the glory as of the Father's only Son, full of grace and truth" (Jn 1:14).

Aloys Grillmeyer states:

"The climax in the New Testament development of Christological thought is reached in John. His prologue to the Fourth Gospel is the most penetrating description of the career of Jesus Christ that has ever been written.

"It is not without reason that the Christological formula of John 1:14, 'And the Word was made flesh and dwelt among us,' could increasingly become the most influential text in the history of dogma.

"The Johannine Christology has a dynamism all its own. Christ appears as the definitive Word of God to man, as the unique and absolute revealer, transcending all prophets" (*Christ in the Christian Tradition*, 1:2c).

PSALM 100: *"Shout joyfully to the Lord, all you lands..."*

One of the treasured memories of my youth was a pilgrimage to the Shrine of St. Anne de Beaupre in Quebec to offer one of my first Masses. The evening before there was a candlelight procession in which the faith and joy of the pilgrims could be felt. It was a truly faith-filled experience.

Psalm 100, designed to be used at a procession into the Temple, expresses that same "joy in the Lord." Joy, gladness and thanksgiving should adorn our worship of God because he has created us out of nothing and formed us into his own "well tended flock." For Jews and Christians this is a cherished image: Yahweh as the tender Shepherd of Israel and Jesus Christ as the Good Shepherd of his Church, his flock.

"Good indeed is the Lord" who shows us steadfast love and fidelity. These are the great covenant promises Yahweh made to Israel and the foundation of their relationship (Ex 34:6-7; Dt 4:35-39). The Hebrew word rendered as "steadfast love" in this translation can actually mean "merciful love" or "loving mercy." This concept, presented as a refrain in Psalm 136, is a deep, rich, tender and all-embracing love.

For centuries Catholics have used this psalm, called the "*Jubilate Deo*" from its first words in Latin, and it has been set to many beautiful musical renditions. It is one of the few psalms used more than once in the monthly cycle in *The Liturgy of the Hours*. It has long been a favorite among Protestants for use at revivals, and it is called, affectionately, "The Old Hundredth." They use a familiar old translation: "All people that on earth do dwell."

Psalm 100 is used by Jews and Christians to express their worship in adoration of God. St. Athanasius comments on Christian worship:

"We do not worship a creature. Far be the thought! Such an error belongs to heathens and Arians. We worship the Lord of creation, Incarnate, the Word of God.

"For if the flesh also is in itself a part of the created world, yet it has become God's body. And we neither divide the body, being such, from the Word and worship it by itself, nor when we wish to worship the Word do we set him apart from the flesh, but knowing, as we said above, the 'the Word was made flesh' we recognize him as God also, after having come in the flesh" (*Letter to Adelphius*, ch. 3).

Our faith in Christ is certainly a cause for joyful worship. Pope St. Gregory the Great wrote:

"What follows is reason for great joy: 'Blessed are those who have not seen and believed' (Jn 20:29). There is here a particular reference to ourselves. We hold in our hearts One we have not seen in the flesh.

"We are included in these words but only if we follow up our faith with good works. The true believer practices what he believes. But of those who only pay lip service, Paul says 'They profess to know God but they deny him in their works'(Tt 1:16). And St. James adds, 'Faith without works is dead' (Jm 2:26)" (*Homily 26*).

Who but Gilbert Keith Chesterton could express the joy and vibrancy of Catholic living any better than in his little verse, *Benedicamus Domino*?

> Wherever a Catholic sun doth shine,
> There's plenty of laughter and good red wine.
> God grant that it be ever so —
> *Benedicamus Domino!*

PSALM 101: *"I sing of love and justice..."*

A literal application of Psalm 101 can lead to some rather weird situations. Nathaniel Hawthorne describes one in *The Scarlet Letter*, where Hester Prynne is condemned to wear a letter "A" to atone publicly for her "adultery." And what Oliver Cromwell did to Ireland in the name of the Puritan religion will be emblazoned in the Irish psyche until the end of time.

Actually, this is an interesting psalm since it describes what is expected of a true and just king. It was probably used during coronation ceremonies and keeps alive the memory of David, the ideal king.

Love and justice, the covenant virtues, are the motif for a good king's reign. Indeed, any study of the Books of Samuel and the Books of Kings demonstrates that when Israel had upright, religious kings the nation and the people prospered. Those who were anything less than zealous in the pursuit of the Law of God seldom prospered.

The king must set the example of integrity in his own life and in his own royal court. Good example is always the great magnet that attracts good-hearted people. Those who speak perversely or act shamefully cannot be a friend, i.e. an official, of the king's. The devious, the arrogant, the proud and slanderers are to be avoided. It would seem that the king expects his officials to be servants of the public, not their lords and masters. What an ideal for all who serve publicly in Church or state!

The king chooses faithful Jews to be his companions, his advisors and his judges. By surrounding himself with the faithful he himself is protected in the performance of his religious and civic duties. He will begin his day by administering true justice to keep the city free from evil (cf. 2 S 15:2).

Christians see in this almost an examination of conscience for the good ruler and the good person. Our Lord said quite simply, "If you love me, keep my commandments" (Jn 14:15). He gave the norm, "Be perfect as your heavenly Father is perfect" (Mt 5:48). Love and justice tempered with mercy are the beginning and the end of the pursuit of spiritual righteousness. This is how God is perfect.

However, the number of crimes that have been committed in the name of religion, historically, is truly frightening. Zealots and fanatics, of the left or the right, are terrorists of the spirit. They are frequently convinced that they are doing God's work, explicitly and without mercy.

It is hard, if not impossible, to justify such things as the excesses of the Crusades, the Spanish Inquisition, the Index of Forbidden Books or the ghetto treatment of the Jews in Europe. Islamic conversion by the sword, the white Protestant settlers in the Old West who could say, "The only good Indian is a dead Indian," and the British slave ships that brought the African slaves to America are a few more examples to show how blind people can be. There is enough blame to go around for all nations and religions.

Thank God, the saints help restore our faith in human nature and what God's grace can do in fallen man. St. John Brebeuf, St. Peter Claver, Blessed Junipero Serra, and St. Martin de Porres were typical of what Catholic missionaries by the thousands did in giving their lives for Native Americans. It has been said that one saint can redeem a generation and Church history demonstrates how many saints God has raised up in each generation.

Saint Louis IX, King of France, has left us a description of a noble Christian king in writing to his son:

"My dearest son, my first instruction is that you should love the Lord your God with all your heart and all your strength. Without this there is no salvation. Keep yourself from everything that you know displeases God, that is to say, from every mortal sin. You should permit yourself to be tormented by every kind of martyrdom before you allow yourself to commit a mortal sin...

"Be kindhearted to the poor, the unfortunate and the afflicted. Give them as much help and consolation as you can. Thank God for all the benefits he has bestowed upon you that you may be worthy to receive greater. Be just to your subjects, swaying neither to the left or the right, but holding the line of justice. Always side with the poor rather than with the rich, until you are certain of the truth. See that all your subjects live in justice and peace...

"Be devout and obedient to our mother the Church of Rome and the Supreme Pontiff as your spiritual father" (*A Spiritual Testament to his Son*).

If Psalm 101 proposes an ideal, we have people in every age who try to inspire us and bring out the best in human nature. Think of Martin Luther King, Jr., and his "I have a dream" where true civil rights and social justice will animate America. And then there is John F. Kennedy's Inauguration Address, "Ask not what your country can do for you, but what you can do for your country."

PSALM 102: *"Lord, answer my prayer..."*

One of the most difficult things a parish priest has to do is preside over the funeral rites for a deceased infant, especially an unbaptized baby. Ranking not far behind this in anguish, is the funeral for a teenager

Penitential Psalm 102 reflects this anguish in the soul of the psalmist who is dying young. God is ending his life when he lived but "half his days." He begins with a prayer to God to come quickly to his aid in phrases often used in the Liturgy: "O God come to my assistance; O Lord make haste to help me!"

His description of his physical condition is almost classic in its stark simplicity. Body, soul and spirit are afflicted with pain and dissolution. Because of stress he has become "skin and bones." His enemies use his name as a curse, as proof of the fury and wrath of God. He is avoided by his friends and the image used is that of the night owl, an unclean bird considered something of a loner.

The middle stanza turns into a lament for the ruin and destruction that has come upon Jerusalem. Devastation has been both personal and civic. The poet is confident that the Lord will restore Zion and give it back its freedom and prosperity. Thus future generations will praise God. This section is so vibrant with hope and confidence in God that some scholars wonder if it isn't really a fragment of some lost psalm. Whatever the answer, its ringing words of the assurance of God's care for the poor and lowly are uplifting and truly comforting.

When Jerusalem was restored, it never regained its former political or economic splendor, but something far greater happened. After the Exile the nation rebuilt its solid belief in the one, true God and monotheism was its great treasure and glory. There was never another mass, national apostasy and when Antiochus Epiphanes tried to suppress the Jewish religion (1 M 1:20-63), Mattathias and his sons were able to rally national support to protect their religious values (1 M 2:1-14).

The Epistle to the Hebrews quotes from this section in commenting on the messianic enthronement of the Son of God:

"At the beginning, O Lord, you established the earth, and the heavens are the work of your hands. They will perish but you will remain; and they will all grow old like a garment. You roll them up like a cloak and like a garment they will be changed" (Heb 1:10-12).

The third stanza returns to the original complaint. In contrast to the shortness of man's life, the eternity of God is proclaimed. The foundations of the earth and the heavens, no matter how old they may be, will "wear out" when compared to God's eternal life — "your years have no end."

Besides the use that the Church has always made of the Penitential Psalms, especially during the penitential seasons of Lent and Passiontide, the Christian can pray this psalm in petition for help in this "vale of tears," and can also use it to praise the majesty of the infinite God.

But the Christian dimension adds meaning to what Palm 102 merely starts. We turn to God for comfort in all our troubles, of course (2 Cor 1:4) but since Christ has given us the bright promise of immortality all the trials and tribulations of this life are as nothing compared to the eternal life and love promised.

"I consider that the sufferings of this present time are as nothing compared with the glory to be revealed for us" (Rm 8:18).

"For this momentary light affliction is producing for us an eternal weight of glory beyond all comparison as we look not to what is seen but to what is unseen; for what is seen is transitory, but what is unseen is eternal" (2 Cor 4:17-18).

The promise and pledge of future immortality bestowed on the Christian by the free gift of the grace of Christ given us by God and implemented in the Sacrament of Baptism color all of our thinking and acting — or should.

"Hope," writes Peter Lombard, "is the certain expectation of future glory, the fruit of divine grace and the preceding merit of Christ" (*Sentences* 3:26).

St. Clare of Assisi certainly caught the rich color of Christian spirituality in these words:

"I pray you, O most gentle Jesus, having redeemed me by Baptism from original sin, so now by your Precious Blood, which is offered and received throughout the world, deliver me from all evils, past, present and to come.

"By your most cruel death give me a lively faith, a firm hope and perfect charity so that I may love you with all my heart and soul and all my strength; make me firm and steadfast in good works and grant me perseverance in your service so that I may be able to please you always. Amen" (*Prayer*).

PSALM 103: *"Bless the Lord, my soul..."*

One of the most beautiful and expressive eucharistic practices in the Latin Rite of the Roman Catholic Church is Benediction of the Blessed Sacrament. Before the eucharistic fasting rules were relaxed so that Mass could again be celebrated in the evening, it was the most common devotion after the Mass.

Psalm 103 begins with the personal exhortation to bless God with all one's human powers and strength. One of the reasons given for this prayerful exercise is the forgiveness that God lavishes on us as individuals. The phrase "your youth is renewed like the eagle's" refers to the belief that when the eagle molted, it received its youthful vigor again. This power also referred to its sexual vitality and from that on to the idea of being blessed with a strong family.

The second stanza goes from the singular to the plural, so that God's favor to Israel is also a cause for blessing, praising, God. He brings justice to the oppressed, a strong attribute of God's; the reference to Moses is that God favored the oppressed Israelites by sending Moses to work his wonders. Zechariah referred to this in the *Benedictus*: "Because of the tender mercy of our God by which the daybreak from on high will visit us" (Lk 1:78).

"Merciful and gracious is the Lord, slow to anger, abounding in kindness" is a refrain that has brought spiritual solace to many a reformed sinner. God doesn't nurse anger against his creation but his generosity far exceeds even his justice.

The third stanza of this psalm contains some of the most tender expressions in the whole Psalter. "As the heavens tower over the earth, so God's love towers over the faithful," a figure of speech to praise God's superlative love. "As far as the east is from the west, so far have our sins been removed from us." In a flat-world concept, no distance could be greater. God, an ideal Father, is the model of compassion for his sons and daughters.

The very frailty of human nature begs God's merciful compassion. Like the flowers of the fields, maybe dandelions for us, we come and go as quickly. One day blossoming, the next day swept away by the wind. "But the Lord's kindness is forever" even to the grandchildren of those who serve God.

The final stanza is a hymn of praise tacked onto this psalm. God in his heavenly sanctuary deserves adoration from all the heavenly inhabitants, all creatures, everywhere, and the final line repeats the first, "Bless the Lord, my soul!"

The rich imagery of adoration and the tender expressions of love and mercy have appealed to Christian believers who use this psalm with devotion. Its appeal for justice to the oppressed is an inspiration for all who work for civil rights and social justice.

Archbishop John Ireland wrote that the mission of the Ameri-

can Church was "to prepare the world, by example and moral influence, for the universal reign of human liberty and human rights"
(*On American Citizenship*).

The U.S. Bishops echoed these sentiment later:

"The heart of the race question is moral and religious. It
concerns the rights of man and our attitude toward our fellow man.
If our attitude is governed by the Christian law of love of neighbor and respect for his rights, then we can work out harmoniously
the techniques for making legal, economic and social adjustments"
(*Pastoral Letter*, 1958).

Psalm 103 is also a favorite for the Feasts of Angels and Archangels because of their mission to praise God (cf. Rv 21 and 22),
but particularly because of the final stanza calling the heavenly host
to bless God. Pope St. Gregory the Great gives us another thought
about the angels: "Personal names are applied to some archangels
to denote their ministry when they come among us. Thus, Michael
mean 'Who is like God?' Raphael is 'God's Remedy' and Gabriel
is 'The Strength of God'" (*Homily 34*).

The Divine Praises, used to conclude Benediction of the
Blessed Sacrament, are a modern expression of the art of blessing
God:

> Blessed be God.
> Blessed be his holy Name.
> Blessed be Jesus Christ, true God and true man.
> Blessed be the Name of Jesus.
> Blessed be his most sacred Heart.
> Blessed be his most precious Blood.
> Blessed be Jesus in the most holy Sacrament of the altar.
> Blessed be the Holy Spirit, the Paraclete.
> Blessed be the great Mother of God, Mary most holy.
> Blessed be her holy and immaculate conception.
> Blessed be her glorious assumption.
> Blessed be the name of Mary, virgin and Mother.
> Blessed be St. Joseph, her most chaste spouse.
> Blessed be God in his angels and in his saints.

PSALM 104: *"Bless the Lord, my soul!"*

Your first view of the ocean, Atlantic or Pacific, is always something awesome. It's as if you've glimpsed infinite power at work. There's nothing like it, not Niagara Falls, the Grand Canyon or the mighty Mississippi.

That is the feeling of awe the poet expresses when he presents us with a magnificent poetic view of the story of creation (Gn 1:1-2:4). Starting with the exclamation "Bless the Lord!" the first two stanzas revel in the power of Yahweh creating. Later Hebrew writings would soften the verb to "Blessed be the Lord!" The feeling of exultation remains.

God is clothed with majesty and glory and robed in light. The clouds, the wind and flaming fire are his messengers. The watery chaos of primeval time obeys God's command to separate into the waters of the firmament, the ocean and the streams and rivers. The Hebrews, a desert and mountain people were properly transfixed by water. The foundations of the world are fixed firmly amidst all this water by God. All told, we have here a satisfying cosmogony that attributes all visible creation to its ultimate cause, God.

The third stanza proclaims that God nourishes and cares for his creation. Wild beasts are provided with food, domestic animals are given the grass they need, and even man is given both bread from the earth and "wine to gladden our hearts." The magnificent cedars of Lebanon, created by God's word, are the homes of the birds of the air.

Then the poet turns his attention to the days and the seasons, governed by the sun and the moon and the heavenly bodies. People use the day for their work and the animals roam at dark, seeking their food from God. "The young lions' roar" is their form of praying.

The poet shows that these heavenly bodies, worshipped by so many of the pagan nations they knew or whose land they had traversed, were actually created by Yahweh and were, indeed, his adornments.

A short stanza repeats the fact that God is the master of the earth and the sea. The fascination with the sea and sailing vessels comes up again. The Hebrews were great and brave soldiers, but they were never a naval force. Leviathan, possibly a whale but more probably a mythical sea creature of immense strength, is also God's creature.

Finally the psalm turns to the creation of life itself. Not only did God create all living things, but he sustains them in being. He breathes life into them, or withdraws his breath and they return to dust, but he can also renew the face of the earth.

The grand finale again praises God the Creator for his power to bring things into being and keep them going. There is also a prayer to remove sin and evil from the world so that the justice of the Creator may be in evidence.

The last phrase repeats the first, "Bless the Lord, my soul!" and adds "Hallelujah!" or Alleluia. This is the first of 23 times that it will now be used in the Psalter. The word combines the plural imperative of "bless" (*hallelu*) with an abbreviated form of Yahweh (*Yah*), thus, "Bless God!" It was a word and concept enthusiastically adopted by the Christians since the writing of the Book of Revelation. An axiom from the patristic period states that Christians are an Easter people "and Alleluia is our song."

Verse 30, "When you send forth your spirit they are created and you renew the face of the earth" became one of the themes for the Christian feast of Pentecost (Ac 2:1-13). If God is to be praised for his work in creating the physical world, he is more to be praised for his work of spiritual re-creation and renewal by sending the Holy Spirit.

"So whoever is in Christ is a new creation" (2 Cor 5:17) because we "were sealed with the promised Holy Spirit" (Eph 2:13). In regard to the idea of God continuing to sustain his creation, St. Paul quotes an ancient pagan author and makes the thought his own: "In him we live and move and have our being" (Ac 17:28).

St. Cyril of Alexandria explains:

"After Christ had completed his mission on earth, it still remained necessary for us to become sharers in the divine nature of the Word. We had to give up our own life and be so transformed that we would begin to live an entirely new kind of life that would be pleasing to God. This was something we could do only by sharing in the Holy Spirit" (*Commentary on John* #10).

St. Augustine writes:

"He who has given us the gift of being gives us also the gift of being good. He gives to those who have turned back to him. He even sought them out before they were converted and when they were far from his ways" (*Commentary on Psalm 104*, 2).

The psalmist's beautiful appreciation of the cedars of Lebanon (vv. 16, 17) puts us in mind of the tribute to nature by Joyce Kilmer:

> I think that I shall never see
> A poem lovely as a tree;
> A tree whose hungry mouth is prest
> Against the earth's sweet-flowing breast
> A tree that looks at God all day,
> And lifts her leafy arms to pray;
> A tree that may in summer wear
> A nest of robins in her hair;
> Upon whose bosom snow has lain,
> Who intimately lives with rain.
> Poems are made by fools like me,
> But only God can make a tree.
>
>   (*Trees*)

PSALM 105: *"Give thanks to the Lord, invoke his name..."*

Epic poetry preserves oral traditions of heroic dimension, notable for their grandeur and sweep. Eventually they were put into written form and we treasure them in such instances as *Beowulf*, the *Iliad* or the *Aeneid*. It should come as no surprise, therefore, that the deeds of the great Patriarchs, Abraham, Isaac and Jacob (Israel), as well as Moses and Joseph, should receive epic treatment in Psalm 105.

This epic poem begins in the grand manner of inviting all the listeners to praise God for his wonderful deeds and the heroic nature of his servants in the setting of Canaan and Egypt (Ham). Three concepts predominate in the telling: promises (covenant), servants (patriarchs) and the land of Canaan, the gift of God as a result of his promise.

The stories of Abraham, Isaac and Jacob are in the grand manner of epic poetry, both heroic and tragic. They are also very human in their virtues and sins. As a matter of fact, this increases their credibility.

The psalm teaches with theological precision that Yahweh entered into an everlasting pact with Abraham, "confirmed by oath to Isaac, and ratified as binding for Jacob, an everlasting covenant for Israel." Equally firm is the teaching that to the Israelites, God gives "the land of Canaan, your own allotted heritage."

Those who received this promise were "few in number, a handful and strangers" wandering in the Canaanite territories. God protected them saying, "Do not touch my anointed, to my prophets do no harm." The Genesis tradition does not consider Abraham, Isaac, Jacob and Joseph as "anointed" or as "prophets" but the generic terms fit admirably. They were especially set apart by God (anointed) and they went before the face of God and spoke for him (prophets).

The fourth stanza treats of the Patriarch Joseph (Gn 40 and 41), sold as a slave by his brothers and transported to Egypt in a slave gang. His interpretation of dreams brings him into prominence and eventually he becomes what we would call Pharaoh's Prime Minister. "He made him lord over his palace; ruler over all his possessions."

The literary epic reaches its heights in stanza five with a detailed retelling of the plagues in Egypt when Moses and Aaron delivered the ultimatum, "Let my people go!" (Ex 5:1). With great poetic license, the writer gives very colorful descriptions of the plagues, in a different order than in Exodus.

The conclusion of the story summarizes the Exodus experience. God led them by a cloud and a pillar of fire, he sent them quail and manna, "bread from heaven," and gave them water in the desert. They entered the Promised Land, Canaan, victoriously with joy and wealth to fulfill their side of the covenant.

The psalm is breath-taking and magnificent in scope, content and the telling. Since this is part of the theology that Jews and Christians share together, we both rejoice over the wonderful works of God and his faithfulness to his promises. It increases the Christian's trust in the promises made in the New Covenant in Christ Jesus. What was foreshadowed in the Old Testament is brought to spectacular fulfillment in the New Testament. The wonders then were passing; the marvels now have fruit in life everlasting.

Christian devotion has transferred whatever is applicable from the Patriarch Joseph to the New Testament Patriarch, St. Joseph, the foster father of the Son of God. Verse 21 is one of the themes for Feasts of St. Joseph, "He made him lord over his palace, ruler over all his possessions." What treasures St. Joseph presided over in the Holy Family! However humble, the home of Joseph of Nazareth was a palace enriched by the presence of the Son of God.

St. Bernardine of Siena writes:

"What is St. Joseph's position in the whole Church of Christ? Is he not a man chosen and set apart? Through him and, yes, under him, Christ was fittingly and honorably introduced into the world.

"Holy Church in its entirety is indebted to the Virgin Mother because through her it was judged worthy to receive Christ. But after her we undoubtedly owe special gratitude and reverence to St. Joseph. God has adorned him with all the gifts of the Holy Spirit needed to fulfill his task" (*Sermon 2 on St. Joseph*).

St. Bernard of Clairvaux also should be heard on the subject:

"God submitting in obedience to a woman is indeed humility without equal; the woman commanding her God is sublime beyond measure. In praising virgins we read that they follow the

Lamb wherever he goes. How can we possibly praise enough the Virgin who leads him?

"Learn, O man, to obey. Learn, O earth, to be subject. Learn, O dust, to bow down. In speaking of our Creator, the evangelist says 'and he was subject to them,' that is, to Mary and to Joseph" (*Missus Est* #1).

> Joseph of Nazareth, you are the man
> Last in the line that rose from David, King,
> Down through the royal generations ran,
> And ends with Jesus Christ.
> Gabriel from heaven came to Mary's side,
> Came with the joyful promise of a King,
> Came to you also, Joseph, to confide
> That God conceived this child
> Guardian and foster-father of the Christ,
> Honor to you, so chosen by our God!
> Husband of Virgin Mary, you are the first man
> To show us Christian love.
>   (Stephen Somerville, *Joseph of Nazareth*)

PSALM 106: *"Give thanks to the Lord, who is good..."*

If you went to a Catholic grammar school, you became very familiar with the great events in the Old Testament in Bible History class. There was the angel who held Abraham back when he was about to sacrifice Isaac, or there were the Israelites dancing around the Golden Calf, or the waters in the Red Sea piling up. It was dramatic, the stuff of an epic poem.

Psalm 106 is the epic poem, retelling the wonders of the Exodus and the Conquest against the background of God's mercy and forgiveness in spite of a people who over and over again "forgot the God who had made them." In the face of all that God had done for them, how could they continue to fall away, again and again? That's what this poem asks.

Beginning and ending with a resounding "Alleluia," the first few verses are a prayer of praise and an invitation to pray and serve the just, all-powerful God. But, "we have sinned like our ancestors; we have done wrong and are guilty." The poet goes on to cite eight incidents in which we have the progression: God's deed, man's rebellion, and God's merciful forgiveness.

In the first incident, despite the wonders God had worked in Egypt to secure the freedom of the people, when the forces of Pharaoh threatened them at the Red Sea, they turned against Moses (Ex 14:11). Nevertheless, God brought them across the waters made as dry "as though a desert." God forgave their infidelity.

The second event concerns their craving for meat in the desert. The people became tired of the manna and demanded meat. They were given quail to eat but God also sent among them a wasting disease and the seraph serpents (Nb 21:6).

The third story concerns the rebellion led by Dathan and Abiram, who challenged the leadership of Moses. Moses took this as a rebellion against God as well as against himself and Aaron, whom God had placed over them, so "the earth opened and swallowed" the rebels and all they owned (Nb 16:31-34).

In the fourth incident, at Horeb, the Israelites made the golden calf to worship (Ex 32:1-35): "They exchanged their glorious God for the image of a grass-eating bull." God would have destroyed them if Moses hadn't "withstood him in the breach to turn back his destroying anger."

In the fifth story, the people finally arrived at the southern entrance to the Holy Land, but they were terrified by the reports the twelve scouts brought back and refused to trust God to bring them in successfully (Nb 13 and 14). For this that whole generation was condemned to wander the desert for the rest of their lives.

The sixth event in this epic occurred near the end of the Exodus. As the Israelites tarried in their passage through the Moabites, many of them succumbed to the women of the land and sacrificed to their god, Baal of Peor. Aaron's grandson, Phinehas, was singled out for his zeal in executing a public law-breaker in this event but God exacted a strict punishment on all the idolaters (Nb 25:1-18).

The seventh incident concerns how Moses was denied entrance into the Holy Land. At the waters of Meribah (Contention; Nb 20:2, 13), Moses seemed to show a lack of faith when he struck the rock twice to bring forth the water God had promised.

The eighth and final action in this epic, and the longest, tells what finally happened when the people entered the Holy Land. God had given them a triumphant entry and ordered them to clear the land of all the pagans there (Dt 7:1). Their obscene worship doomed them to God's wrath. But, "they did not destroy the peoples as the Lord had commanded."

The Israelites mingled with the Canaanites and worshipped their idols. They sacrificed to the idols, seemingly even human sacrifice, a practice that was totally foreign to Yahweh's commands. "They defiled themselves by their actions." Because of this, they were oppressed by the peoples of the land, a history told in agonizing detail in the Book of Judges.

However, God remembered his covenant and had mercy on the people. He "relented in his abundant love." For this reason, the Jews may hope for God's continued protection, particularly in the post-exilic times in which this poem was probably written. It's as if to say, "There's still hope for us." The final verse is the doxology which ends the fourth book of the Psalter.

The Christian who meditates on this dramatic work may be tempted to say "How, in the face of all these divine interventions, could they keep falling away from God?" However, far from feeling superior, we should meditate on ourselves as the modern spiritual Israelites. We not only have the memory of the wonderful works of God, we share in a more truly wonderful work — life in Christ Jesus! The gifts of grace with which God surrounds us, the sacrifice of the Mass, the Sacraments — all of these things make present to us the wonders of God's grace. These aren't merely past events; they are present happenings.

St. Paul refers to many of these Exodus events and reminds us, "These things happened to them as an example, and they have been written down as a warning to us" (1 Cor 10:11).

"Now we find that the Law keeps slipping into the picture

to point the vast extent of sin. Yet, though sin is shown to be wide and deep, thank God his grace is wider and deeper still! The whole outlook changes — sin used to be the master of men and in the end handed them over to death; now grace is the ruling factor, with its purpose of making men right with God and its end the bringing of them to eternal life through Jesus Christ our Lord" (Rm 5:20; Phillips Modern English translation).

St. Sophronius reminds us of these facts:

"By faith we have embraced Christ, the salvation of God the Father, as he came to us from Bethlehem. Gentiles before, we have now become the People of God. Our eyes have seen God Incarnate, and because we have seen him present among us and have mentally received him into our arms, we are called the New Israel. Never shall we forget his presence" (*Sermon 3*).

BOOK FIVE: Psalms 107 - 150

PSALM 107: *"Give thanks to the Lord who is good…"*

Whoever coined the phrase, "There are no atheists in a fox-hole" must have known the spirit of Psalm 107. The poet describes four desperate situations as a composite picture of all that can go wrong in life.

The opening verses are standard invitations to thank God "whose love endures forever." The redeemed are to gather from the four corners of the world, a reference to the Jews in the Diaspora (Greek for "scattered abroad"), a post-exile notion that may have been added to an already existing psalm.

The first "desperate situation" prompting a loving rescue is that of a people wandering aimlessly in a desert. It is tempting to look for specific situations in Israel's history for these events, but they are poetic archetypes of a general nature.

The barren, sterile desert offers no hope to the wanderers so they turn to God for help. "In their distress they cried to the Lord." God then graciously leads them directly to a city with food and water. For this, give thanks to God for such wondrous deeds done in behalf of "mere mortals."

The second distress call comes from those who are in prison. "Darkness, gloom and chains" made prisons in ancient times even worse than what modern critics describe as the "barbarous conditions" to be found in so many jails today. Because the prisoners in this passage "rebelled against God," he humbles them until they turn to him.

They finally appeal to God who snaps their bonds and breaks down "the gates of bronze." This results in joyful thanksgiving, again because God pays attention to mere mortals.

The next distress call comes from the sick bed. Since the connection between sin and sickness was the popularly accepted belief, those who were mortally ill must turn to God for healing. That God would pay attention to such human cries, when he delivers the sick and dying, calls forth sacrifices of thanksgiving.

Finally, sailors must entrust themselves to God's care. In the most powerful description of seagoing in the Old Testament, the poet describes the perils of the sea graphically. The Israelites were not a sea-going power, and so were keenly aware of the terrors of the deep.

The turbulent, swelling menace of a ship at sea in a storm is caught in this psalm with such force that you can almost get sea sick! "Tossed the waves on high... rose up to the heavens, sank to the depths... they reeled and staggered like drunkards... their skill of no avail."

Raging water was a symbol of the chaos of the abyss, which God conquered in his work of creation. With this symbolism in mind, we get some sense of the awe the fishermen/apostles felt when Christ calmed the storm and walked on the water (Mt 8:26; Mk 4:39; Lk 8:24). No wonder all three of the synoptic evangelists recorded it.

But this psalm repeats its rhythm by showing the sailors calling out to God for help and being delivered by him. This demands that mere mortals give praise and witness before all the assembly of the people.

The last eleven verses (33-43) seem to be a hymn fragment that was attached to Psalm 107 both to preserve it and because it has some general relationship to the theme of disaster and deliverance. Some scholars think it poetically refers to the destruction of Sodom and Gomorrah. I bow to their superior wisdom.

The use of verses from this psalm in the New Testament proves that it was a popular prayer at the time of Christ. The Blessed Mother in the *Magnificat* uses verse 9, "The hungry he has filled with good things; the rich he has sent empty away" (Lk 1:53).

St. Peter alludes to verse 20 in his encounter with the gentile, Cornelius. "You know the word that was sent to the Israelites as he proclaimed peace through Jesus Christ, who is Lord of all" (Ac 10:36 and again in Ac 13:26).

The idea of turning to God (gods) in times of trouble and stress is, I think, natural to most religions, so it is hardly surprising that Christians do just that. For the sick, the Sacrament of the Sick has great solace:

"'If anyone among you is sick, let him call the priests and let them pray over him, anointing him with oil in the name of the Lord, and if he has sinned he will forgive him' (Jm 5:14). There is no doubt that this ought to be understood of the faithful who are sick and who can be anointed with the holy oil of the chrism when it is necessary for themselves or their families" (Pope St. Innocent I, *Letter to Decentius*).

In the Roman Martyrology the number of saints who devoted themselves to the relief of prisoners and slaves is legion. St. Peter Claver, S.J., ministered almost his entire priestly life to the slaves at Cartagena, Colombia. He describes in detail their piteous condition as they left the slave ships and how he and his companions ministered to them with works of charity:

"This was how we spoke to them, not with words but with our hands and actions. And in fact, convinced as they were that they had been brought here to be eaten, any other language would have proved utterly useless. Then we sat, or rather knelt, beside them and bathed their faces and bodies with wine" (*Letter to His Superiors*).

Salvation in the desert? The Desert Fathers sought closeness to God in the desert. Catherine de Hueck Doherty, "the Baroness," wrote:

"It seems strange to say, but what can help modern man find the answers to his own mystery and the mystery of him in whose image he is created is silence, solitude — in a word, the desert.

"True silence is the search of a man for God; true silence is the speech of lovers; true silence is the key to the immense, flaming Heart of God; true silence is a suspension bridge that a soul in love with God builds to cross the dark, frightening gullies of its own mind that impede its way to God" (*Poustinia* 1:1).

Charles de Foucauld, the Hermit of the Sahara, wrote:

"God makes me find in the solitude and silence a consolation on which I had not counted. I am constantly, absolutely constantly, with him and with those I love... I see all things in the light of the immense peace of God, of his infinite happiness, of the immutable glory of the blessed and ever tranquil Trinity. Everything loses itself for me in the happiness that is God" (*Letters* 1916).

Psalm 108: *"My heart is steadfast, God..."*

Semper Fidelis (Always Faithful) is the Marine Corps motto and it could well mirror the sentiment in that phrase, "My heart is steadfast." The psalmist proclaims his unswerving loyalty to God, his determination to continue steady and faithful to the Lord.

Verses 2-6 in this psalm are almost word for word identical with Psalm 57:8-12, and verses 7-14 repeat Psalm 60:7-14. There is the admonition to wake the dawn with songs of praise because of the towering love and faithfulness of God. This noble image of God prompts the human response of trying to return it steadfastly, as much as humanly possible.

But facing reality, there are difficulties and crises in our human lives and so, knowing what God can do, this leads to the petition that he will come to our rescue in times of tribulation. Of old, God had promised the lands and the cities of Canaan to the Jews (Dt 9:5), so it is in keeping with Hebrew petition that they remind God of his words and ask him to keep up this protection.

Even when there are some occasional setbacks, the psalmist prays with confidence that God will give the final triumph. The psalm shows a remarkable balance between the need for God's help and the necessity of military strength to keep the land free and prosperous. The blending of the two portions of the older psalms is a felicitous one.

Christians have found many applications of this hybrid psalm. According to the old axiom, "Pray as if everything depended on God, and work as if everything depended on you." St. Benedict could give the practical dictum of *Ora et Labora*, "Pray and Work." The saints during the Counter-Reformation proclaimed "Faith and Good Works" as opposed to Luther's *Sola Fides*, "Faith Alone."

Pope Paul VI spoke of the steadfast work of prayer in and by the Church:

"From ancient times the Church has had the custom of celebrating each day the liturgy of the hours. In this way the Church fulfills the Lord's command to pray without ceasing, both offering its praise to God the Father and interceding for the salvation of the world.

"The hymn of praise that is sung through all the ages in the heavenly places and which was brought by the high priest, Jesus Christ, into this land of exile has been continued by the Church with constant fidelity over many centuries, in a variety of forms.

"The liturgy of the hours has developed into the prayer of the local Church, a prayer offered at regular intervals and in appointed places. It was seen as a kind of necessary complement to the fullness of divine worship that is contained in the eucharistic sacrifice, by means of which that worship might overflow into the daily life of the Church. It is the prayer of the whole People of God" (*Laudis Canticum*).

PSALM 109: *"O God, whom I praise, do not be silent..."*

Psalm 109 contains the "Great Imprecations," curses notable for their vehemence, ingenuity and length. It contains a commentary on the *lex talionis* (the law of retribution), the "eye for an eye, a tooth for a tooth" law (Ex 21:24; Lv 24:20; Dt 19:21).

The psalm begins with the poet begging God's help when his close friends turn against him. They repay "evil for good, hatred for my love." They act like godless men who do not respect people who are God-fearing.

Verses 6 to 19 quote the curses the psalmist's enemies hurl at him. They are attempting to get false witnesses to accuse him in court. They hope that he will have a short life, that his wife may soon be a widow and that his children become orphans, begging for subsistence. They curse his possessions and earnings and want even the remembrance of him erased. They cast aspersions on his parents, accuse him of lying, oppressing the poor and being irreligious.

"May cursing clothe him like a robe... may it seep into his bones like oil," they say. "May it be as near as the clothes he wears, as the belt always around him." In other words, let the curse permeate his very being. Now that's being cursed by a pro!

Instead, in a display of Old Testament retribution, the author asks that these curses be sent to his enemies and turned away from himself. He asks God to show these wicked men that it is God himself who is directing this just retribution. He proclaims his own religious faithfulness, fasting even to the point of looking gaunt. He is sure that God will come to his aid since God always brings merciful justice to the poor and defenseless.

This is one of the few psalms that is not used in the monthly cycle in *The Liturgy of the Hours*. No doubt this is because Christ gave a new commandment:

"You have heard it said, 'An eye for an eye and a tooth for a tooth.' But I say to you, offer no resistance to one who is evil... You have heard that it was said, 'You shall love your neighbor and hate your enemy.' But I say to you, love your enemies and pray for those who persecute you" (Mt 6:38-48).

"I give you a new commandment: love one another. As I have loved you, so you also should love one another. This is how all will know that you are my disciples, if you have love for one another" (Jn 13:34-35).

Before the first Christian Pentecost, St. Peter led the company of Christ's followers in choosing a successor to Judas Iscariot. As part of his argument, Peter quoted Psalm 109:8. "May another take his office" (Ac 1:20). After praying they cast lots and St. Matthias was chosen.

Tertullian has the classical quotation of how pagans took note of the Christians during the time of the great Roman persecutions: "'See,' they say, 'how those Christians love one another,' while they themselves hate one another. 'And how they are ready to die for one another,' while they themselves are ready to kill one another."

PSALM 110: *"The Lord says to you, my lord…"*

Studying what the biblical experts have to say about each psalm, one comes to a great appreciation of their work. Their tireless search for the exact text, their fearless attempt to extract its true meaning, and their careful search for the context of the psalm leave one in amazement.

But even their work pales into insignificance when we see the explanation which the Lord Jesus gives us of a text. Christ uses the first verse of Psalm 110 to explain to the Pharisees that the Messiah may be David's son according to the flesh, but in reality, as David's "Lord" he is something much more besides (Mt 22:41-16; Mk 12:35-37; Lk 20:41-44).

Psalm 110 is one of the most-quoted psalms in the New Testament and one of the few that is used over and over again in *The Liturgy of the Hours.* The consensus of the experts is that it is a royal psalm, used in the coronation ceremonies of a Davidic king. It is certainly a messianic psalm, referring to Christ.

The first verse salutes the crown prince, about to take his throne. Yahweh will give him sovereign power over all the earth starting with Mt. Zion, the center of the earth as far as the Jews were concerned. "Rule over your enemies" refers to the vassals who pledged allegiance to the king, now no longer enemies but subjects. The reference to the footstool presents the picture of a conquering king making his fallen enemies grovel at his feet.

The king was set aside from birth, "before the daystar," i.e. from before the world began. Mysteriously, "like the dew, I begot you," since this water comes on the earth without rain, a scientific mystery for them at that time.

The king will also have priestly power, not that of Aaron and his descendants, but the priestly power exercised by Melchizedek, the King of Salem who was also a priest of the Lord Most High (Gn 14:18-20).

The king rules as the vicar of Yahweh, seated at the right hand of the Lord, but so powerful is the aid God gives that he, God, is considered to be the "right hand" of the king. The "divine right" of kings was probably never so clearly indicated anywhere else.

The last verse of the psalm probably refers to an ancient coronation ceremony where the king went to drink from the spring at Gihon, one of the two principal sources of water for Jerusalem, the life blood of the city. It could also be a poetic image of a warrior king so intent on fulfilling God's justice that he didn't even take time to eat and drink while on the road.

The Epistle to the Hebrews makes the most extensive use of this psalm. When speaking of Jesus, the eternal High Priest, that author quotes, "You are a priest forever according to the order of Melchizedek" (5:7). "This (hope) we have as an anchor of the soul, sure and firm, which reaches behind the veil, where Jesus has entered on our behalf as forerunner, becoming high priest forever according to the order of Melchizedek" (6:19-7:10).

Melchizedek as a type of Christ is the subject of the 7th chapter of this same Epistle. When Abraham came from defeating the kings who had allied themselves against him, he was met by Melchizedek, King of Salem (Peace) who "blessed him. And Abraham apportioned to him a tenth of everything" (7:1-2). "Unquestionably, a lesser person is blessed by a greater," so the priesthood of Melchizedek was greater than that of Aaron's and Levi's, still in their father's loins (7:7-10).

The high priesthood of Aaron and the levitical priesthood depended on physical descent. The genealogy of Melchizedek was unknown. "Without father, mother or ancestry, without beginning of days or end of life, thus made to resemble the Son of God, he remains a priest forever" (7:3). Christ came from a tribe (Judah) and a house (David) which was not a priestly caste, so his spiritual priesthood, according to the order of Melchizedek, is superior and eternal, not depending on ancestry.

Peter Bloisius in the thirteenth century wrote:

"A priest has the primacy of Abel, the patriarchate of Abraham, the government of Noah, the order of Melchizedek, the dignity of Aaron, the authority of Moses, the perfection of Samuel, the power of Peter, the unction of Christ" (*Sermon to Priests* #60).

Father Karl Rahner, S.J., with his customary clarity writes: "We are asking what is the inner reality of the Catholic priesthood? It is, briefly, the continuation of the priesthood of Christ" (*The Priesthood*, 9:3).

Psalm 110 is used for all the principal Feasts of the Lord, Christmas, Epiphany, Transfiguration, Trinity Sunday, the Triumph of the Cross, Corpus Christi, Sacred Heart, Easter, Ascension, and the Presentation of the Lord. It is used as well for the Annunciation and the Feast of All Saints, and for 2nd Vespers (Evening Prayer II) on all Sundays.

PSALM 111: *"I will praise the Lord with all my heart..."*

Those of us who grew up in the pre-Vatican II Church have fond memories of Benediction of the Blessed Sacrament. Many families went to the High Mass on Sunday morning and returned in the early evening for Benediction. Mid-week evening devotions always concluded with Benediction.

The familiar Latin songs and the rolling Divine Praises led up to that glorious conclusion, a hearty rendition of "Holy God We Praise Thy Name." We didn't realize it, of course, but that hymn was a true descendant of the many psalms of praise. Psalm 111 begins a series of psalms which sing the praises of God's greatness.

Beginning with, or titled Alleluia, the psalm is an alphabetical, or acrostic poem, each half verse beginning with the succeeding letter of the Hebrew alphabet. Here, the people have been called together, usually in the Temple, to sing the praises of Yahweh.

The reasons are stated, the great Exodus events, and even to recite them is to recall the delightful, powerful protection God extended to his people. The majestic and glorious deeds proceed from the wisdom of the divine plan. The gift of manna was a high point in the story, as is the conclusion, when Joshua led the people into the Promised Land. The liturgical celebration of these deeds and the observance of the precepts that God gave them in his wisdom at Sinai will ensure their everlasting remembrance.

The last verse is particularly important, "The fear of the Lord is the beginning of wisdom." "Fear" in this instance is akin to "serving the Lord," or "the service of the Lord." "Fear of the Lord" was a Hebrew synonym for "religion."

To fear God, literally, because he will judge justly and punish promptly is perhaps the lowest form of religion, but it may be all some people can muster. "Perfect love casts out all fear" (1 Jn 4:18) because then the person is serving God and neighbor for a higher reason. This should be our Christian motivation. Human love makes us fear to do anything to offend the beloved, because we want as perfect a relationship as possible.

Because of the reference to the manna, the bread from heaven, Christians see a sign of the "true bread that comes down from heaven" (Jn 6:32-33), the Holy Eucharist which is the Real Presence of the Risen Christ. Christ proclaims, "I am the bread of life" and again, "I am the living bread that came down from heaven" (Jn 6:49-51). For this reason, Psalm 111 is used for the Feast of Corpus Christi and the Feast of the Sacred Heart.

St. Augustine, in his commentary, writes of this psalm:

"Diligently our Lord manifested in his promises and prophecies the way in which we would arrive at our final goal. He promised human beings divinity, mortals immortality, sinners justification and the poor a rising in glory.

"Whatever he promised, he promised to those who were unworthy. Thus it is not a case of a reward being promised to workers but of grace (*gratia*) being given as a gift, as its name indicates" (*Commentary on Psalm 110/111*).

The Hebrew psalmist praised God for the past events of history, the Exodus. The Christian — here, the poet Nicetas of Remesiana — praises God for the mysteries that effected our salvation and the wonderful mystery of the Incarnation and its continuing effects in our souls:

You are God: we praise you;
You are the Lord; we acclaim you...
You, Christ, are the king of glory,
The eternal Son of the Father.
When you became man to set us free
You did not spurn the Virgin's womb.
You overcame the sting of death,
And opened the kingdom of heaven to all believers.
You are seated at God's right hand in glory.
We believe that you will come, and be our judge...

(Te Deum)

PSALM 112: *"Happy are those who fear the Lord..."*

Pious platitudes are those religious sentiments which seem to state the obvious. However, sometimes they are called for, indeed even necessary. Psalm 112, an acrostic, alphabetical psalm, continues the thinking of Psalm 111 by showing how the righteousness of God is shared by the righteous man.

Those are happy who fear the Lord because they take delight in fulfilling God's commands. Since we are on pilgrimage, it is necessary to know where we are going and how to get there. By observing God's ways, we have the perfect road map for the journey. Instead of viewing them as a series of "Thou shalt not's" we are glad to have them as signposts and guides.

In the Jewish philosophy of immediate reward and punishment in this life, the just believers can expect good family connections, wealth and riches, stability in their lives and inner peace. The enjoyment of wealth means that they can afford to be generous to the poor and lowly which, while an obligation, is also a great privilege and joy. They don't have to worry about bad news, "ill reports," because they trust God to protect them. "Their horn shall be exalted" signifies virility, vitality and honor.

"All goes well for those gracious in lending, who conduct their affairs with justice." While this reflects a completely different economic system from the one we have, the principles of justice and equity are certainly basic to both.

When St. Paul was appealing for alms for the afflicted in Jerusalem, he quotes from this psalm:

"God loves a cheerful giver. Moreover, God is able to make every grace abundant for you so that in all things, always having all you need, you may have an abundance for every good work. As it is written, 'He scatters abroad, he gives to the poor; his prosperity shall endure forever'" (2 Cor 9:8-9).

St. Paul also alludes to verse 4 when he writes:

"For you were once darkness but now you are light in the Lord. Live as children of light, for light produces every kind of goodness and righteousness and truth" (Eph 5:8-9).

The question of wealth for the Christian has always posed a problem. Christ lived as a poor man; Mary and Joseph were certainly "people of the land," and Christ's message was accepted by the poor in spirit. Christ gave the example of poverty but he did not bless poverty understood as destitution. Most of his miracles helped the poor. Poverty of spirit is a virtue, far from the affliction of dire poverty.

The classical evangelical virtues, poverty, chastity and obedience, insofar as they are charisms, gifts, are a voluntary response to God's invitation.

Since the Christian is working for an eternal reward, he counts the sufferings of this world as nothing in comparison to the glorious reward in store (Rm 8:18; 1 P 5:10). Christ invited us to take up our crosses daily and follow him so that we can identify ourselves with him ever more closely (Mt 16:24).

But the question of wealth and the Christian still remains. Clement of Alexandria takes a very pragmatic view of it:

"Riches which benefit our neighbors are not to be thrown away. They are possessions and goods inasmuch as they are useful and provided by God for the use of men. The Lord so enjoins the use of property as to add that it be shared, that the thirsty be given drink, the hungry bread, the naked clothes and the homeless shelter. It is not possible to supply these needs without substance" (*On the Rich Man*).

The modern Popes, from Leo XIII and his social encyclical *Rerum Novarum*, to the present, have turned their attention to the social and economic order since this framework is governed by the same principles of justice, truth and charity as govern individual action.

The Second Vatican Council issued a serious call for social action:

"To satisfy the demands of justice and equity, strenuous efforts must be made, without disregarding the rights of persons or the natural qualities of each country, to remove as quickly as possible the immense economic inequalities, which now exist and in many cases are growing and which are connected with individual and social discrimination...

"In economic affairs which today are subject to change, as in the new forms of industrial society in which automation, for example, is advancing, care must be taken that sufficient and suitable work and the possibility of appropriate technical and professional formation are furnished. The livelihood and the human dignity, especially of those who are in very difficult conditions because of illness or old age, must be guaranteed" (*Gaudium et Spes* #66).

PSALM 113: *"Praise, you servants of the Lord..."*

(Editorial note: Psalms 113-118 are called Hallel Psalms, songs of praise to be used on the great feasts.)

Nomen est omen, the name is a prophecy, a prediction, a portent, according to an ancient Latin saying. In all ancient cultures, names had profound significance, whether it was the name of a god, a man or woman, or a child. We see this in the names used in the Old Testament, in names used in the Native American societies and in the giving of saints' names in the Sacrament of Baptism.

The change in the names of Abram and Sarai to Abraham and Sarah (Gn 17:5) and from Jacob to Israel (Gn 35:10) showed a significant development in the relationships of the Patriarchs to Yahweh. When Christ changed Simon's name to Peter (Mt 16:18), the Apostles would have immediately recognized the great significance of the action.

So, in Psalm 113, the charge to praise the name of the Lord would be a call to profound adoration. A psalm that begins and ends with the exclamation "Alleluia!" was an invitation to concentrate on the divinity of Yahweh, "from the rising of the sun to its setting." This could mean from sunrise to sunset, or from east to west, or here, probably both.

God, who rules all creation from his throne in heaven, stoops down to care for the needs of mankind, especially the poor and the needy. He exalts the lowly believer with princely rewards. A barren woman was considered cursed but God also has mercy on her. The barren Elizabeth could cry out, "So has the Lord done for me at a time when he has seen fit to take away my disgrace before others" (Lk 1:25). Hannah prayed to the Lord at Shiloh to take away the curse of her barrenness (1 S 1:11).

After the birth of Samuel, Hannah exulted, "He raises the needy from the dust; from the ash heap he lifts up the poor, to seat them with nobles and make a glorious throne their heritage" (2 S 2:8). The Blessed Virgin Mary quotes the same verses in her *Magnificat* before the birth of Christ: "He has thrown down the rulers from their thrones but lifted up the lowly" (Lk 1:52).

It is for this reason that the Common for Feasts of the Blessed Virgin Mary in *The Liturgy of the Hours* employs Psalm 113 and it is used again for the Feast of the Annunciation.

In fact, with its call for universal adoration of the one, true God, this is one of the psalms most used in the Liturgy. It is included at Christmas, Christ the King, Transfiguration, Trinity Sunday, Sacred Heart, Presentation, Ascension and Pentecost. Besides its use for Feasts of the Blessed Mother, it is used in the Commons for Pastors, Virgins, Holy Men and Holy Women.

The ancient Hebrew idea of God in his mercy stooping down to help mankind is brought to exquisite fulfillment in Christ Jesus: "Though he was in the form of God, [Jesus] did not regard equality with God something to be grasped. Rather, he emptied himself, taking the form of a slave, coming in human likeness; and found human in appearance, he humbled himself, becoming obedient to death, even death on a cross. Because of this, God greatly exalted him and bestowed on him the name that is above every name, that at the name of Jesus, every knee should bend... and every tongue confess that Jesus Christ is Lord" (Ph 2:6-11).

Listen to St. Hilary of Poitiers:

"We believe that the Word became flesh and that we receive his flesh in the Lord's Supper. How then can we fail to believe that he really dwells within us? When he became man, he actually clothed himself in our flesh, uniting it to himself forever. In the Sacrament of his Body he actually gives us his own flesh, which he has united to his divinity. That is why we are all one, because the Father is in Christ and Christ is in us" (*On the Holy Trinity*, Bk. 8).

In the words of St. Bernard:

"The circumcision proves, beyond a shadow of a doubt, the fact of Christ's humanity; the name indicates the majesty of his glory. He was circumcised because he was truly a son of Abraham; he was called Jesus, that name that is above all names, because he is truly the Son of God" (*On the Circumcision* #1).

The Incarnation of the Son of God is truly the reason that Christians must praise the name of the Lord "both now and forever. Alleluia!"

PSALM 114: *"When Israel came forth from Egypt..."*

There are some events in history that are so momentous that they leave an indelible impression on the psyche of a people. The Holocaust of Nazi Germany, the Black Plague in medieval Europe, the disgraceful treatment of the Native Americans in the American West, the introduction of African slavery into the South — these are events that clamor for attention.

The Exodus event colored all subsequent Jewish history. The

direct intervention of Yahweh on their behalf was ever before their eyes.

Psalm 114 is a lovely ballad that commemorates that event with delightful poetic license. It is probably an ancient commemoration since Jacob and Israel are treated as synonyms for a united country. Judah is praised as the place of central, national worship.

For the poet, when Israel left the place of slavery, Egypt, they immediately met the challenge of the waters of the Red Sea and the crossing of the Jordan. He conveniently ignores the long, dreary forty years of wandering in the desert with only a passing mention of giving the exiles water in an arid land, in the last verse.

The waters of the Red Sea and the Jordan fled before Israel like defeated soldiers fleeing a battlefield. Nature itself is pictured, in a delightful metaphor, as welcoming Israel with the mountains skipping like rams and the hills gamboling like lambs of the flock. These images may also refer to earthquakes, with the earth "trembling before the Lord." Under both images, Yahweh is the supreme Lord of nature.

Yahweh gave life and freedom to the Israelites through the Exodus event, leading them through the waters of sea and river. The Church, the New Israel of God, has been given life and freedom through the waters of Baptism. God has called us to be "a chosen race, a holy nation, a people all his own so that you may announce the praises of him who called you out of darkness into his own wonderful light" (1 P 2:9).

St. Justin Martyr reminds us of the importance of Baptism as initiating us into the Christian way of life:

"No one may share the Eucharist with us unless he believes that what we teach is true, unless he is washed in the regenerating waters of Baptism for the remission of sins, and unless he lives in accordance with the principles given us by Christ... We hold our common assembly on Sunday because it is the first day of the week, because on that day our Savior, Jesus Christ, rose from the dead" (*First Apology* #66).

St. Thomas Aquinas is even more direct:

"In Baptism, Christ's passion works a regeneration; a person dies entirely to the old life and takes on the new. Therefore Baptism washes away the whole guilt of punishment belonging to the past" (*Commentary on Romans* 2:4).

Abbot Columba Marmion writes:

"When we were created, the Holy Trinity said, 'Let us make man to our own image and likeness'; when adoption was conferred on us at Baptism, the Holy Trinity engraved on our souls the very features of Christ. And that is why when the Eternal Father sees us clad in sanctifying grace, making us like to his divine Son, he cannot but grant us what we ask of him — not in our own name but in that of the One in whom he is well pleased.

"Such is the grace and power that Baptism bestows; it makes us, by supernatural adoption, brothers and sisters of Christ, capable in all truth of sharing his divine life and everlasting inheritance.

"O Christian, when will you understand your greatness and dignity? When will you proclaim by your works that you are of a divine race? When will you live as a disciple of Christ?" (*Christ the Life of the Soul*, p. 168).

This hymn of praise is used in the Office for Trinity Sunday, Easter Sunday and Pentecost.

PSALM 115: *"Not to us, Lord, not to us..."*

God made us to his own image and likeness but the temptation is to turn this notion around and remake God in our own image and likeness. It is always difficult to worship an invisible God, especially when he names himself, "I am who am" (Ex 3:13).

This may have been one of the reasons why the Israelites seemed so prone to fall into idolatry. The nations around them had something concrete to worship. Even knowing that we are made in the image and likeness of God, that we have an intellect that seeks truth and a free will that allows us to love, the Incarnation which brought Christ in the flesh is a tremendous help to our poor human needs. We can visualize the human Christ.

The opening verse of Psalm 115 is beautiful in Latin, *Non nobis, Domine, non nobis, sed nomini tuo da gloriam*, but it is even more poignant in English: "Not to us, O Lord, not to us, but to your name give glory." Whether in the Holy Land, surrounded by enemies, or in the Diaspora, surrounded by successful pagans, the Jews had to remind themselves that glory was due to this invisible God. In response to the taunt, "So, where is your god; what does he look like?" the honest answer was, "Our God is in heaven; whatever he wills he does."

The second stanza is a delightful "spoof" of the idol makers and worshippers. No matter how precious the metal the idols are made of, no matter how artistic the maker, their senses are only for show. Eyes that do not see; ears that do not hear, feet that cannot move — how could anyone believe in them! They are powerless to help and those who trust in them are bound to be betrayed.

The concluding stanza is a series of praises and blessings that show the true religious sentiment of a real Israelite. "The house of Israel" means all the people. "The house of Aaron" refers to the priestly caste. "Those who fear the Lord" are converts who are not direct descendants of the twelve patriarchs, like the centurion Cornelius (Ac 10:2).

God is the strength and hope of all his people. He will fill them with blessings in abundance, increase and bless their posterity and give them true happiness. God, ruling from his "heaven of heavens" or highest heaven, has given the earth to his people to be used, as a blessing.

The shadowy belief in some vague sort of afterlife made the enjoyment of the earth even more precious, even more of a blessing. It wasn't until the second century before Christ that a more positive belief in immortality with God became the common belief among the Israelites. Even then, the Sadducees rejected the idea of an afterlife (Ac 23:7-10).

Christians certainly join the Jews in proclaiming that glory belongs to God and that all blessings come from him. We also are at one with them in disapproving of idolatry, but the idols of our times do not usually come in the form of golden calves and the like. No, our idols are more likely to be the drive for power and dominance, the love of wealth and possessions, the "body beautiful" and phony sophistication.

Many people, in their search for meaning in life, follow a variety of false gods. The Fathers of Vatican II had some pertinent words to say about this:

"The truth is that the imbalances under which the modern world labors are linked with that more basic imbalance which is rooted in the heart of man. For in man himself many elements wrestle with one another. Thus, on the one hand, as a creature he experiences his limitations in a multitude of ways; on the other hand he feels himself to be boundless in his desires and summoned to a higher life.

"Pulled by manifold attractions he is constantly forced to choose among them and renounce some. Indeed, as a weak and sinful being, he often does what he would not, and fails to do what he would (cf. Rm 7:14). Hence he suffers from internal divisions, and from these flow so many and such great discords in society. No doubt many whose lives are infected with a practical materialism are blinded against any sharp insight into this kind of dramatic situation, or else, weighed down by unhappiness they are prevented from giving the matter any thought.

"Thinking they have found serenity in an interpretation of reality everywhere proposed these days, many look forward to a genuine and total emancipation of humanity wrought solely by human effort; they are convinced that the future rule of man over the earth will satisfy every desire of his heart. Nor are there lacking men who despair of any meaning to life and praise the boldness of those who think that human existence is devoid of any inherent significance and strive to confer a total meaning on it by their own ingenuity alone" (*Gaudium et Spes* #10).

The "theology" of materialistic humanism is as bankrupt as the idolatry of any ancient pagan, just a little more sophisticated!

Speaking of Christian unity, St. Dionysius of Alexandria wrote using this analogy:

"For this a man ought to suffer anything and everything, rather than divide the Church of God, and it is no less glorious to incur martyrdom to avoid schism than to avoid idolatry; in fact, in my opinion it is more so. For in one case a man is a martyr for the sake of his own single soul, but in the other for the sake of the whole Church" (*Letter to Novatian*).

PSALM 116: *"I love the Lord who listened to my voice..."*

"One act of thanksgiving when things go wrong with us," wrote Blessed John of Avila, "is worth a thousand thanks when things are agreeable to our inclinations" (*Letter*).

Psalm 116, despite its sometimes threatening tone, is a powerful thanksgiving song. The author, faced with death, dreading it in accord with the belief that there is no afterlife, or a shadowy one at best, turns to God with loud cries of petition. God looks on the lowly and the needy and saves them, and so he rescues the poet. (Editorial note: The Greek Septuagint and the Latin Vulgate translations divide some of the psalms in this fifth book of the Psalter, including this one, differently from that used in the Hebrew version which modern translations follow, so there can be much confusion in quoting from these psalms by number.)

Freed from the danger of death and despair, the psalmist breathes a sigh of relief; he will walk again in the land of the living. Since this phrase is also used of the Temple, he will go again to worship there.

In the depths of his panic, he had turned against his fellow men and almost lost faith in God. How to repay? He will offer a sacrifice of thanksgiving. The death of a faithful servant is too costly for God to allow. Indeed, he admits to being a house-born slave, the lowest of the low, a person with absolutely no rights, a servant of God in every respect. He will sing his Alleluias in the presence of all the people in the Temple.

The Christian application of this psalm is manifold. It is used during Holy Week, at Easter and on the Feasts of All Saints, Apostles, Martyrs and the Triumph of the Holy Cross.

The death that is "costly" to the psalmist is precious, indeed, to the Christian. The Roman Martyrology salutes the triumphant death of the martyrs as courageous heroes and heroines of Christ.

St. Augustine reminds us:

"We, the Christian community, assemble to celebrate the memory of the martyrs with ritual solemnity because we want to be inspired to follow their example, share in their merits and be helped by their prayers... But the veneration strictly called worship, *latria*, that is, the special homage belonging only to divinity, is something we give and teach others to give to God alone" (*Against Faustus* #20).

"I will take up the cup of salvation" is used in the Tridentine Latin Mass at the time of Communion from the chalice, the redeeming Blood of Christ being the true source of our salvation. In the words of St. Alphonsus Liguori:

"Jesus Christ wished that the price of his Blood, shed for the salvation of all, should be applied to us in the Sacrifice of the Altar; in which the victim offered is the same, though it is there offered differently from what it is on the Cross, that is, without the shedding of blood" ("The Sacrifice of Jesus Christ" in *The Holy Eucharist*).

"I am your servant, the child of your maidservant" is reflected in Mary's *Magnificat*, "For he has looked upon his handmaid's lowliness; behold, from now on all generations will call me blessed" (Lk 1:48). Mary is quoted only seven times in the Gospels, but as St. Bernardine of Siena remarked, "Whenever she spoke, she spoke seven words filled with wisdom" (*Sermon on the Visitation*).

But it is perhaps in the celebration of the Paschal Mystery, the Passion, Death and Resurrection of Christ, that this psalm shines best. Christ suffered before his death in the Agony in the Garden; he knew that his life was about to end in his crucifixion; he called to God his Father and was glorified, through his Death, in the Resurrection. At every Mass, the true "sacrifice of thanksgiving," we recall these things.

"When we eat this bread and drink this cup, we proclaim your death, Lord Jesus, until you come again in glory!" (Proclamation of the Mystery of Faith in the Liturgy of the Mass).

PSALM 117: *"Praise the Lord, all you nations..."*

The concept of the divinity of Yahweh was a subject of continuing revelation. First he was a patriarchal God, then a territorial God, later a tribal and national God and finally the God of all creation and of all peoples.

This shortest of psalms celebrates Yahweh's universal love and mercy, his faithfulness, to all of his creation, and his special predilection for those whom he had created in his own image and likeness. St. Paul quotes this psalm when he celebrates the fidelity and mercy of God, who confirms the promises made to the patriarchs that then overflow in mercy to the Gentiles in the universal, salvific work of Christ (Rm 15:7-13).

The liturgy of the Church uses it to salute that mercy at work in the Feasts of Christ the King, the Transfiguration, and the Ascension. On Feasts of the Apostles we honor them for being the instruments who brought the Good News to all the nations.

St. Ignatius of Antioch writes of this universal salvation:

"By his Resurrection, Christ raised up a standard over his saints and faithful ones for all time, both Jews and Gentiles, in the one body of his Church. For he endured all this for us, for our salvation; he really suffered and just as truly rose from the dead" (*Letter to the Church at Smyrna* #3).

In the old concluding Benediction Hymn we all learned to lift up our voices in singing God's glory:

> Holy God we praise your Name!
> Lord of all we bow before you!
> All on earth your scepter claim,
> All in heaven above adore you!
> Infinite your vast domain,

Everlasting is your reign.
(Ignaz Franz, *Holy God We Praise Your Name*, v. 1)

PSALM 118: *"Give thanks to the Lord who is good..."*

This story is told, however apocryphal it may be. After the death of Pope St. Pius X, Cardinal Giacomo della Chiesa was elected as Pope Benedict XV. Cardinal Merry del Val, the Cardinal Secretary of State, had been responsible for exiling della Chiesa to an obscure diocese in Italy. It was widely believed that del Val would succeed Pius X as Pope.

When del Val came up to make his obedience to the new Pope, the Pope is reputed to have said, "The stone which the builders rejected has become the cornerstone" (Ps 118:22). Without missing a step, del Val replied, "By the Lord has this been done and it is marvelous in our sight" (Ps 118:23).

As the Romans say, "If it isn't true, it should be!" Whatever the case, Psalm 118 has been used extensively by Christians and Jews alike.

It is a triumphant processional hymn to commemorate great victories, national as well as personal in scope. It begins with the usual words of praise, inviting the priests, people and converts to pay tribute to the enduring and merciful love of God.

In the second stanza the psalmist expresses the greatest confidence in God's protection and blessing for the just man. If the Lord is on our side, "what can mortals do against me?" With the Lord as protector there is no need "to put one's trust in princes."

The psalm goes on to recognize the fact that Israel has always been surrounded by hordes of hostile nations. "In the Lord's name I crushed them." They may be as pesky as walking into a swarm of bees or as deadly as fire blazing through thorny brush. "The Lord, my strength and my might, came to me as savior."

The shouts of victory ring through the camp, rejoicing in the triumph and acknowledging God's strong right hand as the true cause of the victory. A soldier in danger of death is snatched back from disaster. "I shall not die but live and declare the deeds of the Lord." Even if wounded, "the Lord chastised me harshly but did not hand me over to death."

Psalm 118 reaches poetic heights in the fifth stanza. "The stone the builders rejected has become the cornerstone" (v. 22). This became a proverb to be used in many instances. That which the world considers insignificant can be raised to the greatest heights by God's intervention (v. 23). The New Testament interpreted this as directly referring to Christ's Death and Resurrection (Mt 21:42; Lk 20:16-18; Ac 4:11).

"This is the day the Lord has made; let us rejoice in it and be glad" (v. 24). The day the Lord has made is the day of triumph, of victory. It is right and good to cheer it on. That is why this psalm figures so large in the Christian joys of the Easter and Pentecost Feasts. It also marks the victory of the Martyrs on their Feasts. In *The Liturgy of the Hours* it is used each week in the four week cycle of psalms.

"Lord, grant salvation! Lord, grant good fortune!" (v. 25). The Hebrew word for "grant salvation" is Hosanna and the Hosannas of Palm Sunday (Mt 21:9; Mk 11:9-10) join the Alleluias of the whole Easter season. Hosanna, coupled with "Blessed is he who comes in the name of the Lord" (v. 26), is sung or said at every Mass after the Preface of the Mass in the Latin Rite of the Roman Catholic Church.

Easter, the day the Lord has made, is truly the day Christians triumph in their Savior and Redeemer. Frank Sheed shares some of his thoughts on the subject:

"Of what happened on that first day, Easter, and on the forty days in which he came and went among them before his Ascension, the Evangelists selected from their own memories and the accounts of others, incidents which they saw as specially significant, with no attempt to harmonize them. But all four give the same outline. There was the tomb found empty on the Sunday morning; there were appearances to various women, disciples, apostles" (*What Difference Does Jesus Make?*, p. 192).

Père LaGrange gives an interesting sidelight:

"Pious children of the Church entertain no doubt that the newly risen Savior appeared first of all to his most holy Mother. She had fed him at her breast, she had guided him in his childhood years, she had, so to say, introduced him to the world at the marriage feast at Cana, and beyond that she hardly appears in the Gospel until she stands at the foot of the cross.

"But to her alone, with Joseph, Jesus had devoted the thirty years of his hidden life and would he not have reserved for her alone also the first moments of his new life?" (*The Gospel of Jesus Christ*, ch. 7).

Pope St. Gregory the Great gives us an Easter hymn:

Hail Day! in which the Trinity
First formed the earth by sure decree;
The Day its Maker rose again,
And vanquished death and burst our chain.
Away with sleep and slothful ease!
We raise our hearts and bend our knees
And early seek the Lord of all,
Obedient to the prophet's call.

(*Primo Die, Quo Trinitas*)

PSALM 119: *"Happy are those whose way is blameless..."*

Psalm 119, the longest in the Psalter, is an appreciation of God as the founder and guarantor of the moral order. Pope John Paul II in *Veritatis Splendor* finds a firm basis for right and wrong, good and bad in morality.

Psalm 119 has its own unique poetic construction, too. It is an acrostic psalm with 22 stanzas each beginning with successive letters in the Hebrew alphabet. Each stanza has eight verses beginning with the same letter. There are eight key words for "law" or "instruction in the law" that are used in almost every stanza — law, edict, command, precept, word, utterance, way, decree and a ninth, teaching.

This psalm has been likened to an anthology of all the various forms and many of the themes used in the other psalms. It is not a priestly song, nor does it rely on historical themes such as Mt. Sinai, Mt. Zion, the Temple, etc. Its theology is based on the deuteronomic tradition. The work lends itself to instruction, exhortation and meditation. It would have been useful in instructing the young and converts.

The poet certainly expresses his joy in treasuring the law of God, the laws that come from a knowledge of God and a personal, I-Thou relationship with God. His tears are shed for those who despise the law or persecute its ardent followers. The rewards for staying close to God and his way are numerous, both interior and exterior: peace of mind, prosperity, protection from the wicked, etc.

From this psalm, St. Benedict and many monastic founders took the order of their liturgical "hours" — praying seven times a day and rising in the night to pray (v. 164). In *The Liturgy of the Hours* this psalm is used by stanzas, and at least one is used almost every day.

To read the whole 176 verses at one time may make the psalm seem boring and excessively repetitious. Despite its lack of poetic or dramatic heights, it has some very thoughtful lines: "I have more insight than my elders because I observe your precepts" (v. 100). "Your word is a lamp for my feet, a light for my path" (v. 105). "The revelation of your words sheds light, gives understanding to the simple" (v. 130).

The medieval Schoolmen taught that the ultimate norm of morality is an informed conscience. With this in mind, this meditation on morality has many Christian dimensions.

"Loving God means keeping his commandments" (1 Jn 5:3). And what are the most basic of all commandments for the Christian? "Love the Lord your God with all your heart, with all your soul and with all your mind. This is the greatest and first commandment. The second is like it. You shall love your neighbor as yourself. The whole law and the prophets depend on these two commandments" (Mt 22:37-40; Mk 12:30-31).

St. Paul's description of the way of love, "a more excellent way" (1 Cor 12:31) has become a part of our classic human heritage:

"If I speak with the tongues of men and angels but do not have love, I am a resounding gong or a clanging cymbal. And if I have the gift of prophecy and comprehend all mysteries and all knowledge; if I have faith enough so as to move mountains, but do not have love, I am nothing. If I give away everything I own, and if I hand my body over to be burned but do not have love, I gain nothing.

"Love is patient, love is kind, love is not pompous, it is not inflated, it is not rude, it does not seek its own interests; it is not quick tempered, it does not brood over injury; it does not rejoice over wrongdoing but rejoices with the truth.

"It bears all things, believes all things, hopes all things, endures all things. Love never fails... Faith, hope and love remain; but the greatest of these is love" (1 Cor 13:1-13).

St. Cyprian tells us:

"Charity is the bond of brotherhood, the foundation of peace, the steadfastness and firmness of unity; it is greater than faith and hope; it surpasses both good works and suffering for the faith; and, as an eternal virtue, it will abide with us forever in the kingdom of heaven" (*On Patience*, ch. 15).

The poet Jessica Powers (Sister Miriam of the Holy Spirit, O.C.D.) gives us this reflection:

> The heart can set its boundaries
> On mortal acres without fear.
> Descent of skies, cascade of seas
> Are not to be expected here.
> The heart can take a human love
> To feed and shelter, if it will,
> Nor think to see its cities move
> In avalanches down a hill.
> Only when God is passing by
> And is invited in to stay
> Is there a split of earth and sky.
> Boundaries leap and rush away.

And wound and chaos come to be
Where once a world lay still and small,
But how else could infinity
Enter what is dimensional.

(*Boundaries*)

PSALM 120: *"The Lord answered me…"*

(Editorial note: Psalms 120-134 are titled Psalms of Ascent, or, in the older versions, Gradual Psalms. They may have been used on pilgrimages, as the travelers wound their way up to Jerusalem, or may have been sung on the fifteen steps leading into the Temple. Despite their brevity, they contain examples of all the psalm forms. It seems that this was a popular collection, much loved by all the people.)

How many times have we used these tired old expressions with deep feeling: "Home, Sweet Home!" "Be it ever so humble, there's no place like home," or even "Show me the way to go home."

That's the spirit of Psalm 120. It is the heartfelt prayer of a man who has lived in exile too long and found it a rough existence. The Jews were used to being looked at with jaundiced eyes, but those lying lips and the treacherous tongues finally took their toll on the author of this psalm.

God has delivered him from the venom of his enemies, but he is led to heap a biblical curse on them, "May God do thus and thus to you — and more besides." Their punishment will be like a wound from a warrior's sharp arrow, or be intense as the heat from desert charcoal.

The exile felt like an alien, whether in the far north, such as Meshech near the Black Sea, or in the nomadic south, Kedar, among the Arabians. He speaks for all who are far from home. He longs for Jerusalem, his homeland, and searches for peace, a way to distance himself from the war-loving natives of foreign lands.

The Gradual Psalms have been used extensively in Christian

liturgies. They sum up so many basic human feelings; they express such deep human longings. In *The Liturgy of the Hours*, still popularly called "The Divine Office" or "the Breviary" they are used for the Complimentary Psalmody.

The longing for peace expressed in Psalm 120 strikes a beautiful note. Christ, the Prince of Peace, foretold by the prophets, announced by the angels, proclaimed by the Church, answers our need for eternal peace.

But peace is not merely the absence of war; in the classic expression, it rests on the tranquillity of order.

Pope St. Leo the Great expressed it this way:

"But what can we find in the treasure of the Lord's bounty but that peace which was first announced by the angelic choir on the day of his birth? That peace, from which the children of God spring, sustains love and mothers unity; it refreshes the blessed and shelters eternity; its characteristic function and special blessing are to join to God those whom it separates from the world" (*Sixth Sermon on Christmas*).

Pope John XXIII exhorted us in modern times to work for peace:

"The world will never be the dwelling place of peace, until peace has found a home in the heart of each and every man, until every man preserves in himself the order ordained by God to be preserved. That is why St. Augustine asks the question, 'Does your mind desire the strength to gain the mastery over your passions? Let it submit to a greater power and it will conquer all beneath it. And peace will be in you — true, sure, most ordered peace. What is that order? God as ruler of the mind; the mind as ruler of the body. Nothing could be more orderly'" (*Pacem in Terris* #165).

PSALM 121: *"I raise my eyes toward the mountains..."*

A large international airport has a rather prominent Catholic chapel. In the early days of passenger travel, a priest was always on call to give absolution to nervous, first-time flyers. Flight insurance, also, used to be a major source of profit at many airports.

Travel in biblical days was even more dangerous. Psalm 121 contains a blessing for someone starting out on a journey, more than likely a Temple pilgrim about to return home. Looking toward the mountains showed apprehension, for bandits lurked in the high places waiting to swoop down on travelers. The shrines of pagan gods were also in the high places so there was spiritual danger as well.

Looking back at "the" mountain, Zion, reminded the pilgrim that blessings, protection and guidance came from Yahweh. "My help comes from the Lord who made heaven and earth" was a reassuring blessing common to Jews and Christians.

Unlike pagan deities, God never slumbers or sleeps. He is always watchful over the ways of his faithful and goes with them on their way. The ravages of the cruel sun during the day and the terrors caused by the moon (hence, lunatic) cannot touch one watched over by God. The traveler leaves with the security of knowing that "the Lord will guard your coming and going, both now and forever."

Christian devotion considers this earthly life a pilgrimage, and indeed a perilous journey through life. The constant guidance provided by Christ as shepherd and guide is the greatest consolation and source of motivation for us.

St. Augustine reminds us that:

"The Church recognizes two kinds of life as having been commanded to her by God. One is a life of faith, the other a life of vision; one is passed on pilgrimage in time, the other a dwelling place in eternity; one is a life of toil, the other of rest; one is spent on the road, the other in our homeland" (*Commentary on the Gospel of John* #124).

The reference to the mountains is recalled in the Feast of the Transfiguration. Christ took Peter, James and John with him up Mt. Tabor and showed them a glimpse of his risen glory (Mk 2:8; Mt 17:1-8). An allusion to the revelation of Yahweh to Moses on Mt. Sinai is highly likely (cf. John L. McKenzie, *Dictionary of the Bible*, p. 897).

Pope St. Pius V used this passage in an unusual way:

"Jesus Christ crucified, Son of the most holy Virgin Mary! Incline your Sacred Heart and listen to my petitions and sighs, as you listened to your eternal Father on Mt. Tabor. Jesus Christ crucified, Son of the most holy Virgin Mary! Open your Sacred Eyes and look on me as you looked on your holy Mother from the cross" (*Prayer to Christ Crucified* ##1 and 2).

In the Book of Revelation, St. John pays tribute to the first Christian martyrs, those who have survived the great times of distress and washed their robes white in the blood of the Lamb:

> For this reason they stand before God's throne
> and worship him day and night in his temple.
> The one who sits on the throne will shelter them.
> For they will not hunger or thirst any more,
> nor will the sun or any heat strike them.
> For the Lamb who is in the center of the throne
> will shepherd them
> and lead them to springs of life-giving water,
> and God will wipe away every tear from their eyes.
> (Rv 7:15-17)

PSALM 122: *"I rejoiced when they said to me…"*

In the Introduction to his *Canterbury Tales*, Chaucer tells how the coming of April's rains turns the minds of men and women to pilgrimages. The three great feasts of the Jews, Unleavened Bread (Passover), Weeks (Pentecost), and Booths or Harvest (cf. Dt 16:16) turned their minds to thoughts of a pilgrimage to the Temple in Jerusalem.

These pilgrimages were frequently arduous affairs for those who came from any distance and their object was definitely spiritual. "No one shall appear before the Lord empty-handed" (Dt 16:17). As a friar in Chaucer's "Summoner's Tale" says, "Whoso will pray, he must fast and be clean, and fat his soul and make his body lean."

Psalm 122 reflects both the joy and the seriousness of the pilgrimage to Jerusalem. The poet expresses that joy at the very thought of it. And, when he finally arrives, he exults at the beauty and the size of the city. By our standards, the cities of ancient times were hardly more than fortified towns, bound by their walls to limit their size. Their density and their filth would probably turn us off.

But the psalmist exults in what he sees and what it means — the tribes witnessing to Yahweh, the king's power and his meting out justice, and the promises made to the house of David, notably of a Messiah.

The second stanza turns into a prayer for Jerusalem which the poet loves intensely. "May those who love you prosper," may peace and blessings descend on you. The second longest of the Ascent Psalms ends with tender power: may blessings descend on the house of the Lord.

Psalm 122 is also the Ascent Psalm most used in Christian liturgy and devotion. We are reminded of the pilgrimages that Christ himself made to Jerusalem: his presentation in the Temple (Lk 2:23), his first Passover pilgrimage (Lk 2:41-51), his final journey to Jerusalem before his Passion (Lk 9:51), and his triumphant entry there (Lk 19:28-40).

The Epistle to the Hebrews describes two great assemblies, that of the Israelites at Mt. Sinai to finalize the covenant and the assembly of the Christians celebrating the new covenant sealed in the Blood of Christ:

"You have approached Mount Zion and the city of the living God, the heavenly Jerusalem and countless angels in festal gathering, and the assembly of the firstborn enrolled in heaven, and God the judge of all, and the spirits of the just made perfect, and Jesus, the mediator of a new covenant, and the sprinkled blood that speaks more eloquently than that of Abel" (Heb 12:22-24). The blood of Abel cried out for vengeance; the blood of Christ brings salvation.

The love that the psalmist has for Jerusalem is reflected in the Christian who has a tender love for the Church. Listen to Julian of Norwich who shares her vision with us:

"God showed the very great pleasure he takes in all men and women who mightily and wisely receive the preaching and teaching of the Church. For he is Holy Church, he is its ground, its substance, its teaching. He is its teacher. He is the end and the reward toward which every kind soul travels... By this vision he showed me how to grow in its teaching, that I might, by his grace, increase and rise to more heavenly knowledge and higher loving" (*Revelation*).

The theologian Matthias Scheeben wrote:

"What high, supernatural dignity is attained by man when he becomes a member of the Church, how astounding the union into which he enters with Christ, and through Christ with God, and at the same time with all his fellow members in the Church!

"What a tremendous mystery lies even in simple membership in the Church! It is a mystery as great as the mystery of the Mystical Body of Christ, as the mystery of the Eucharist in which it culminates, as the mystery of the Incarnation upon which it is based, as the mystery of grace which is its fruit" (*The Mysteries of Christianity*, 19:78).

PSALM 123: *"To you I raise my eyes..."*

As part of the philosophy of Alcoholics Anonymous and allied programs that use the Twelve Steps, one has to be completely down and out and recognize that he can do nothing without the help of a Higher Power, in order to make a comeback.

The author of this psalm is in that very position, whether writing for himself or speaking on behalf of the nation. Things couldn't be worse, he acknowledges, and he turns in confidence to Yahweh, enthroned in heaven.

The figure of speech then used is poignant and touching in its total sincerity. "Like the eyes of a servant on the hands of his master, like the eyes of a maid on the hands of her mistress" acknowledges complete dependence on the will and command of

God. They await the will of God as a slave waits for the master's next action, eyes riveted on him.

Treated with contempt, insulted and put down by the arrogant, their only hope is that God will show his favor again. The psalm ends with a note of quiet hope that God will so act. Reliance on the Lord is the only recourse that the downtrodden have.

How often Christ responded to those who appealed to his pity and mercy. There were the two blind men near Jericho who cried out, "Lord, Son of David, have pity on us!" (Mt 20:30), the Canaanite woman near Tyre and Sidon who begged for her daughter, "Lord, Son of David, have pity on me" (Mt 15:22), the leper who pleaded "Lord, if you wish, you can make me clean" (Lk 5:12), and the beautiful scene at Nain, where the bereft woman didn't even have to ask (Lk 7:11-17). The examples could be multiplied many times.

St. Paul vividly expresses the power of Christ's humanity:

"Have among yourselves the same attitude that is also yours in Christ Jesus who, though he was in the form of God did not regard equality with God something to be grasped. Rather he emptied himself, taking the form of a slave, coming in human likeness; and found human in appearance, he humbled himself becoming obedient to death, even death on a cross.

"Because of this, God greatly exalted him and bestowed on him the name that is above every name, that at the name of Jesus every knee should bend of those in heaven and on earth and under the earth, and every tongue confess that Jesus Christ is Lord to the glory of God the Father" (Ph 2:5-11).

The Incarnation itself, then, is the prime example of Christ identifying with stricken mankind. Pope St. Leo teaches:

"Christ took the nature of a servant without stain of sin, enlarging our humanity without diminishing his divinity. He emptied himself; though invisible, he made himself visible; though creator of all things, he chose to be one of us mortal men.

"Yet this was the condescension of compassion, not the loss of omnipotence. So he, who in the nature of God had created man, became in the nature of a servant, man himself" (*Letter 28 to Flavius* #3).

Mary Stuart, Queen of Scots, had a real feeling for this example of compassion:

> Keep us, O God, from pettiness.
> Let us be large in thought, word and deed.
> Let us be done with fault-finding and leave off self-seeking.
> May we put away all pretense and meet each other
> > face to face
> without self-pity and without prejudice.
> And, O Lord God,
> Let us not forget to be kind. Amen.
> > (*Prayer for Generosity*)

PSALM 124: *"Had not the Lord been with us..."*

An old joke insists that the Ten Lost Tribes of Israel ended up in Ireland. It is not by accident or chance, however, that Israel survived throughout its turbulent history. Plagued by hostile native tribes during the time of the Judges, tossed between two aggressive world powers after David and Solomon, the nation survived purely and simply through the mercy, power and strength of God.

The thanksgiving theme that runs through Psalm 124 is firmly grounded on those historical facts. The fury of their enemies is likened to the chaotic floods of creation whose seething waters could have drowned them; this is also possibly a reference to the passage through the Red Sea. The fury of the mythic fire-breathing dragon could have burned them or swallowed them alive.

But the Lord always came to their rescue. Saved from the fury of Pharaoh, and saved from recurrent danger, the people sing of the blessings of God. Again there is a poignant expression of freedom: "We escaped with our lives like a bird from the fowler's snare; the snare was broken and we escaped."

The final verse has become a common expression in both Jewish and Christian worship: "Our help is in the name of the Lord, who made heaven and earth."

We can draw a parallel between the physical dangers that surrounded the Jews, and the spiritual dangers that flail away at the spiritual life. As the old penny catechism taught, these temptations come from the world, the flesh and the devil.

Worldly opposition to Christianity was present from the very beginning as Christ had predicted (Mt 10:17). St. Paul reminded his disciples, "Five times at the hands of the Jews I received forty lashes, minus one. Three times I was beaten with rods, once I was stoned" (2 Cor 11:24-25). When St. Paul settled in Corinth, Our Lord had to encourage him: "Do not be afraid. Go on speaking and do not be silent, for I am with you" (Ac 18:9-10).

The so-called Ten Great Persecutions in the Roman Empire, up to the time of Constantine, were based on the law *Christiani non sint.* Christians may not be, they may not exist, let there be no Christians!

Christian saints through the centuries have also acknowledged this spiritual warfare:

"Keep us, O Lord Jesus, through the day by the merits and intercession of the Blessed Virgin Mary and all your saints, from all vicious and unruly desires, from all sins and temptations of the devil, and from sudden and unprovided death and the pains of hell" (St. Edmund of Abingdon, *Prayer*).

"Everyone cannot become a genius, but the path of holiness is open to all... It is untrue that the saints were not like us. They, too, experienced temptation, they fell and rose again; they experienced sorrow that weakened them and paralyzed them with a sense of discouragement... They did not trust themselves but placed all their trust in God" (St. Maximilian Kolbe, *First Editorial*).

For many years, the prayers after Low Masses included this powerful prayer:

St. Michael the Archangel, defend us in battle.
Be our protection against the malice and snares of the devil.

May God rebuke him, we humbly pray,
And do you, O Prince of the heavenly hosts,
By the power of God cast into hell Satan
And all the other evil spirits who prowl about the world
Seeking the ruin of souls. Amen.

PSALM 125: *"Like Mt. Zion are they who trust in the Lord..."*

If there is a church anywhere in Christendom more ugly than
the Church of the Holy Sepulchre in Jerusalem I can't imagine
where it might be. Yet, the Christian pilgrim soon forgets this as
he becomes immersed in the biblical world there.

There is the world of the Old Testament, venerable with age.
The world of the New Testament comes alive from Bethlehem to
Nazareth to Calvary and the empty Tomb. The relics of the Crusaders' Latin Kingdom are a tribute to a faith which, perhaps, witnessed too militantly. And the modern State of Israel is vibrant
with life.

Psalm 125 brings the ancient pilgrim into the City of David,
Jerusalem, and up to Mt. Zion and the Temple. What confidence
it inspired, based on the promise of God! And it was physically
impressive as well. "As the mountains surround Jerusalem, the Lord
also surrounds his people both now and forever."

The second stanza proclaims that the "scepter of the wicked"
will not prevail — and this covers foreign aggressors or local tyrants. The poet prays that the wicked will be overcome so that they
do not contaminate the faithful who live in "the land of the just."
Literally it is "the land of the lot," the way the Holy Land was
divided among the tribes (Nb 26:55-56).

The final stanza contains a beautiful blessing for the upright
of heart and an imprecation against those "who turn aside to wicked
ways." The final line is an exclamation, "Peace upon Israel!"

The Christian sees the Church as the New Israel of God and
finds protection for the faith in the Church, the body of Christ,
firmly founded on the Rock. As St. Paul remarked:

"But may I never boast except in the cross of our Lord Jesus Christ, through which the world has been crucified to me, and I to the world. For neither does circumcision mean anything nor does uncircumcision, but only a new creation. Peace and mercy to all who follow this rule and to the true Israel of God" (Gal 6:14-16).

Let us turn to one of the bishops of Jerusalem, St. Cyril, for his thoughts about the Church:

"The Church is called Catholic or universal because it has spread throughout the entire world, from one end of the earth to the other. Again, it is called Catholic because it teaches fully and unfailingly all the doctrines which ought to be brought to men's knowledge, whether concerned with visible or invisible things, with the realities of heaven and the things of earth.

"Another reason for the name Catholic is that the Church brings all classes of men into religious obedience, rulers and subjects, the learned and the unlettered. Finally it deserves the word Catholic because it heals and cures unrestrictedly every type of sin and because it possesses within itself every kind of virtue" (*Catechesis* #18).

This confidence we have in the Church is expressed by St. Ambrose:

"The Church of the Lord is built upon the rock of the Apostles among so many dangers in the world; it therefore remains unmoved. The Church's foundation is unshakable and firm against the assaults of the raging sea. Waves lash at the Church but do not shatter it. Although the elements of the world constantly beat upon the Church with crashing sounds, the Church possesses the safest harbor of salvation for all in distress" (*Second Letter*).

The Fathers of Vatican II wrote:

"Christ instituted this new covenant, the new testament, that is to say, in his blood, calling together a people made up of Jew and Gentile, making them one, not according to the flesh but in the Spirit. This was to be the New People of God" (*Lumen Gentium* #9).

PSALM 126: *"When the Lord restored the fortunes of Zion..."*

In Psalm 126 the Babylonian Exiles have returned to Jerusalem and the joy was so great that "we thought we were dreaming." They sang and danced for joy because God had liberated them. "Oh, how happy we were!"

Then, the reality of life in the ruined city became apparent to them. The city walls were in ruins, the Temple a disaster, and the fertile fields abandoned and dried up. They turned to God for help in restoring the land. They dreamed of irrigation like that which flooded the dry river beds in the Negeb during the brief rainy season. Just bringing enough water into Jerusalem was an almost superhuman task.

Yet their confidence in God is inspiring. "Those who sow in tears" — the sweat of hard labor — will be rewarded with a rich harvest when they "will reap with cries of joy." Primitive as their agricultural methods were, the work of hand sowing will produce a harvest of bundled sheaves to cause them joy.

Christ often used agricultural similes to explain his doctrine. When the disciples urged him to eat as he sat at Jacob's well in the Samaritan town, he told them, "I have food to eat of which you do not know... My food is to do the will of the One who sent me and to finish his work. Do you not say, 'In four months the harvest will be here'? I tell you, look up and see the fields ripe for harvest. The reaper is already receiving his payment and gathering crops for eternal life" (Jn 4:32-38).

The parable of the Sower who went forth to sow his seed is an extended discourse on the spiritual harvest and the response the Christian must make in generosity (Mk 4:1-20). "Ask the harvest master to send laborers into the harvest" (Mt 9:37-38).

St. Paul also used these figures of speech. "I planted, Apollos watered, but God caused the growth" (1 Cor 3:6). "Our hope for you is firm, for we know that as you share in the sufferings, you also share in the encouragement" (2 Cor 1:7).

St. Augustine saw us as spiritual exiles when he wrote his commentary:

"Clearly the Jerusalem on high is also eternal but the one that existed on earth was only a shadow of the other. The earthly one lasted during the time when the Messiah was announced; the other one enjoys the eternity of our restoration. During this life, we are exiles from this Jerusalem on high" (*Commentary on Psalm 125/126*).

Exiled as we are in this vale of tears, the Church recommends us in a special way to the Blessed Mother:

> Hail, Holy Queen, mother of mercy,
> Our life, our sweetness and our hope.
> To you do we cry, poor banished children of Eve.
> To you do we send up our sighs,
> Mourning and weeping in this Valley of Tears.
> Turn then, most gracious Advocate,
> your eyes of mercy towards us,
> And after this, our exile,
> Show us the fruit of your womb, Jesus!
> O clement, O loving, O sweet Virgin Mary!
> (*Salve Regina*, Herman Contractus)

PSALM 127: *"Unless the Lord build the house..."*

"Vanity of vanities," says the wise man, "Vanity of vanities! All things are vanity!" (Ec 1:2). As he looked at what motivated the men of his age, he found them chasing after insubstantial things that, eventually, perish. Only the search for things of eternal value is worth man's real attention.

Psalm 127 expresses this same thought in two ancient Wisdom proverbs. The first stanza points out that only God can establish a "house," that is, a family name that will endure. Modern men and women endow universities, libraries and museums to perpetuate their family names but how soon some youngster asks, "Who were they?"

It is vain, says the poet, to work morning, noon and night and think that this will perpetuate the house and its prosperity.

Only God can assure the peaceful possession of property and repu-tation. When one is at peace with God, he can enjoy his rest at night and expect that his work will be fruitful.

The second stanza carries this a step further. Children are a gift from the Lord, those who will inherit the name and the dream and carry it to further heights. To be blessed by the fruit of the womb while still young means that the children will probably in-herit more health and vigor, will be able to defend the goods of the family, and will be around to care for their parents in their old age. What an ideal pro-life picture this makes!

The last verse refers to lawsuits which were tried at the city gates. A man can approach the judges with much more assurance if he is surrounded by numerous, strong sons.

The Church discerns a feminine undercurrent in this psalm. In the liturgy, this psalm is used for Feasts of the Blessed Mother who brought the house of David to its fulfillment in Christ Jesus, her Son, and of all Virgins and Holy Women since these saints are the glory of the House of God.

The reference to children reminds us of Christ's love for the little ones. "Unless you become like little children you cannot enter the kingdom of heaven" (Mt 18:3). When the children were brought for his blessing and some objected, he said, "Let the chil-dren come to me for the kingdom of heaven belongs to such as these" (Mt 19:14-15).

St. Augustine begins his commentary on the psalm in this manner:

"'Unless the Lord builds the house the builders labor in vain.' Who are they who labor to build it? All those who in the Church preach the word of God, the ministers of God's Sacraments. But unless the Lord builds the house, the laborers labor in vain. We speak from without; he builds from within. It is he who builds, counsels, inspires fear, opens your minds and directs them to the faith" (*Commentary on Psalm 126/127* #1).

Finally, to avoid the vanity of vanities, worldly glory and plea-sure, we read in the work of Boethius these reflections:

"We must agree that the most high God is full of the highest and most perfect good. But we have already established that perfect good is true happiness; therefore it follows that true happiness has its dwelling in the most high God" (*The Consolation of Philosophy* 3:10).

PSALM 128: *"Happy are all who fear the Lord..."*

Had I been around to review Psalm 128 when it was first published, I would have decided that it offers a touching, if too brief, look at the ideal Jewish family in late biblical days. Those who serve the Lord and "fear" him, in the sense of following him with reverence, can expect to prosper through the works of their hands and enjoy happy family life.

The wife and mother is the heart of the family, as Msgr. Knox translates it, and the children will play around the table like vigorous olive shoots, plants already full of life. The blessing that the pilgrim takes back with him from Zion is one of peace and prosperity and a long life to enjoy the grandchildren. The closing "Peace upon Israel!" is meant to be a blessing for the whole community.

Jean Gerson, Chancellor of the University of Paris in the fifteenth century, wrote:

"Though I have spent years in reading and prayer, yet I could never find anything more efficacious, nor, for attaining to mystical theology, more direct, than that the spirit should become like a little child, and a beggar, in the presence of God" (*Letter*).

The Fathers of Vatican II wrote:

"Authentic married love is caught up into divine love... By virtue of this sacrament: spouses fulfill their conjugal and family obligations, advance the perfection of their own personalities, and guide their children to human maturity, salvation and holiness" (*Gaudium et Spes* #48).

The 1964 ritual used for Marriages in the United States has a powerful exhortation addressed to the Bride and Groom:

"Because God himself is the author of marriage, it is of its very nature a holy institution, requiring of those who enter into it a complete and unreserved giving of self...

"It is a beautiful tribute to your undoubted faith in each other that you are nevertheless so willing and ready to pronounce these vows. Therefore it is most fitting that you rest the security of your wedded life upon the great principle of self-sacrifice...

"Whatever sacrifices you may hereafter be required to make to preserve the common life, always make them generously. Sacrifice is usually difficult and irksome. Only love can make it easy and perfect love can make it a joy. We are willing to give, to sacrifice, in proportion as we love. And when love is perfect, the sacrifice, the giving, is complete...

"If true love and the unselfish spirit of perfect sacrifice guide your every action, you can expect the greatest measure of earthly happiness that may be allotted to man in this vale of tears" (*Collectio Rituum*, pp. 289-291).

PSALM 129: *"Much have they oppressed me from my youth..."*

The charm of the heroine in the musical *The Unsinkable Molly Brown*, is the fact that she is a true survivor. No matter how many hard knocks life deals her, she comes out ahead. When she books passage on the maiden voyage of the *Titanic*, we know that somehow she will get back to Denver.

The author of Psalm 129 pictures Israel as a survivor. From Egyptian slavery through the Babylonian Exile, through all the countless lesser violations, God has always come through and saved Israel.

Brief as the psalm is, it contains two powerful figures of speech, one for Israel and one for her oppressors.

Israel is the slave bound and beaten. The welts on his back are like furrows in a field to be planted. One can almost feel the whips as they trace "long furrows" on Israel's back. The Christian is reminded of Christ being flogged during his Passion (Mt 27:26; Mk 15:15; Lk 23:22; Jn 19:1).

For the oppressors, the picture is quite different. They are likened to the shallow-rooted grass that would spring up on the mud roofs of the poor during the spring rains. Then, since it had no depth, as soon as the scorching summer sun hit it, it would shrivel up and die. No reaper would ever harvest it and there would be no happy exchange of blessings among harvesters.

The Church, the New Israel, has also witnessed more than its share of suffering and martyrdom. Every age, indeed, every generation, glories in its saints, many of whom were martyrs. Before the accession of the Emperor Constantine, every Pope died a martyr, without exception (*Catholic Almanac*). St. Theophane Venard in Indochina, SS. John de Brebeuf and Isaac Jogues in North America, St. Charles Lwanga in Africa are just more heroes in the list of martyrs who cover every century and continent.

St. John Fisher, the martyred Bishop of Rochester, England, wrote with feeling on this psalm, tying together the blood of the tortured slave with the sacrifice of Christ on the cross and its application to us, daily, in the sacrifice of the Mass:

"Our high priest is Jesus Christ, our sacrifice is his precious body which he immolated on the altar of the cross for the salvation of all mankind. The blood that was poured out for our redemption was not that of goats or calves (as in the old law) but that of the most innocent lamb, Jesus Christ our Savior...

"Christ first offered sacrifice here on earth when he underwent his most bitter death. Then clothed in the new garment of immortality, with his own blood he entered the Holy of Holies, that is, into heaven. There he also displayed before the throne of the heavenly Father that blood of immeasurable price which he had poured out on behalf of all sinful mankind...

"Moreover, the sacrifice is eternal. It is offered not only each year (as with the Jews) but also each day for our consolation, and indeed at every hour and moment as well" (*On Psalm 129*).

The Blessed Mother, who stood at the foot of the cross (Jn 19:25-27) is commemorated by Jacopone da Todi, in this thirteenth century hymn:

At the cross her station keeping,
Stood the mournful Mother weeping,
Close to Jesus to the last.
Through her heart his sorrow sharing,
All his bitter anguish bearing,
Now at length the sword has passed....
Bruised, derided, cursed, defiled,
She beheld her tender Child,
All with bloody scourges rent;
For the sins of his own nation,
Saw him hang in desolation,
Till his spirit forth he sent.

(*Stabat Mater*, vv. 1, 4)

PSALM 130: *"Out of the depths I call to you, Lord..."*

Of the Seven Penitential Psalms, the *Miserere*, Psalm 51, and the *De Profundis*, Psalm 130, are the most poignant and human, and the most used in the liturgy of the Catholic Church.

The psalm opens on a note of the deepest anguish of soul and a feeling of total misery. Totally overwhelmed by his sense of his sins, the poet cries out to God for an audience. If God were to make a list of our wrongs like a court indictment, we would have no chance at all. Instead, we revere God for his mercy and forgiveness. In the face of such power our sense of awe and wonder grow. We understand St. Peter's response to the miraculous catch of fish, "Depart from me, O Lord, for I am a sinful man" (Lk 5:8).

The second half of the poem contains another of those happy figures of speech that abound in the Ascent Psalms. With great confidence, we wait for God to act, knowing that he will respond with mercy and "plenteous redemption."

We wait like sentinels, longing for the dawn, like watchmen who know that darkness encourages wrong-doers, like Levites in the Temple, waiting to call out the dawn prayers. The longest and most anxious hour of the night is the one before dawn.

The confident conclusion is that since God has always saved Israel from their sins, we can be sure that God will forgive the sincere, repentant sinner. The Christian sees this brought to its complete fulfillment in Jesus, whose very name means "Savior." As St. Gabriel announced to St. Joseph, "You are to name him Jesus because he will save his people from their sins" (Mt 1:21).

St. Alphonsus Liguori, who founded the Congregation of the Most Holy Redeemer (Redemptorists), chose his motto from this psalm, *Copiosa apud eum Redemptio*, v. 7: "With him is fullness of redemption."

The extensive use of Psalm 130 in the Office for the Dead and in devotions for the Poor Souls in Purgatory is at the heart of the theology of Purgatory. If we die owing anything to the justice of God there is a place of cleansing to prepare the soul, already saved, for entrance into the presence of God to enjoy the Beatific Vision.

Christians in the earliest centuries prayed for their dead to help pay what they might owe in justice to God. Prayers for the dead were scribbled on the walls of the catacombs. St. Augustine noted, in passing, that prayers for the dead were an ancient and pious Christian practice. Today, at the turn of the twenty-first century, the practice is just as pious and a bit more ancient.

Thomas of Celano, one of the first followers of St. Francis of Assisi, wrote the classic hymn that describes the Final Judgment, "That day of wrath, that dreadful day, when heaven and earth shall pass away" and God's justice will be acknowledged by the whole human race:

> Good Lord 'twas for my sinful sake,
> That thou our suffering flesh did take;
> Then do not now my soul forsake.
> In weariness thy sheep was sought;
> Upon the cross his life was bought,
> Alas, if all in vain were wrought.
> Thou who didst Mary's sins unbind,
> And mercy for the robber find,
> Dost fill with hope my anxious mind.

Oh, on that day, that tearful day
When man to judgment wakes from clay,
Be thou the trembling sinner's stay,
And spare him, God, we humbly pray.
Yes, grant to all, O Savior Blest,
Who die in thee, the saints' sweet rest.
                    (*Dies Irae, Dies Illa*, vv. 9, 10, 13, 18)

PSALM 131: *"Lord, my heart is not proud..."*

The classic explanation of contemplation is the image of the mother who is rocking her first-born in her arms, not saying a word, just caught up in loving the child. In one of the shortest psalms in the book, Psalm 131 has offered us another beautiful figure. The weaned child snuggles contentedly in the mother's arms, a perfect picture of humility and trust.

The author is not looking for a position of power and authority. He is not investigating theological mysteries that are beyond his understanding. The simplicity of his approach to God is an outstanding example of why Israel and the Israelite should have faith and hope in God for all time.

For the Christian interpretation of this psalm we turn to Our Lord's assessment of his own relationship to the poor:

"Come to me, all you who labor and are burdened, and I will give you rest. Take my yoke upon you and learn from me, for I am meek and humble of heart; and you will find rest for yourselves. For my yoke is easy and my burden light" (Mt 11:28-30).

Humility basically is truth. It is not so much a state of mind as a realization of our relation to God the Creator, we mere creatures, and our relationship to one another. As we read:

"In your relations with one another, clothe yourselves with humility, because God is stern with the arrogant but to the humble he shows kindness. Bow humbly under God's mighty hand, so that in due time he may lift you high. Cast all your cares on him because he care for you" (1 P 5:5-7).

St. John Bosco takes up the thought:

"This was the method that Christ used with the apostles. He put up with their ignorance and roughness and even their infidelity. He treated sinners with kindness and affection so that he caused some to be shocked, others to be scandalized, and still others to hope for God's mercy. And so he commanded us to be gentle and humble of heart" (*Letter to His Companions*).

Gilbert Keith Chesterton had an interesting sidelight to this quotation:

"We have all heard people say a hundred times over that the Jesus of the New Testament is indeed a most merciful and humane lover of humanity, but the Church has hidden this human characteristic in repellent dogmas and stiffened it with ecclesiastical terrors till it has taken on an inhuman character.

"That is, I venture to repeat, very nearly the reverse of the truth. The truth is that it is the image of Christ in the Church that is almost entirely mild and merciful. It is the image of Christ in the Gospels that is a good many other things as well" (*The Everlasting Man*, ch. 2 #2).

The Church has always proposed the Blessed Mother as a model of humility. St. Alphonsus Liguori comments:

"God having determined to become man, that he might redeem lost souls, and thus show the world his infinite goodness, and having to choose a Mother on earth, he sought among all women the one that was the most holy and the most humble.

"Among all of them there was one whom he admired, and this was the tender Virgin Mary, who, the more exalted by her virtues, so much the more dove-like was her simplicity and humility and the more lowly she was in her own estimation" ("The Annunciation" in *The Glories of Mary*).

PSALM 132: *"Lord, remember David..."*

The Passion Play at Oberammergau is one of the most famous in the world, but typical of a genre that goes back many centuries. It is the dramatic representation of the Passion, Death and Resurrection of Christ. It is also a type of liturgical dramatization that was once quite popular in Catholic countries.

Psalm 132 was a liturgical dramatization of one of the most solemn times in the life of King David, the transfer of the Ark of the Covenant from a forest area to Jerusalem. The Philistines had captured the Ark (1 S 4:11) and after suffering a minor plague, they turned it loose and the cart brought it, via Beth-shemesh, to Kiriath-jearim, where it remained for twenty years.

Soon after David became King of a united Israel, he captured Zion and made Jerusalem his capital. This was a politically wise move, since no tribal city was favored. David wanted to bring the Ark of the Covenant there to consolidate the religious unity of the people as well.

The procession to bring the Ark back ran into difficulties and it was left temporarily in the home of Obededom. After three months David brought the Ark into the city amid great rejoicing, where he danced for joy before the Ark (2 S 6:14).

When David settled down in his own palace, he became very concerned about building a Temple to replace the Tent in which the Ark was housed. God sent the prophet Nathan to tell David not to build the Temple but to leave it for his son (Solomon) to build (2 S 7:13).

On this occasion God swore to David that his dynasty would be mighty, and everlasting, if his sons kept the Covenant (2 S 7:11). David's response was to go and sit before the Ark and offer a prayer that is remarkable, exemplary, for its attitude of humility and gratitude (2 S 7:18-19).

This is the history of what Psalm 132 dramatizes, with some permitted poetic license. The oath David swore, not to sleep until he had a home for the Ark seems to be pure fiction. It may express David's attitude, but we have no record of it.

While David was in Ephrathah, the region around his home town, Bethlehem, he gathers his men around him and says, "Let's go and bring the Ark to Jerusalem!" Again, good drama. They proceed to "the fields of Jaar," Kiriath-jearim and bring the Ark back amid great regal and liturgical pomp. Thus was reenacted the triumph of David and the people in a liturgical ceremony.

The second stanza of the drama concerns the relationship between God and David because of this act. God promises an everlasting dynasty to David and his posterity, if they are faithful. It also proves that God wants his resting place to be Mt. Zion. If there seems to be some politics mixed in here, there probably is. This proclaims that David is the legitimate king and that Jerusalem is where Yahweh wants to be worshipped. Very neat politics and drama!

Because of that, God will bless Zion with material prosperity and religious purity. There David's horn will sprout legitimate descendants and heirs who will be an anointed lamp for the people. David's foes, military or political, will be put to shame and the crown will belong to David and to his seed.

For Christians, Jesus Christ is this eternal sprout from the house of David who will rule forever, in a fashion more literal than an Old Testament psalmist could possibly imagine. Christ was born of Mary, a virgin "of the house of David" (Lk. 1:32). Zechariah prophesies of his son, John the Baptizer, that he will be the messenger to go before the One that the God of Israel will "raise up as a horn for our salvation within the house of David, his servant, even as he promised through the mouth of his prophets of old" (Lk 1:69-70).

St. Peter in his speech on the first Christian Pentecost refers with confidence to this promise, that David's descendant has come in the person of Jesus to fulfill the ancient prophecies (Ac 2:29-36). St. Stephen weaves this into the speech before his martyrdom (Ac 7:45-46).

The figure of the Temple also has a Christian dimension. St. Paul wrote, "Your bodies are temples of the Holy Spirit" (1 Cor 6:19). And again, "You are the temple of the living God" (2 Cor 6:16). Christ's Mystical Body, the Church, is a temple built of the faithful (cf. Eph 2:19-22).

Or, as St. Augustine teaches:

"The Church is the Body of Christ and his Temple and House

and State. So he who is the Head of the Body dwells in his House, sanctifies his Temple and is King of this State. As the Church is all of these, so too is Christ.

"What then have we promised to God, except that we be God's temple? We can offer him nothing that is more pleasing than to say to him: 'Possess us!'" (*Commentary on Psalm 131, 132*).

PSALM 133: *"How good it is, how pleasant..."*

Of all the classical friendships recorded in world literature, one of the finest is the relationship between David and Jonathan. "Jonathan entered into a bond with David because he loved him as himself" (1 S 18:3). In succeeding chapters that friendship proved itself when Jonathan saved David from the wrath of King Saul.

When Saul and Jonathan were both killed in a battle with the Philistines, David sang an elegy for them. Of Jonathan he sang, "I grieve for you, Jonathan my brother! most dear have you been to me. More precious have I held love for you than love for women" (2 S 1:26). The value of true friendship is rare and precious.

Psalm 133 extends that notion to family unity and by extension to national unity. How much can be accomplished when people work together in fraternal love.

The psalmist uses two beautiful figures of speech in this regard.

Scented ointment was a very necessary part of good grooming, especially in a country where water was not plentiful. Pouring oil over the face and beard would have been most refreshing to one who had been exposed to the cruel ravages of sun and wind. Referring to the blessed oil used in the "consecration" of a High Priest gives a spiritual dimension to this familial unity (Ex 20:22-33).

Since water was such a precious commodity in the Holy Land, the dew that descended on the crops in the waterless season was a special blessing and a special way to refer to unity. Hermon was the name of a high snow-capped mountain in the north of Palestine, the source of the Jordan river, and so it symbolized the water needed near Jerusalem.

A family or country that was united in cooperation, especially around Jerusalem, could expect the lavish blessings of a full life.

The Psalm-prayer for Psalm 133 sums up so much of this for Christian use: "Pour out over your Church, Lord, the spirit of brotherly love and a longing for your peace. May this precious oil of the Holy Spirit flow over us with your gracious benediction" (*The Liturgy of the Hours*).

Christian charity is the norm for our unity, as St. John wrote: "Let us love one another, for love is of God" (1 Jn 4:7). It should spur on our efforts for Christian unity, ecumenism. So much of the First World seems bent on a destructive course of post-Christian aimlessness.

If ever the Christian message with its values, priorities and direction were needed, it is now. It wouldn't take much of a modern Jeremiah to point out the evils that beset us from urban crime, from poverty, from discrimination and so forth. A strong, united Christian voice could give firm and loving direction.

In its *Decree on Ecumenism*, the Second Vatican Council declares, "The restoration of unity among all Christians is one of the principal concerns of this Council" (*Introduction*). It states that division among Christians "openly contradicts the will of Christ, scandalizes the world and damages the holy cause of preaching the Gospel to every creature" (*ibid.*).

After identifying Catholic ecumenical principles the Fathers of the Council declare, "Unity in essentials and proper freedom for diversity of gifts, spiritual life, liturgy and theology, all in charity, best express the authentic catholicity and apostolicity of the Church" (#4).

In pursuing Christian unity they remind us that we must get our own house in order, first: "The faithful should remember that the more effort they make to live holier lives according to the

Gospel, the better will they further Christian unity and put it into practice" (#7).

While full Christian unity must await the power of the Holy Spirit, the Council points out that there are many areas in which divided Christianity can still benefit by closer cooperation. Such cooperation would have many near-term advantages:

> Christian cooperation should contribute:
> to a just evaluation of the dignity of the human person,
> to peace,
> to the application of the Gospel principles to social life,
> to the advancement of the arts and sciences,
> to the relief of affliction, illiteracy, poverty, housing
> shortages and the equal distribution of wealth,
> and to a better knowledge of each other (#12).

Prince Demetrius Gallitzin, working as "Father Smith" in the American frontier before the Civil War, wrote:

"Whatever differences on points of doctrine may exist among the different denominations of Christians, all should be united in the bonds of charity, all should pray for one another, all should be willing to assist one another; and when we are compelled to disapprove of our neighbor's doctrine, let our disapprobation fall upon his doctrine, not upon his person" (*Letter*, 1836).

PSALM 134: *"Come, bless the Lord..."*

Has anyone ever figured out why nurses wake up their patients, before dawn, with some innocuous phrase such as, "Are you awake?" Or, why is it that travel agents always book you on a plane that makes you rush to the airport at dawn? In biblical days when the pilgrims traveled on foot, leaving at the break of day made sense so that the people could make as many miles as possible during the day.

So, it is fitting that the last of the Ascent Psalms ends with an evening service. This would be the last service the pilgrims would attend before leaving the Temple for home. It is basically a type of the priestly blessing that God commanded Moses to give to Aaron (Nb 6:22-27).

"Come, bless the Lord" means publicly acknowledging God's greatness. Those who serve in the Temple, worshipping night after night, the priests and Levites, would praise the Lord and call his blessings down on the people. Prayer with upraised hands was common to Jews and Christians alike (1 Tm 2:8). The Temple, the throne of God's glory on earth, was meant to be a source of blessings.

The second shortest psalm in the Psalter, after Psalm 117, Psalm 134 has been popular in the liturgy. It is used for Compline in most monastic breviaries and it is used in *The Liturgy of the Hours* in Night Prayer for Sundays.

The Temple was a house of prayer (Mt 21:13) and Christ gave us the example of praying (Lk 5:16) night and day. Twentieth century authors were just as diverse and ingenious in their approach to prayer as were the Fathers and Doctors of the Church already quoted in this work.

Caryll Houselander offers us these thoughts:

"The prayers of the Church are the age-long poetry of mankind, lifted above the perfection of poetry, for they are the prayer of Christ on earth. This is what ritual means, with its ordered movements, its wide encircling gesture of love, its kiss of peace, its extended arms of sacrifice" (*Guilt*).

Pierre Teilhard de Chardin, S.J., brings us to different heights:

"To adore — that means to lose oneself in the unfathomable, to plunge into the inexhaustible, to find peace in the incorruptible, to be absorbed in defined immensity, to offer oneself, and to give of one's deepest to that whose depth has no end. Whom, then, can we adore? O Jesus, show yourself to us as the Mighty, the Radiant, the Risen!" (*The Divine Milieu*, 3:2).

Finally, Solanus Casey, O.F.M. Cap., brings us back to earth:

"Your plan may prove to be sublime, if you'll await God's plan. We cook up plans but turn ill with too much flavoring of self-will. If this idea comes from heaven, be patient, it will grow like leaven.

"God descends to use our powers, if we don't spoil his plan with ours. We do God's work best when we obey, and crucify self-will each day.

"We seek God's glory, not our own. Then let us honor him alone. No matter if I preach or pray or sweep the floors or mow the hay, the angels watch to recompense my loving, prompt obedience" (*Letters*, 1937).

PSALM 135: *"Praise the name of the Lord..."*

Anthologies have always been popular in public libraries since they bring together various literary pieces, such as essays, poems, short stories and the like, frequently on a related theme. Sometimes they will bring together unusual or shorter pieces by a single author. Dorothy Day, Catherine de Hueck Doherty, G.K. Chesterton and Hilaire Belloc have been the object of various collections. The O. Henry annual collections of short stories were popular volumes for decades.

Bracketed between two Alleluias, Psalm 135 is an anthology of verses singing the praises of God and giving reasons for that praise. The verses are taken from other psalms and from other books of the Old Testament. In liturgical and devotional services it is often used with Psalm 136.

The introduction is a typical call to praise and a reminder that "the Lord who made heaven and earth" sends his blessings from the Temple on Mt. Zion. He, the Creator, is the great God, greater than all those false gods worshipped by the nations. "Whatever the Lord wishes, he does," including the wonders of nature that depend on him. Wind and storms, lightning and rain are from his storehouse.

For the Israelite, the salvation history of God's dealing with his special nation is more than reason enough to praise God. In setting Israel apart, God sent the plagues on Egypt, especially the slaughter of the firstborn, "human and beast alike."

Before Israel crossed over the Jordan, the first Canaanite kings who opposed them were Sihon, king of the Amorites (Nb 21:21-24), and Og, king of Bashan (Nb 21:31-34). With poetic license the conquest is made to seem quick and easy. However, the Holy Land eventually became, in fact, the special heritage of Israel and God showed special mercy to them.

Verses 15-18 are brought over from Psalm 115, expressing again the incredulity that the Jews felt over worshipping idols of silver and gold. If these images couldn't take care of themselves, how could they help those who worshipped them? It was the senseless worshipping the insensate!

The blessing from Psalm 118 closes the psalm, the beautiful invitation for the house of Israel, the house of Aaron, the house of Levi and all who serve the Lord to acknowledge publicly (bless) Yahweh who reigns from Mt. Zion in Jerusalem. Then there is the closing Alleluia — "Praise Yahweh!"

While considering the Christian dimension of this psalm, it might be well to say something about the use of Christian art in worship. Many converts from "Bible alone" denominations are not used to the centuries old tradition of its use or the richness of its theological value in teaching.

For many centuries the common people were mostly illiterate. Stained glass windows showing the miracles of Christ and his parables spoke volumes to the people. Pictures and statues were of great value in teaching Christian truths.

Anthony Wilhelm, who spent many years teaching adult converts, found that they accepted the great theological dogmas, but raised many questions about the practices of Catholicism. He treats the use of statues under the heading of "Sacramentals":

"Statues, pictures, etc., are not prayed to as having power of themselves; rather they remind us of God's presence. God commanded the Jews long ago, 'Make two cherubim of beaten gold... which you shall then place on top of the Ark' (Ex 25:18-20).

Christian art from the early centuries has used images of Christ and the saints to stimulate devotion.

"A sacramental is a reminder, but it is also something more: it is a special way of putting ourselves in Christ's presence, asking his help and blessing" (*Christ Among Us*, p. 180).

When the Israelites complained against God and Moses, God sent saraph snakes to punish the complainers. God commanded Moses to make a bronze image of a saraph snake, mount it on a pole and have the people gaze on it for a cure (Nb 21:4-9).

In the eighth and ninth centuries, the Church in the Byzantine Empire underwent the scourge of the iconoclasts, literally, the "icon blasters." The veneration of statues and images of Christ and the saints was vigorously denied by the Emperors and the military. St. John Damascene became the champion of the true Catholic position which encourages the use of Christian art as an aid to devotion and an educational tool.

Now let us turn to St. Thomas Aquinas who speaks of eternal life and praise in the Christian context:

"The first point about eternal life is that man is united with God. God himself is the reward and end of all our labors. Next it consists in perfect praise. It also consists in the complete satisfaction of desire, for the blessed will be given more than they wanted or hoped for. Again, eternal life consists in the joyous community of all the blessed" (*Minor Conferences* #2).

Praise on the lips of St. Francis of Assisi becomes a special song:

> Most high, omnipotent, good Lord,
> Praise, glory, honor, benediction, all are thine.
> To thee alone do they belong, most High,
> And there is no man fit to mention thee.
> Praise be to thee, my Lord, with all thy creatures,
> Especially to my worshipful Brother Sun,
> Which lights up the day; through him dost thou
>   brightness give;
> Beautiful is he and radiant with splendor great;
> Of thee, most High, signification gives.
>
> (*Canticle of the Sun*: Intro.)

PSALM 136: *"Praise the Lord, who is so good..."*

(Editorial note: Psalm 136 is called the Great Hallel, Great Praise. Psalms 113-118 are the Lesser Hallel, or the "Egyptian Hallel.")

"A litany is a form of prayer in which the leader prays a series of praises and petitions and the people reply with a set refrain. It has always been popular with Christians, the oldest being the Litany of the Saints, the most popular being the Litany of Our Lady (of Loreto). The *Kyrie Eleison* and the *Agnus Dei* from the Mass are short examples of a litany" (Dollen, *Listen, Mother of God!* p. 9).

Psalm 136 is the only lengthy example of a litany in the Psalter. The refrain, repeated twenty-six times, is: "For his mercy endures forever," or, in the newer translation, "God's love endures forever." The Hebrew word combines an uplifting idea of God's merciful love or loving mercy that is faithful to the covenant.

The reason for this outpouring of love is that God is so good, that he is "the God of gods," in the sense of "he is certainly God, he is truly the Lord."

The psalmist goes on to describe with great poetic imagination God's work of creation as described in Genesis. He made the heavens with the sun to rule the day and the moon and stars to rule the night. He spread out the earth upon the waters with great skill.

Then in a fashion familiar to all the Hebrews, the praises go on to demonstrate how God shows his mercy and love in the historic exodus event, from the great plague against Egypt, to the parting of the Red Sea and the grueling task of crossing the desert.

Moving into the Holy Land, the nomadic Israelites had to overcome fierce opposition from such warlike leaders as Sihon of the Amorites and Og of Bashan. Fighting for his people, God gave them the land of Canaan as a perpetual inheritance.

In a short stanza, the prayer commemorates God's triumph in settling the people in the days of the Judges, and possibly, at least in usage, the return from the Babylonian Exile. The last verse repeats the glorious theme, "Praise the God of heaven, God's love endures forever."

The notion of praising God is certainly common to Christians, Jews and Moslems among the great world religions. The motive for praising God will differ, however, from the understanding of how God loves us.

"See what love the Father has bestowed on us in letting us be called children of God! Yet that in fact is what we are. The reason the world does not recognize us is that it never recognized the Son. Dearly beloved, we are God's children now; what we shall later be has not yet come to light. We know that when it comes to light we shall be like him, for we shall see him as he is" (1 Jn 3:1-3).

We recognize that God the Creator has done marvelous works. He has transformed us into his own image and likeness and through Christ given us a share in his life. Yet the Church acknowledges that even more wonderful is the fact of God's forgiveness in pardoning sinners who rebel against him (Psalm Prayer 136, *The Liturgy of the Hours*).

St. Paul's classic description of Christian love, "a still more excellent way" urges our response to the great love God has shown us:

"If I speak with the tongues of men and angels, but do not have love, I am a resounding gong or a clashing cymbal. If I have the gift of prophecy and comprehend all mysteries and all knowledge; if I have the faith to move mountains, but do not have love, I am nothing...

"Love is patient, love is kind... It bears all things, believes all things, hopes all things, endures all things. Love never fails... So faith, hope and love remain, these three; but the greatest of these is love" (1 Cor 13:1-13).

St. Margaret Mary Alacoque wrote of this blending of love and mercy as being at the center of devotion to the Sacred Heart of Jesus:

"It seems to me that the Lord's earnest desire to have his Sacred Heart honored in a special way is directed toward renewing the effects of the redemption in our souls.

"From this divine heart, three streams flow endlessly. The first is the stream of mercy for sinners; the second is the stream of charity which helps all in need; the third stream sheds love and light for his friends who have attained some perfection" (*Letter*).

PSALM 137: *"By the rivers of Babylon…"*

Television has become the great bond that is gradually making us realize how true it is that we are a global village. Cultural events are exchanged, movies are shared and above all, news is flashed around the world so that all can be informed.

The plight of the homeless, the despair of the exiles, the gruesome effects of famine and the like, all are brought into our homes. They tear at the hearts of, and beg for the charity from, all men and women of good will. The Fathers of the Second Vatican Council urged this work on priests (*Presbyterorum Ordinis* #8) and the laity (*Apostolicum Actuositatem* #8).

Psalm 137 is a heart-rending psalm that goes right to the heart of human misery. The peaceful setting, by the rivers of Babylon, *super flumina Babylonis*, the Tigris and Euphrates, belies the misery in the exile's soul. When he thought back to Jerusalem he lost all heart.

The poet, evidently a musician, can not take his harp or lyre down to sing the songs of Zion, the psalms that spoke of the glory of the city, the Temple and the God-given promise of peace and security if the people were faithful to the covenant.

The request, "Sing for us now the songs of Zion" was a taunt, equivalent to the question, "Where is your God?" How could they sing the joyful songs of Zion in a foreign, that is, an unclean land? It was unthinkable!

The psalmist pledges never to forget Jerusalem. What is most important to a musician, his hands to play the instrument, his tongue to sing the words, should be sacrificed before the memory of Zion would fail.

Then, showing the stress of exile and oppression, the poet

curses those who destroyed Jerusalem. The Babylonians tore down Jerusalem (2 K 25) and the Edomites looted the fallen region. The poet, with an "eye for an eye" sense of justice, demands that they suffer the same punishment that they meted out.

The final line seems appalling to us moderns, even though we live in the shadow of the Holocaust and the gas ovens of Nazi prison camps. "Happy those who seize your children and smash them against a rock." The atrocities of war are enough to make pacifists of us all. This imprecation, this curse, was probably a heartfelt response to the exile and the events leading up to it, the stress of the situation — and perhaps prophetic, that God would actually bring these enemies to a dreadful end.

St. Hilary reminds us that the Babylonian Exile is a type of our own spiritual captivity. We are a pilgrim Church on the journey home to heaven. We suffer all the hardships of a long, tiresome journey. It is so easy to be drawn into the passing currents of the world around us, to be lured down paths of worldly pleasure, greed and materialism. We must never forget the heavenly Jerusalem, realizing that "Here we have no lasting city" (Heb 13:14).

Pope Leo XIII gives us this reminder:

"In God alone can the human will find absolute and perfect peace. God is the only end of man. All our life on earth is the truthful and exact image of a pilgrimage.

"Now Christ is the Way, for we can never reach God, the supreme and ultimate Good, by this toilsome and doubtful road of mortal life, except with Christ as our leader and guide.

"How so? First and chiefly by his grace, but this would remain 'void' in man if the precepts of his law were neglected" (*Tametsi Futura* #6).

Abbot Columba Marmion expands on this:

"Christ Jesus is the sublime ideal of all holiness, the Divine Model presented by God himself to the imitation of his elect. Christian holiness consists in the complete and sincere acceptance of Christ by faith, and in the expansion of this faith by hope and charity; it implies the stable and total hold exercised by Christ upon our activity through the supernatural influence of his Spirit.

"Christ Jesus, the Alpha and Omega of all our works, becomes by the communication of his own life, the very life of our souls: 'For me to live is Christ' (Ph 1:21)" (*Christ the Ideal of the Monk*, Preface).

PSALM 138: *"I thank you, Lord, with all my heart..."*

In the United States, "thanksgiving" is associated with Indians, Pilgrims, turkeys, pumpkin pie and over-eating. Despite the legends of early New England, our national, annual Thanksgiving Day was started by a presidential decree of Abraham Lincoln's on Oct. 3, 1863.

The name "Eucharist" (thanksgiving), to designate the Sacrifice of the Mass and the Sacrament of Holy Communion, was first used in the *Didache*, a first century document, and by St. Ignatius of Antioch and St. Justin. For the Christians, this was something to be truly grateful for (cf. John L. McKenzie, *The Dictionary of the Bible*, p. 249).

Psalm 138 begins the last series of psalms with the name of David in the title (138-145). It is a thanksgiving psalm of both a personal and a communal nature. As a personal prayer it begins with the exultant, "I thank you with all my heart."

The next line gives the scholars trouble: "Before the gods to you I sing." This is a literal translation. The older versions spoke of praise and thanking God "in the presence of the angels." The sense is that God, reigning in his heavenly court, is the one to whom I make my thanksgiving.

The psalmist has obviously been saved from some great trial or affliction and he bows in prayer towards God's holy Temple from which all blessings flow. "By your graciousness, you have exalted your name over all," he prays.

The rest of the psalm brings in the community. When God

is good to Israel, the surrounding nations also have to acknowledge God's goodness and greatness. At least they should. This is an obvious truth to the poet and he optimistically and idealistically prays that it be so.

The imagery is typical: God ruling on high but caring for the lowly, the strong right hand that saves, and the protection that God gives while enemies rage around Israel. The elements of enthusiasm and exultation give this prayer of thanksgiving a real lilt.

By using the older translation of the second line, this psalm fitted into the Feasts of the great Archangels, Michael, Gabriel and Raphael. In the Book of Revelation, angels are mentioned at least fifty times so we do know that they are present in the heavenly court. I would hate to try to count the number of times the angelic company is mentioned in the Scriptures.

The difference between the thanksgiving theme in the Psalter and its use in the Catholic world is quite marked. The Hebrew poet is thanking God for a past event or events and prays with confidence for future help. In the Eucharist, we thank God for this continuing wonder and his personal closeness. Even when we commemorate past events we make them present liturgically. We are not archaeologists or antiquarians; we have a present, living Sacrifice and Communion.

"And on the Lord's Day, after you have come together, break bread and offer the Eucharist, having first confessed your sins, so that your sacrifice may be pure" (*Didache*, ch. 14).

St. Cyril of Jerusalem teaches us:

"Do not, then, regard the eucharistic elements as ordinary bread and wine. They are in fact the body and blood of the Lord, as he himself has declared. Whatever your senses may tell you, be strong in faith.

"You have been taught and are firmly convinced that what looks and tastes like bread and wine is not bread and wine but the body and blood of Christ" (*Catechesis* #22).

St. Gaudentius of Brescia writes from the fourth century:

"The heavenly sacrifice, instituted by Christ, is the most gracious legacy of his New Covenant. On the night he was delivered up to be crucified, he left us this gift as a pledge of his abiding presence.

"This sacrifice is our sustenance on the journey of life. By it we are nourished and supported along the road of life until we depart from this world and make our way to the Lord" (*Sermon* #2).

PSALM 139: *"Lord, you have probed me, you know me..."*

St. Thomas Aquinas "puts this all succinctly and beautifully when he says that God is in the world, in everything and everyone in the world by his essence, causing all things, by his presence, all things being naked and open to the eye of this intelligent cause, by his power on which everything depends, to which everything is subject" (Walter Farrell, *Companion to the Summa*, v. 1, p. 64).

When the ancient Hebrew poet wanted to talk about the omniscience and omnipotence of God, he wasn't capable of the abstract philosophical analysis of St. Thomas Aquinas. The ancient Israelites weren't interested in systematic philosophy. But when they did talk about the attributes of God, they came up with something as beautiful and expressive as Psalm 139.

"You have probed me" — you know me thoroughly, inside and out, my thoughts words and deeds. You know my thoughts from afar and all my travels. "Even before a word is on my tongue, you know it, Lord." I am safe in the encircling power of your presence. Such knowledge is beyond me! It's too much for me to comprehend.

If this frightened me and I wanted to hide from you, where would I go? If I were to fly to the heavens or descend to the depths, you are there. Can I hide in the darkness — but that's the same as light to you.

When you created human nature, it was another of your wonderful works. You knew me body and soul, from conception to the grave. All my days were present to you before I began to live them. If I tried to number your designs and deeds I would have to be eternal, like you are, so vast and unlimited are they.

The only thing that can keep us from happiness with God is sin. In your justice Lord, punish sin and take wickedness from among us. Your enemies are my enemies.

Then the initial refrain returns, "Probe me, God, know my heart; try me; know my concerns" and if I stray, lead me back to the true path.

St. Paul expresses the Christian meaning of this marvel:

"Oh, the depth of the riches and knowledge of God! How inscrutable are his judgments and how unsearchable his ways! 'For who has known the mind of the Lord or who has been his counselor?' 'Or who has given him anything that he may be repaid?' For from him and through him and for him are all things. To him be glory forever. Amen" (Rm 11:33-36).

The marvelous power of God has come to us in the Incarnation of Christ Jesus, as St. Gregory of Nyssa tells us:

"Paul teaches us the power of Christ's name when he calls him the power and wisdom of God, our peace, the unapproachable light, where God dwells, our expiation and redemption, our great High Priest, our pastoral sacrifice, our propitiation; when he declares him to be the radiance of God's glory, the very pattern of his nature, the Creator of all ages, our spiritual food and drink, the cornerstone, the visible image of the invisible God.

"He goes on to speak of him as the mighty God, the Head of his body, the Church, the firstborn of the new creation, and the Mediator between God and man, the only-begotten Son crowned with glory and honor" (*On Christian Perfection*).

St. Maximus the Confessor shares this maxim:

"We do not know God in his essence but by the grandeur of his creation and the action of his providence, which presents to us, as in a mirror, the reflection of his infinite goodness, wisdom and power" (*Centuries on Charity*, 1:98).

And how do we respond? Listen to St. Bernard of Clairvaux:

"You wish to hear from me why and how God should be

loved? I respond: the reason for loving God is God himself; the way to love him is beyond measure" (*On the Love of God*, ch. 1).

PSALM 140: *"Deliver me, Lord, from the wicked…"*

Psalm 140 repeats several themes and images that we have seen frequently in the various psalms of lament, prayers for deliverance from individual or community woes.

The wicked, the violent, those who plot evil day after day were the stuff of horror themes for the psalmist. How often he returns to the idea of the men with serpent-like tongues who stir up trouble as if they had the "venom of asps upon their lips." Half-truths, lies, slander and calumny can cause great tragedy in a small community. On the world stage, the propaganda of the great lie reached vast proportions during the two World Wars and the Cold War which followed. "Disinformation" became an art form.

So here the poet uses, again, the image of the hunter setting hidden traps and camouflaged nets to describe the way the arrogant trap the just. On the other hand, we have the now familiar figure of God coming to the aid of the poor and lowly like a battle helmet in time of peril and the idea of letting the evil plot of one's enemies fall back on the plotters themselves. Wasn't it Shakespeare who coined the phrase, "hoist with his own petar"? (*Hamlet*, Act III, Scene IV).

The image of the burning coals falling on the wicked is no doubt a reference to the destruction of Sodom and Gomorrah (Gn 19:23-29). The psalm confidently predicts that God will restore justice and give secure protection to the needy, the poor, the just and the upright.

St. Paul combines ideas from this and similar psalms when he discusses the universal bondage of sin: "Their throats are open graves; they deceive with their tongues; the venom of asps is on their lips; their mouths are full of bitter cursing" (Rm 3:13-14). This leads to his theological explanation of justification not through the works of the Law but through faith in Christ. Note that St.

Paul does not teach "faith alone" as Luther thought. Paul denies the need for the Law's working, but certainly not the necessity of the works of charity (cf. 1 Cor 13 ff.).

Pope St. Gregory the Great also had some reflections on evil words:

"It is the wisdom of this world to conceal the heart with stratagems, to veil one's thoughts with words, to make what is false appear true and what is true appear false.

"On the other hand, it is the wisdom of the just never to pretend anything for show, always to use words to express one's thoughts, to love the truth as it is and to avoid what is false, to do what is right without reward and to be more willing to put up with evil than to perpetrate it, not to seek revenge for wrong, and to consider as gain any insult for truth's sake" (*Moral Reflections on Job*, Bk. 10).

St. Louis IX, the King of France, applied this to royal actions:

"My son, if you come to reign, do that which befits a king, that is, to be so just as to deviate in nothing from justice, whatever might happen to you. If a poor man goes to law with one who is rich, support the poor rather than the rich until you know the truth, and when the truth is known, do what is just" (*Instruction to His Son*).

PSALM 141: *"Lord, I call to you..."*

Incense was burned in the Temple to symbolize prayer rising to heaven just as the smoking incense floated aloft. Its sweet smell became a symbol of the sweetness of prayer going into God's presence. What more suitable a gesture for the one praying than to lift up his hands toward heaven?

That is the background of the beginning of Psalm 141, where the one praying is in great need of speedy assistance. He asks to be kept from sin and the company of sinners. He does not want to be enticed by the wealth that their wickedness could afford, rich foods and aromatic oil. Only the truly wealthy could afford such luxuries, and wealth often came through the oppression of the poor.

The experts all puzzle over the text of vv. 5-7. The best they can do is give the sense of them, in context. It seems to be that correction which comes from just and holy people is actually a blessing, and those, especially leaders, who try to lead people astray deserve terrible punishment. It reminds me of the story of Susanna and her two accusers, elders who should have helped her instead of trying to seduce her (Dn 13).

The psalms ends, something like Psalm 140, with a prayer for help and protection and a plea to God that the evildoers who plot against the psalmist will fall into their own traps.

The heavenly worship described in the last book of the New Testament strongly resembles the worship in the Temple, but here the throne of God is approached through Jesus Christ, the Lamb of God. Incense figures prominently in that worship as well (Rv 8:3-5; 14:18).

St. Luke begins his Infancy Narrative with the ministrations of the priest Zechariah who goes to the altar of incense in the Temple and receives the visit of the angel who announces the birth of John the Baptizer (Lk 1:9-11).

As soon as the Church was freed from persecution, it developed its own ritual of worship. The historian, Eusebius of Caesarea, wrote:

"(When Constantine granted peace to the Church) our bishops performed religious rites with full ceremonial, priests officiated at the liturgy — the solemn ritual of the Church, chanting psalms, proclaiming the other parts of the God-given Scriptures, and celebrating the divine mysteries. Baptism was also administered, the sacred symbol of the Savior's passion" (*Ecclesiastical History*, Bk. 10).

St. Charles Borromeo, one of the leaders of the Counter-Reformation tells us that:

"In her concern for our salvation, our loving mother the Church uses the liturgical seasons to teach us through hymns, canticles and other forms of expression, of voice and ritual, used by the Holy Spirit. She shows us how grateful we should be for our blessings" (*Pastoral Letter*).

A more modern author, Father Gerald Vann, O.P., adds another notion:

"The way back to God is the way of worship. If all that we are and become and do in our many-leveled life could be made one in worship, we should be saints. Some think that Christian morality is no more than a series of Don'ts; others, a little less ill-informed think of it as no more than a series of Do's. These things are included, for being and doing are interdependent; but it is being that comes first in importance; and Christian morality tells us first of all not what we should do, still less what we should not do, but what we should be" (*The Heart of Man: Vision of the Way*).

PSALM 142: *"With full voice I cry to the Lord..."*

In Psalm 142, the author describes himself as a prisoner, whether actually or metaphorically, and he pleads with God for acquittal since he proclaims himself innocent. In a loud voice he pleads so that his complaint and his distress will be known. He is beset with the traps his enemies have hidden along his path.

He pictures himself in a court of law where his friends have abandoned him. Looking to his right hand where his best friend or advocate should have been to help, he sees no one. Then he turns to the Lord for help and vindication. No matter how strong his accusers — his pursuers — are, God can provide for him.

The last verse involves a vow of thanksgiving sacrifices and works of praise in the Temple where the freed man can proclaim God's goodness to him.

While there is little that is original in this psalm, it does provide a lament from the heart, a cry of distress that can be used in many different situations. The title refers to David's flight before the anger of Saul and his taking refuge in caves in the wilderness, but the appeal of the prayer is more universal.

The Christian, beset by the dangers and enticements of this world, can use this psalm to beg for help in times of difficulty. Martyrs who pay the price of their blood when imprisoned for Christ can look forward to the most complete of vindications, as St. Edmund Campion wrote:

"Be it known to you that we have made a league, all the Jesuits in the world, cheerfully to carry the cross you lay upon us, and never to despair your recovery, while we have a man left to enjoy your Tyburn, or to be racked with your torments, or consumed with your prisons.

"The expense is reckoned, the enterprise begun; it is of God, it cannot be withstood. So the Faith was planted: so it must be restored" (*Letter to the Council* [*Campion's Brag*]).

St. Hildegard of Bingen wrote:

"But I am constantly filled with fear and trembling, for I recognize no security in myself through any kind of personal ability. Then I lift up my hands to God that I may be held by God" (*Book of Divine Works* #39).

As for the injustices in prison life itself, listen to another poet:

> This too I know — and wise it were,
> If each could know the same —
> That every prison that men build,
> Is built with bricks of shame,
> And bound with bars, lest Christ should see
> How men their brothers maim.
>   (Oscar Wilde, *The Ballad of Reading Gaol*)

PSALM 143: *"Lord, hear my prayer…"*

The last of the Seven Penitential Psalms, Psalm 143 has been very popular in liturgical usage. In some of the Eastern Rite liturgies it is used daily in Morning Prayer and in the Roman Catholic liturgy it is used at least once a week in Night Prayer.

The poet begs God to hear him and gives the two fundamental reasons for calling on him: God's faithfulness and his justice. Do not judge me harshly, he prays, because "before you no living being can be just." In our human condition, we fall prey to all sorts of enemies that could easily destroy us.

One of the reasons for hope is that God has so often and so wonderfully demonstrated his care, for Israel and for individuals. When it seems that we have been left to darkness, "like those long dead," we can await the dawn when God will answer us with the new light of another day.

Verse 10 has a remarkable spiritual message: "Teach me to do your will, for you are my God. May your kind spirit guide me on ground that is level." Dante's much quoted phrase echoes that sentiment: "In his will is our peace."

The psalm ends with a powerful plea for present life and future protection. Once again, it is God's justice and kindness that anchor our hope.

When St. Paul speaks of the need for justification through Christ, he points out that all men "are under the domination of sin" and that "no man can be justified in God's sight" (Rm 3:9, 20; Gal 2:16), a direct reference to this psalm.

The Psalm Prayer draws a direct contrast between the darkness of sin and death, and the dawn of Easter Sunday when the Resurrection of Christ gives us hope (*The Liturgy of the Hours*).

St. Irenaeus states quite directly, "To believe in God means to do his will" (*Against Heresies* 4:6).

St. Elizabeth Ann Seton elaborates a little more:

"What was the first rule of our dear Savior's life? You know it was to do his Father's will. Well, then, the first end I propose in our daily work is to do the will of God. Secondly, to do it in the manner he willed, and finally, to do it because it is his will" (*Spiritual Conferences*).

Msgr. Robert Hugh Benson also gives us some reminders:

"Divine truth must always be extreme: it must, so to speak, always overlap at both ends, just because it is divine, and therefore much too big for this world...

"Religion must at least touch the will: for however small our will may be, it is always large enough to be united to the will of God" (*Christ in the Church*).

Throughout the Psalter, the authors refer to the wonderful works God has done in Israel's past. St. Clement Mary Hofbauer reminds us of the wonderful works God has done for Christians, the New Israel:

"Remember your mercies of old. Turn your eyes in compassion upon the vineyard planted by your own right hand, and watered by the tears of the Apostles, by the precious blood of countless martyrs, and made fruitful by the prayers of so many confessors and innocent virgins" (*Prayer*).

PSALM 144: *"Blessed be the Lord my rock..."*

Retreat masters often urge retreatants to keep a spiritual journal of their thoughts and ideas, garnered from the religious exercises. It would usually just be a string of phrases that would help the retreatant recall high points in the spiritual exercises.

Psalm 144 seems to have grown that way. Except for the last few verses, almost every verse is borrowed from some other psalm. If it has any unity, it would seem to be a prayer of a king who has many thoughts on his mind.

The image of God as rock is full and familiar. As a foundation, rock would give stability to the building. As a high place easily defended, it would give protection. A mountain fastness could provide safe shelter for those hunted or it could be the place to launch an attack on passers-by.

"Rock" in this psalm expresses the notion of God's strength provided to the king, which guides him on to victory. Man himself is really quite insignificant on a cosmic scale and unless God rises to man's help he would be powerless before his enemies. These enemies can be armed forces or lying and deceitful courtiers.

Verses 12-15 are so distinctive that many experts consider them a separate psalm, or the introduction of the "new song" mentioned in verse 9. It begs God's blessings on the country, blessings that include strong sons and beautiful daughters, prosperous farms and abundant cattle. It includes peace with the nations that surround them and urban peace and happiness. "Happy the people so blessed; happy the people whose God is the Lord."

This interesting pastiche of biblical ideas contains many themes that are familiar to the praying Christian. The "new song" at the conclusion would certainly touch the heart strings of any fervent mother or father.

The idea of "rock" however, strikes another note as well. When Christ changed the name of the Apostle Simon to Peter, Rock (Mt 16:18), it seems evident that Our Lord fully intended all the various symbolism attached to the "rock" to be applied to St. Peter, *mutatis mutandis.* The symbolism distinct to divinity was obviously not intended, but the rest of the rich symbolism must have been.

St. Thomas Becket wrote:

"The Roman Church remains the head of all the churches and the source of Catholic teaching. Of this there can be no doubt. Everyone knows that the keys of the kingdom of heaven were given to Peter.

"Upon this faith and teaching the whole fabric of the Church will continue to be built until we all reach the full maturity in Christ and attain the unity in faith and knowledge of the Son of God.

"All important questions that arise among God's people are referred to the judgment of Peter in the person of the Roman Pontiff" (*Letter 77*).

The Council of Trent solemnly taught this as well:

"This Church has but one ruler and one governor, the invisible one, Christ whom the eternal Father has made head over all the Church which is his Body (Eph 1:22); the visible one who, as the legitimate successor of Peter the prince of the Apostles, fills the apostolic chair. That this visible head is necessary to establish and preserve unity in the Church is the unanimous accord of the Fathers" (*Catechism* #1).

This is how St. Robert Bellarmine expresses it:

"The one and true Church is the community of men brought

together by the profession of the same Christian faith and con-
joined in communion of the same sacraments, under the government of the legitimate pastors and especially the one vicar of Christ
on earth, the Roman Pontiff" (*On the Church*).

In a burst of exuberance, the English Catholic apologist of
the last century, Wilfrid G. Ward, once exclaimed, "I should like
a new papal bull served every morning with my *Times* at break-
fast."

PSALM 145: *"I will extol you, my God and king..."*

The Feast of Jesus Christ the King was established by Pope
Pius XI in 1925 at a time when it seemed that some European
monarchies might be restored. Now some preachers have a difficult time making the powerful point which the feast proclaims
regarding the absolute power of Jesus Christ since what few kings
and queens remain have a story-book quality about them. The
lesson, for the most part, is lost on our contemporaries.

However, in biblical times absolute regal power and impe-
rial prerogatives were an ever present reality. Psalm 145 takes ad-
vantage of that to praise the mighty power of Yahweh. This is an
acrostic poem, with each verse beginning with successive letters
of the Hebrew alphabet. This forces some artificiality upon the
poem but does not diminish its beauty and strength. It is also the
last of the "David" psalms.

Almost every other verse calls upon us to worship God and
the next verse gives some motivation for praising God. There is
praise for God's covenant faithfulness and justice and his open-
handed mercy in providing what the people need.

Tradition is important, in which "one generation praises your
deeds to the next," and hands on the good news of God's works.
"The Lord is gracious and merciful, slow to anger and abounding
in love," when dealing with his people.

Prayer is also an important part of worship since, "You, Lord,
are near to all who call upon you, to all who call upon you in truth."

God is constantly alert to the needs and desires of the faithful and the repentant.

In some Jewish traditions this psalm is recited thrice daily at morning, noon and night. In others it is treated as a litany with the phrase, "Blessed be the Lord and blessed be his name for ever and ever," added to each verse. In many Christian monastic traditions part of it is used at the blessing before meals. And, of course, it is used on the Feast of Christ the King.

The title "king" is given to Christ by the Magi: "Where is the newborn king of the Jews?" (Mt 2:2); it is attributed to him during the triumphal entry into Jerusalem: "Your king comes to you meek..." (Mt 21:5) and Pilate contributes to it by asking: "Are you the king of the Jews?" (Mt 27:11) and then placing the title on the crucifix, "Jesus of Nazareth, King of the Jews" (Jn 19:19).

In the O Antiphons used during the Advent Season, we pray "O Emmanuel, our King and Lawgiver, the expectation of all the nations and their savior: come and save us, O Lord our God" (*The Liturgy of the Hours*).

Hugh of Fleury wrote in the early part of the twelfth century:

"The chief powers by which the world is ruled are two, the royal and the priestly. Both powers Our Lord Jesus Christ willed to bear in his person alone in a holy and mysterious way, for he is both King and Priest: King because he governs us; Priest because he has cleansed us by the immolation of his own body from the sordidness of our sins and reconciled us to his Father" (*Treatise on Royal Power* 1:2).

A more recent theologian, Francis X. Durrwell, tells us that:

"For Christians Christ was the divine King-Messiah. The earliest Palestinian communities called him '*Maran*' (Our Lord) and the Greek communities proclaimed him '*Kyrios*.' In the first public profession of faith in Christ we read 'Let all the house of Israel know most certainly that God has made both Lord and Christ this same Jesus whom you have crucified' (Ac 2:36). In St. Peter's mind the two terms are even more closely joined: God has made Jesus the Lord-Messiah" (*The Resurrection* 4:1).

St. Francis Xavier is believed to be the author of this hymn:

Then why, O Blessed Jesus Christ,
Should I not love You well,
Not for the sake of winning heaven,
Or of escaping hell —
Not with the hope of gaining anything
Nor seeking a reward;
But as You yourself have loved me,
O ever-loving Lord?
Even so I love You and will love
And in your praise will sing,
Solely because You are my God,
And my eternal King.

                    (*O Deus, Ego Amo Te*, vv. 5-7)

PSALM 146: *"Praise the Lord, my soul..."*

(Editorial note: The last five psalms of the Psalter begin with the title, and end with the word Alleluia! They all have the characteristics of anthologies, leaning heavily on earlier psalms. They are replete with exuberant, enthusiastic praise.)

The monks of Prince of Peace Benedictine Abbey in Oceanside, California are models of liturgical and ritual correctness for all the surrounding area. It is a glorious experience to attend their monastic Sunday liturgies where you can almost feel the praises of God ascending on high. This is true of other Abbeys, I am sure.

In Psalm 146 the author dedicates his life to praising the Lord. He contrasts serving God with the service of men. Princes, whether of the royal line or the wealthy, are powerless to offer salvation and they die just as surely as their clients.

The majority of the verses then go on to praise God for his concrete actions in helping mankind. This is a far different treatment from that given by the Scholastics in the Middle Ages. The philosophers enjoyed the abstract; the Jewish poet sees things in the present.

The omnipotent God who creates and maintains his creation

ties worship very strongly into the realm of social justice. He "secures justice for the oppressed, gives food to the hungry... sets prisoners free," helps the sick, protects the alien, sustains orphans and widows. These thoughts, present in many other psalms, reach a crescendo of approbation in Psalm 146.

The conclusion then is to praise God through all generations since he will reign forever.

Psalm 146 has been very popular in Christian use. It is used in the Office for the Feast of the Sacred Heart, in the Common Offices for Pastors and for Holy Men, and in the Office for the Dead. The common thread seems to be that by performing works of charity and mercy, we most imitate the goodness of God at work in the world. "Write 'Blessed are the dead who die in the Lord... for their works follow them'" (Rv 14:13).

Church history demonstrates that the Church in various ages and in various places has always tended to emphasize some aspect of the Christian message. The Church in the United States in our time has been noteworthy for its dedication to social justice.

Who could count the untold thousands of women religious who gave themselves totally to the education of the poor, the health of the sick, the feeding of the poor and the like? Later, they and countless other Catholics joined millions of Americans in working to end racial discrimination, poverty and homelessness and the like.

It seems like an endless task, since Our Lord reminded us, "The poor you will always have with you" (Mt 26:11). But the very struggle itself is worth it. "Blessed are they who hunger and thirst for righteousness, for they will be satisfied" (Mt 5:6).

Many rights which we today take for granted were hotly contested earlier in this century. Cardinal William O'Connell had to write:

"Capital has a right to a just share of the profits, but only a just share... Anyone who possess a natural right may make use of all legitimate means to protect it and to safeguard it from violation... The worker has the right to refuse to work, that is, to strike, and to induce, by peaceful and lawful methods, others to strike with him" (*Letter on Workers' Rights*).

It seemed radical when Father John Augustine Ryan wrote:

"Just as the woman worker who lives with her parents has a right to a wage sufficient to maintain her away from home, so the unmarried adult has the right to a family living wage.

"If only married men get the latter wage, they will be discriminated against in the matter of employment. To prevent this obviously undesirable condition, it is necessary that a family living wage be recognized as the right of all adult workers. In a competitive regime, the standard wage for the married and the unmarried is necessarily the same.

"No other arrangement is reasonable in our present industrial system" (*Distributive Justice*, ch. 23).

The U.S. Bishops wrote:

"The heart of the race question is moral and religious. It concerns the rights of man and our attitude toward our fellow man. If our attitude is governed by the great Christian law of love of neighbor and respect for his rights, then we can work out harmoniously the techniques for making legal, economic and social adjustments" (*Pastoral Letter*, 1958).

The words of the old Negro "spiritual" signify what a long and bitter battle it will be:

> We shall overcome —
> We shall overcome —
> We shall overcome some day.
> Deep in my heart,
> I do believe,
> We shall overcome, some day.

PSALM 147: *"How good to celebrate our God in song…"*

The stories told about St. Cecilia may be true or not, but as it has been said, "If not, they should be!" They tell us that she always sang to God in her heart, and that was enough to make her the patron saint of music and musicians.

Music seems to be a natural extension of religious worship from Gregorian chant to the classical Masses of the Great Age of Western Music. It was certainly an important part of the rites in the Temple of Solomon on Mt. Zion. From the drums of Africa to the guitars of the Folk Masses to the magnificent organs in Europe, musical instruments have always accompanied praise.

How natural then, for Psalm 147 to begin with the reference to fitting praise given to God in song. According to another ancient axiom whose origins are attributed to St. Augustine, "Whoever sings well prays twice." Each of the three stanzas of this psalm begin with a call to praise God, twice by singing.

The first stanza praises God for restoring Jerusalem and probably refers to the return of the Jews from the Exile in Babylon. With all the wisdom and power this suggests, God does not forget the poor and the brokenhearted. Particularly beautiful is the thought in verse 4. He — this powerful, thoughtful, caring God — "numbers all the stars and calls each of them by name." It's almost as if they were his pets!

In the second stanza we sing to the Lord with thanksgiving because in his providence he cares for the natural needs of the earth. He provides rain for the earth, makes the grass grow and provides food for the animals. Yet his pleasure is especially reserved, not for the strong or athletic, but for the devout.

The third stanza, treated in some important translations as a separate psalm, continues the theme of praise and thanksgiving for God's care of Jerusalem and its inhabitants. It contains a highly poetic version of winter and spring in the Holy City. More important, God has provided for the spiritual instruction of the house of Jacob, a spiritual sustenance that is more important than mere food and water.

The Church uses this psalm over and over again in its regular liturgies and on some Feasts. Among the Feast Days, it is used for Christmas, Corpus Christi, the Triumph of the Holy Cross and All Saints Day. It is found in the commons for Feasts of the Blessed Virgin Mary, the Apostles, Virgins and Holy Women.

Verse 14 which praises God for filling his people with the

finest wheat has occasioned many eucharistic hymns, since the bread of Christ, made the body of Christ, is the finest that wheat could be. St. Thomas Aquinas wrote:

> And in faith the Christian hears
> That Christ's Flesh as bread appears,
> And as wine his Precious Blood;
> Though we feel it not or see it,
> Living faith indeed decrees it,
> All defects of sense makes good.
>
> (*Lauda Sion Salvatorem*, v. 6)

The theme for the Office and the devotion to Our Lady of Guadalupe was taken from Psalm 147:20: "God has not done thus for any other nation." Some in Rome protested that this seemed to be an extravagant claim. The Mexicans replied that her apparition to Blessed Juan Diego as a native Mexican Indian (Aztec) in the garb of a pregnant woman was truly an extraordinary event, and they were allowed to keep the motto.

St. Augustine comments on the fact that we should praise God at all times:

"You are praising God when you do your day's work. You are praising him when you eat and drink. You are praising him when you rest on your bed. You are praising him when you are asleep. So, when are you not praising him?" (*Commentary on Psalm 147* #2).

PSALM 148: *"Praise the Lord from the heavens..."*

The various natural sciences tell the devout person the "scientific facts" of the world around us. When they thought the earth was flat, prayers echoed that. Dante's vision of the universe in the Divine Comedy is beautiful for its poetry and its theology, but hardly accurate from, say, an astronomer's point of view today. Galileo and St. Robert Bellarmine were bound to be friends, differ as they might on a scientific point as yet unproved.

So, Psalm 148 magnificently summons all of creation to the

worship of God, all creation as the poet then understood it. The first stanza takes up the call, starting with the heavenly viewpoint. First the angels must praise God, then the sun, the moon, the stars and the rain waters stored in the heavenly vaults. They praise God by doing the tasks he assigned them.

The second stanza reverses the order, starting with the lowest of earthly creatures, from the sea monsters in the deepest waters. Then we climb the ladder: inanimate objects such as rain and hail, mountains and hills and then animate ones, wild and tame animals and whatever crawls and flies. Finally we get to humans, kings and princes, boys and girls, men and women.

All are called to praise the name of the Lord for he is "majestic above earth and heaven." He has shown special love for Israel, lifting high their horn, so special praise is expected from them.

The *Benedicite* (Dn 3:52-90), the song of the three young men in the fiery furnace, used often in Christian liturgies, seems to be an expansion of the categories of Psalm 148. Many of the expressions of worship and praise in the Book of Revelation also make use of this and the other Alleluia psalms (e.g., Rv 5:13).

The themes of praise resound in Catholic worship, devotion and practice. St. Benedict would have his monks work "so that God would be glorified in all things." St. Ignatius urged his Jesuits to go forward "for the greater glory of God."

Father Gerard Manley Hopkins, S.J., really understood this particular psalm as only a poet could:

> Glory be to God for dappled things —
> For skies of couple-colour as a brinded cow;
> For rose-moles all in stipple upon trout that swim;
> Fresh-firecoal chestnut-falls; finches' wings;
> Landscape plotted and pieced — fold, fallow, and plough;
> And all trades, their gear and tackle and trim.
> All things counter, original, spare, strange;
> Whatever is fickle, freckled (who knows how?)
> With swift, slow; sweet, sour; adazzle, dim;
> He fathers-forth whose beauty is past change;
> Praise him.   (*Pied Beauty*)

PSALM 149: *"Sing to the Lord a new song..."*

Body language and facial expressions often communicate ideas more eloquently than words. Dancing, a form of expression that is found in all major cultures, has had little impact on the worship services in the Judaeo-Christian traditions. The rubrics for Masses, especially on more solemn occasions, do resemble a choreographic work of art, but it would be difficult to call it "dancing" as such.

Psalm 149 is a curious "new song" that proclaims the glory of God in singing, dancing and just warfare. "Let them praise his name in festive dance, make music with tambourine and lyre." It is as if the Lord came down to mingle with the poor when they celebrate victories.

The psalm then turns to the divine vengeance that God demands from evildoers. Israel is the two-edged sword that God uses to bring down the just and fierce retribution for sins. As was said of Judas Maccabeus, they were "fighting with their hands and praying in their hearts" (2 M 15:27).

God's faithful people praise him by doing his will, whether in the Temple or out on the battlefield. So strong is this message that Psalm 149 is used for Morning Prayer on Feasts and Solemnities in *The Liturgy of the Hours*.

The image of the two-edged sword was popular with some writers. "Indeed the word of God is living and effective, sharper than any two-edged sword, penetrating even between soul and spirit, joints and marrow, and able to discern reflections and thoughts of the heart. No creature is concealed from him, but everything is naked and exposed to the eyes of him to whom we must render an account" (Heb 4:12-13).

In the last book of the New Testament, we read, of the one like the son of man, that "a sharp two-edged sword came out of his mouth and his face shone like the sun at its brightest" (Rv 1:16).

"To the angel of the church in Pergamum, write this: 'The one with the two-edged sword says this: "I know that you live where Satan's throne is, and yet you hold fast to my name and have not denied your faith in me..."'" (Rv 2:12-13).

St. Jane Frances de Chantal has another sidelight on this:

"There is another type of martyrdom, the martyrdom of love. Here God keeps his servants present in this life so that they may labor for him, and he makes them martyrs and confessors as well.

"Divine love takes its sword to the hidden recesses of our inmost soul and divides us from ourselves. I know one person whom love cut off from all that was dearest to her, just as completely and effectively as if a tyrant's blade had severed spirit from body" (*Memoirs*).

Many of the saints invited God to use this sharp, two-edged sword to cut out from their lives whatever was not conformable to his will. Thus, St. Gemma Galgani's *Prayer*:

"Assist me, my Jesus, for I desire to become good whatever it may cost; take away, destroy, utterly root out all that you find in me contrary to your will. At the same time, I pray you, Lord Jesus, to enlighten me that I may walk in your holy light."

St. Frances Xavier Cabrini also prayed:

"Fortify me with the grace of your Holy Spirit and give your peace to my soul that I may be free from all needless anxiety, solicitude, and worry. Help me to desire always that which is pleasing and acceptable to you so that your will may be my will" (*Prayer*).

Discerning the will of God, according to Abbot Marmion, is at the heart of holiness. Conforming ourselves to it joyfully, peacefully and sincerely puts us on the road to holiness (*Christ the Life of the Soul*, p. 6).

PSALM 150: *"Praise God in his holy sanctuary..."*

The doxology, "Glory to the Father, and to the Son, and to the Holy Spirit: as it was in the beginning, is now, and will be forever. Amen" is said at the conclusion of almost all the psalms and canticles used in *The Liturgy of the Hours*. It is a fitting way for

Christians to express praise to God through the fundamental mystery of Christianity.

Psalm 150 is the appropriate doxology to Yahweh in the Psalter. Thirteen times Alleluia — Praise — is said in adoration. God is to be praised in the Temple and in the Sanctuary of Heaven. He is to be praised because of his deeds and his glory.

All the musical instruments that were used by the Jews are to unite in crying out the praises of God. All the dancing and excitement of solemn liturgies is summoned up in this holy activity. The conclusion is all inclusive, "Let everything that has breath give praise to the Lord! Alleluia!"

This psalm has been very popular with Christians and is frequently used in the liturgies. It is included in the Office for the Dead, since all creation is called on to give glory to God.

St. Irenaeus reminds us that "Life in man is the glory of God; the life of man is the vision of God" (*Against Heresies* 4:21). And again, "The glory of God is man fully alive…" (*ibid.* 6:20).

One last time, we turn to a Christian poet to help us savor the intent of a psalm:

> O worship the king, all glorious above;
> O gratefully sing his power and his love;
> Our shield and defender, the ancient of days,
> Pavilioned in splendor and girded with praise.
> O tell of his might, O sing of his grace;
> Whose robe is the light, whose canopy space;
> His chariots of wrath deep thunder-clouds form.
> And dark is his path on the wings of the storm.
> Frail children of dust, and feeble as frail,
> In thee do we trust, nor find thee to fail;
> Thy mercies how tender, how firm to the end,
> Our maker, defender, redeemer and friend.
> O measureless might, ineffable love,
> While angels delight to hymn thee above,
> Thy humbler creation, though feeble their lays,
> With true adoration shall sing to thy praise.
> (Robert Grant, *O Worship the King*, vv. 1, 2, 5, 6)

Author Index

(The numbers refer to the Psalms, not the page.)

Scripture Index

(The numbers refer to the Psalms, not the page.)

Subject Index

(The numbers refer to the Psalms, not the page.)

Aaron 67, 77, 105, 106, 110, 115, 134, 135
Abba 92, 96
Abel 110
Abimelech 34
Abiram 106
abortion 58
Abraham 32, 47, 72, 76, 80, 82, 89, 105, 106, 110, 113
Abram 113
absolution 121
acolytes 43
accusations 35
Achish 34
acrostic psalms 9, 25, 34, 37, 111, 112, 119, 145
actions 64
Adam 66, 85
Adonai 68
adoption 26, 67, 114
adoration 92, 95, 96, 100, 103, 113, 134, 150
adultery 36, 51, 101, 109
Advent 145
Advocate 65
Aeneid 105
affections 42, 131
afflictions 25, 70, 71, 77, 82, 85, 101, 102, 112, 138
Africa 101, 114
aged 71, 90, 99, 112, 127
agony 79, 85
agriculture 65
African-American 85, 101, 114, 147
airport 121, 134
Alcoholics Anonymous 123
alien 90, 120, 146
All Saints 110, 116, 147
All Saints, festal use 8, 15, 16, 110, 113, 110, 116, 147
Alleluia 104, 106, 111, 113, 116, 118, 135, 146-150
alms 70, 112
Alpha 137
altar 43, 80
Amalek 83
ambassador 76
ambition 39, 55
Ammon 83
Amorites 135, 136
anawim 56, 112
anchor 110

angels 18, 29, 56, 91, 103, 106, 119, 120, 124, 134, 136, 138, 148, 150
anger 30, 55, 69, 80, 103
anguish 35, 55, 56, 64, 69, 77, 79, 85, 88, 89, 102, 130
Anima Christi 69
animals 38, 41, 50, 57, 104, 119, 148
Annunciation 19, 72, 86, 110, 113
Annunciation, festal use 2, 19, 45, 110, 113, 130, 147
anointed 67, 105, 107, 133
Antioch 89
Antiochus Epiphanes 102
antiquarians 138
Apollos 126
apostasy 102
apostles 48, 55, 64, 65, 79, 97, 107, 116, 117, 118, 131, 144, 147
Apostles, festal use 19, 64, 97, 116, 117, 126, 147
appreciation 22
Arabia 63, 72, 120
Arameans 76
archaeologists 138
archangels (see angels)
architect 95, 97, 135
ardor, 42, 63
Arians 100
Ark of the Covenant 24, 47, 57, 68, 78, 91, 96, 132
army 21, 60, 76
Arnold, Benedict 55
arrogant 12, 26, 36, 52, 75, 94, 101, 123, 131
arrow 7, 18, 57,120
art 22, 97, 135, 149
Asaph 42
Ascension 19, 41, 47, 68, 110, 113, 117, 118
Ascension, festal use 8, 19, 68, 113, 117
Ascent Psalms 120-134
ascetical theology 51
Ash Wednesday 44, 51
asp 91, 140
Assyria 83
Astarte 16
astronomy 148
atheist 14, 38, 40, 53, 107
Athens 44, 87
athlete 19
Atlantic Ocean 104

293